丁文江海外书信集初编

A Collection of V. K. Ting's Oversea Correspondences

张雷 编著

学苑出版社

图书在版编目（CIP）数据

丁文江海外书信集初编 / 张雷编著 . -- 北京：学苑出版社，2017.10
ISBN 978-7-5077-5360-8

Ⅰ. ①丁… Ⅱ. ①张… Ⅲ. ①丁文江（1887-1936）—书信集 Ⅳ. ① K826.14

中国版本图书馆 CIP 数据核字 (2017) 第 260725 号

责任编辑：	杨　雷
编　辑：	张敏娜
封面设计：	陈　曦
出版发行：	学苑出版社
社　　址：	北京市丰台区南方庄2号院1号楼
邮政编码：	100079
网　　址：	www.book001.com
电子信箱：	xueyuanpress@163.com
联系电话：	010-67601101（销售部）67603091（总编室）
经　　销：	新华书店
印 刷 厂：	北京建宏印刷有限公司
开本尺寸：	1/16
印　　张：	22.875
字　　数：	400千字
版　　次：	2017年11月第1版
印　　次：	2017年11月第1次印刷
定　　价：	480.00元

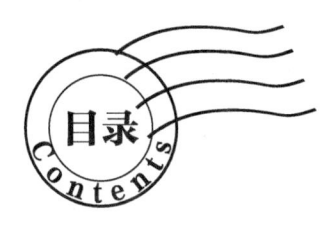

丁文江的国际交游网络	001
编著说明	011
丁文江通讯人物简介	013
书信影印件及文本	015
1910年	016
1911年	026
1913年	040
1914年	052
1915年	054
1916年	056
1917年	063
1919年	081
1920年	084
1921年	101
1922年	128
1923年	141
1924年	157
1925年	185
1926年	197
1927年	200
1928年	226
1929年	246

1930年	251
1931年	253
1932年	288
1933年	303
1934年	307
1935年	317
1936年	325
1955年	347
附　录	353
后　记	358

丁文江格拉斯哥大学实习照

丁文江格拉斯哥大学注册卡－1910年

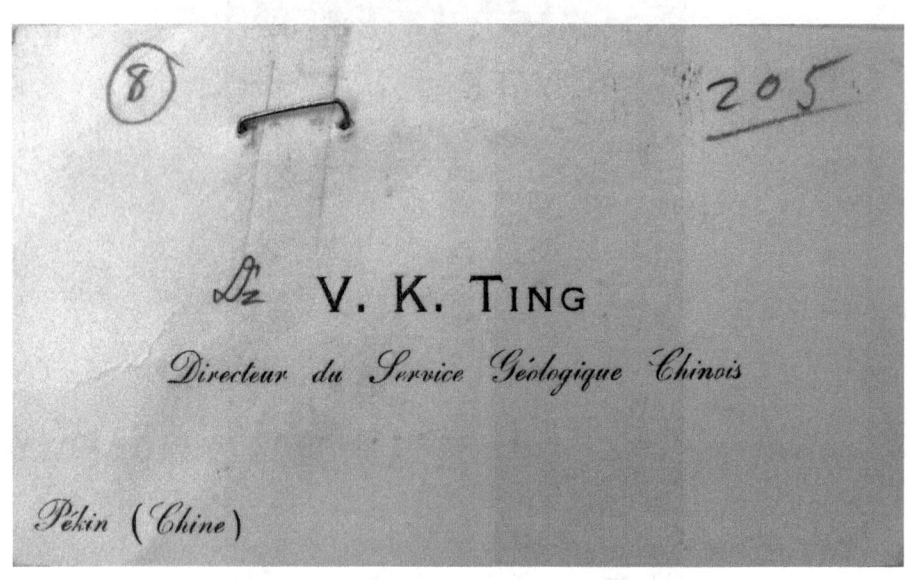

丁文江的法文名片

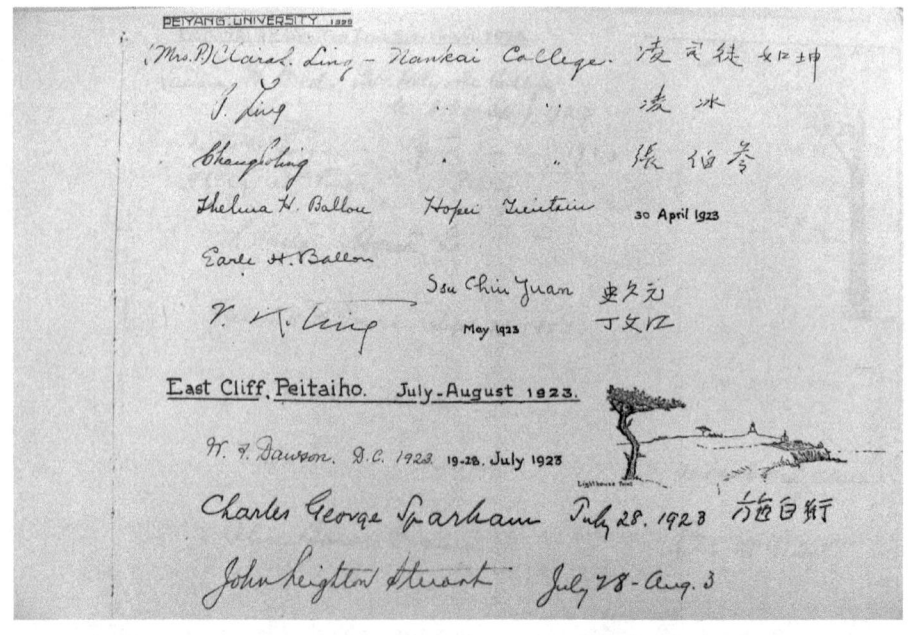

丁文江、史久元夫妇在巴尔博访问簿上的签名－1923年5月

[序言]

丁文江的国际交游网络

丁文江（1887-1936），字在君，江苏泰兴人，1911年毕业于英国格拉斯哥大学（Glasgow University）地质系，一生以地质事业为己任。丁文江不仅是民国地质学的重要缔造者，而且还为民国学界的干才，他曾任中国地质调查所所长、中央研究院总干事等职。丁氏虽英年辞世，但仍不啻民国学术史上的重要人物。

丁文江一生交游甚广，与胡适、翁文灏、傅斯年等都相知甚深。学界对于丁文江已有相当的理解和论述，传记年谱以及文集均有面世。[1] 然而，丁文江负笈英伦七年，是"一个欧化最深的中国人，一个科学化最深的中国人。"[2] 他谙熟中西，其海外交游网络同样广阔，而这方面的资料、文集面世很少。

丁文江海外交游人群大致可以分为三类，一是在华工作的外国学者；二是来华考察的外国学者；三是外国驻华机构的代表。丁文江的交游在范围上跨越地质学、考古学、人类学等。在时间上前期以英国为主，后期以美国为主。丁文江的交游是民国学术国际合作的一种重要模式，同时也可窥民国学术的国际网络。

---

1 （美）费侠莉著《丁文江——科学与中国新文化》（丁子霖等译），北京：新星出版社2006年；欧阳哲生《丁文江文集》，长沙：湖南教育出版社2008年；宋广波《丁文江年谱》，哈尔滨：黑龙江教育出版社2009年。

2 胡适《丁文江这个人》，《独立评论》第188号，1936年2月15日。

一、丁文江与在华工作的外国学者

1. 丁文江与巴尔博

民国地质学是中国最具有世界声誉的学科之一，这固然与本土学者的苦心经营息息相关，但也不能无视一批在华外国地质学者的贡献，其中一是以安特生（Johan Gunnar Andersson, 1874-1960）为代表的瑞典地质学者；一是以葛利普（A.W. Grabau, 1870-1946）为代表的美国地质学者。

丁文江与在华外国地质学者均保持密切互动，形成地质学研究的北京学派。曾任瑞典地质调查所长的安特生，1914年受聘来华担任农商部矿政顾问，丁文江与之合作进行了数次野外考察。而美国哥伦比亚大学地质系教授、古生物学及地层学权威葛利普正是由丁文江聘请来华工作的。丁文江与他们的交往始于中国，持续终生，是他海外交游网络的重要构成。丁文江与巴尔博的交往可为此类的代表。

巴尔博（George Brown Barbour, 1890-1977），英国地质学者，曾任燕京大学地学系教授和美国辛辛那提大学教授。巴尔博生长于苏格兰，而丁文江曾在苏格兰攻读四年，因此他与巴尔博有一种天然的亲近。1921年，在燕京大学执教的巴尔博就收到丁文江的来函，邀请他为地质调查专刊写一篇关于济南地质调查的文章。[1]而巴尔博对丁文江评价甚高，时常与丁氏会餐长谈。巴尔博的会客录中也数次出现丁文江的身影。例如1923年5月，丁文江携夫人史久元拜访巴尔博夫妇。[2]

1932年巴尔博离开中国之后，两人仍保持密切联系。1933年丁文江做苏俄之旅，在华沙致信巴尔博描绘其此行的所见所闻。[3]1934年10月，巴尔博向丁文江请教云南的地质问题。丁文江详细作答并邮寄他在《独立评论》上发表的两篇相关论文。[4]1936年丁文江不幸逝世，巴尔博在英国《地质学会会刊》（The Journal of Geology Society）撰写悼文，盛赞丁文江的一生。[5]

---

[1] Ting to Barbour, 1921/4/30, George B Barbour, In China when…, Cincinnati: University of Cincinnati Press, 1975, p.26

[2] Barbour's Guest book, George B. Barber Papers, Box 12, Cincinnati University Special Collection

[3] Ting to Barbour, 1933/10/4 George B. Barber Papers, Box 14, Folder1, Cincinnati University Special Collection

[4] Ting to Barbour, 1934/11/1, George B. Barber Papers, Box 14, Folder1, Cincinnati University Special Collection

[5] G. B. Barbour, Dr. V. K. Ting, 1887-1936, The Quarterly Journal of the Geological Society of London, vol. xcii, 1936, pp. xcv-xcix.

2. 丁文江与毕士博

虽然丁文江往来的在华外国学者以地质学者为主，但绝不限于地质学，与地质学相关的在华考古学者以及人类学者，丁文江也有结交，例如毕士博（Carl W. Bishop，1881-1942）考古学家，美国史密斯森学会弗瑞尔美术馆（Freer Gallery of Art, Smithsonian Institute）馆长，1923-1934年间，他主持弗瑞尔美术馆先后与清华大学、中央研究院史语所合作考古发掘。在华期间，毕士博关注中国的早期文明，而丁文江的研究也涉及早期人类，因此两人有共同的学术旨趣，经常探讨学术。如1923年，丁文江给毕士博解读长江流域早期的铸剑术资料。[1] 此后两人又探讨战国时期的炼铁、地名地图等问题。在两人通信中，丁文江曾数次推荐李济及其工作。1925年，毕士博聘请李济参与合作发掘殷墟。[2]

1927年，毕士博因中国局势避乱华盛顿，而丁文江曾在1915年委托史密斯森学会鉴定他云南考察带回的化石。作为回报，斯密斯森学会获得一份复制品。但是原件在邮回中国的途中出现部分丢失，毕士博帮助丁文江重新获取一份复制件。[3] 1928年，政治失势的丁文江赋闲大连，他计划写一本关于中国文明之书。毕士博表示了极大的兴趣，并帮助在美国寻找出版商。[4] 在与中国学术机构合作问题上，毕士博也经常向丁文江请教，如与中研院史语所的安阳发掘合作问题以及山西发掘的问题，丁文江均给予具体建议。两人往来直至丁文江逝世。

二、丁文江与来华访问、考察的外国学者

清末以来，西方地质学者先后对中国进行了多次考察。民国时期，在丁文江等人努力下，北京

---

[1] Ting to Bishop, 1923/11/23, Freer Gallery of Art and Arthur M Sackler Gallery Field Expedition Records, 1914, 1923-1934, Box 10, Folder 9, Smithsonian Institution Archives, Washington, D. C

[2] 李济《对于丁文江所提倡的科学研究几段回忆》，李济《感旧录》，台北：传记文学出版社，1967年，第57-58页。

[3] Ting to Bishop, 1927/5/17, Freer Gallery of Art and Arthur M Sackler Gallery Field Expedition Records, 1914, 1923-1934, Box 10, Folder 9, Smithsonian Institution Archives, Washington, D. C

[4] Bishop to Ting, 1928/5/17, Freer Gallery of Art and Arthur M Sackler Gallery Field Expedition Records, 1914, 1923-1934, Box 10, Folder 10, Smithsonian Institution Archives, Washington, D. C

成为新石器时代文明的研究中心，进而吸引更多学者来华考察与访问。因为共同的学术兴趣或追求，访华学人成为丁文江海外交游的重要组成部分。访华学者大致可分两类：一类是来华考察的外国学者，另一类是来华访问的外国学者。

1. 来华考察的外国学者

1.1 丁文江与安竹斯

安竹斯（Roy Chapman Andrews,1884-1960），美国探险家，曾任美国自然历史博物馆馆长，以20世纪初对中国及蒙古的科考而知名。1916-1917年，安竹斯曾在云南福建考察。1922-1930年间，他率领美国自然历史博物馆科考队先后对蒙古进行五次考察，发现大量恐龙和其他大型哺乳动物化石，而安竹斯的成就是与丁文江分不开的。

1919年，安竹斯前来北京拜会中国地质调查所长丁文江，商讨考察中国及蒙古的地质之事。丁文江非常支持并协助办理考察手续和文件，但希望他不必将中国地质调查所已经考察的北方五省及东北地区纳入科考范围，以避免重复工作。[1] 同年，丁文江利用美国游历之际，在纽约自然历史博物馆回访安竹斯并商谈科考之事，但是不久事起波澜。1920年，安竹斯为了突出自己科考的意义，在《亚细亚杂志》发表文章，指出中国没有国立机构能用新方法研究和展览自己的历史材料，没有能促进指导科学工作的人。丁文江闻知，当即向自然历史博物馆馆长奥斯朋（Henry F. Osborn,1857-1935）提出抗议，要求安竹斯做出没有恶意的声明。[2] 奥斯朋接丁文江函后，与安竹斯分别致电丁文江致歉，且表示到华后诸事当与地质调查所商酌，决不竞争。

在中国地质调查所协助下，1922年安竹斯开始科考，同时将考察所发现的所有化石，复制一份给中国地质调查所，并帮助在北京建立自然历史博物馆。[3] 在北京期间，丁文江主持欢迎安竹斯率领的考察队的会议，并邀请安竹斯在中国地质学会发表讲演。[4] 此后，安竹斯先后对中国及蒙古进行

---

[1] 1920年4月11日丁文江致外交总长颜惠庆，台湾"中央"研究院近代史所档案馆藏，馆藏号：03-03-043-02-49，转引：宋广波《丁文江年谱》，哈尔滨：黑龙江教育出版社2009年，第141页。

[2] Ting to Osborn, 1920/12/9, Paper of Ales Hrdlicka, Box 63, Correspondence, Ting, V. K, National Anthropological Archives, Smithsonian Institution, Washington, D. C

[3] Ting to Andrews, 1923/1/6, Central Asiatic Expeditions, 1921-1930, Box 5, Folder 18, American Museum of Natural History, Special Collection, New York

[4] 《顺天时报》1922年10月2日。

了五次考察。丁文江将安竹斯的考察列为近代美国三次重要中国地质考察之一，而安竹斯也不遗余力地为在北京建立自然历史博物馆而奔走。1921年，他趁小洛克菲勒访问北京之际将丁文江介绍给他，寻求资助。[1]而美国自然历史博物馆长奥斯朋也于1923年前来北京拜会丁文江，他甚至请求美国退还庚款在北京创建一座自然历史博物馆。[2]

1.2 丁文江与维里士

维里士（Bailey Willis, 1857-1949）美国地质学家，斯坦福大学教授。1903年9月至1904年6月，在卡内基研究所支持下，维里士一行曾对中国进行地质考察。回美之后出版三卷本《中国的调查研究》（Research in China）。这部著作汇集了中国考察的地质地理资料，对震旦系的划分以及中国地质构造的研究都有重要价值。

1913年为了培养中国的地质人才，丁文江等创办地质研究班招收学生。1916年第一批学生毕业，丁文江决定选派部分优秀学生出国深造，并为之提供两年经费。此时，适逢维里士的朋友宾福士（Harry Foster Bain, 1872-1948，后为美国矿务局局长）访问上海。丁文江在他引荐下结交维里士，并致函推荐留学生。[3]维里士表示非常希望为中美两国的教育与科学奉献微薄之力，他所在的斯坦福大学愿意接受一名学生，学习地形学。[4]1917年，谢家荣进入斯坦福大学地质学学习，1948年当选中央研究院第一届院士。1926年维里士再次访问中国，时任淞沪商埠督办的丁文江在上海予以款待。[5]

此外，丁文江与芝加哥菲尔德自然历史博物馆（Field Museum）东方部主任劳费尔也有往来。劳费尔（Berthold Laufer, 1874-1934），美国人类学家，东方语言学家，精通汉、日、藏等语，从1901至1923年间多次在中国考察。1924年丁文江的一位朋友在《说苑·善说篇》中发现一首越女歌曲。此曲对于研究长江流域古代文化的性质与起源有着独特的语言学价值，丁文江将此曲以及英文翻译邮寄给劳费尔，希望劳费尔利用自己的语言知识，帮助解读歌曲。[6]

---

[1] Ting to G. R. Vincent, 1921 undated, CMB RF. RG4.1 Box 85, Folder 1982, Rockefeller Archive Center, New York

[2] Osborn to Sze, President Coolidge, Secretary Hughes, Aug. 11, Nov. 24, 1924; RSG, 17/460-467, 50/2098 转引：杨翠华《中基会对科学的赞助》，台湾"中央"研究院近代史所专刊，1991年，第10页。

[3] Ding to Willis, September 17, 1917, Box 8, Folder 62, Papers of Willis Bailey, Special Collection, Huntington Library, California

[4] Willis to Ding, October 19, 1917, Box 8, Folder 62, Papers of Willis Bailey, Special Collection, Huntington Library, California

[5] 1926年12月9日翁文灏致丁文江函，台湾"中央"研究院史语所丁文江档26-39，转引：宋广波《丁文江年谱》，哈尔滨：黑龙江教育出版社2009年，第303页。

[6] Ting to Laufer, 1924/1/20, Paper of Berthold Laufer, Series I: Correspondence, Box 5, Field Museum Archives, Chicago.

2. 来华访问的外国学者

2.1 丁文江与赫尔德利奇卡

赫尔德利奇卡（AlešHrdlièka, 1869-1943），美国人类学家，美国国家博物馆体质人类学部主任，他曾提出印第安人源自亚洲说。赫尔德利奇卡与北京协和医院解剖系的步达生（Davidson Black, 1884-1934）相熟。1920年，他应步达生之邀到访中国。在北京访问期间，赫尔德利奇卡赠给中国地质调查所图书馆美国民族学局的通讯，并发表演讲。丁文江感谢赫尔到访，希望地质调查所与美国国家博物馆体质人类学部建立交流机制，同时回赠中国地质调查所的出版物。[1]

2.2 丁文江与罗素

除地质学学者之外，丁文江结交的学者还有罗素。罗素（Bertrand A. W. Russell, 1872-1970），英国著名哲学家、数学家。罗素于1920年10月至1921年7月来华讲学十个月，是为民国学界的一件盛事。罗素在华期间，留英七年的丁文江作为翻译和总招待随侍左右，深受罗氏思想影响。罗素认为中国问题的根本解决方法是教育，他另一个著名观点是中国的前途在于少数精英。这是后来对丁文江影响至深"少数人的责任"政治思想的来源。[2]

在中国期间，罗素深奥超前的思想并未如预想地引起共鸣，以致《北京导报》（Peking Leader）发表社论声称罗素思想不为中国青年欢迎，未能产生深远影响。[3] 服膺罗素哲学的丁文江挺身而出为罗素辩护，表示正是罗素使中国人第一次认识到哲学应该是对所有科学进行综合的结果，社会改造必须以丰富的知识和深思熟虑为前提，罗素在哲学和社会科学方面必将在中国造成深远影响，因此丁文江要求撤回社论。[4]

1921年罗素回国之后，丁文江向他邮寄在中国演讲的纪念册，以示并未忘记罗素的访问，丁

---

[1] Ting to Hrdlička, 1920/10/26, Paper of AlešHrdlička, Box 63, Correspondence, Ting V. K, National Anthropological Archives, Smithsonian Institution, Washington D. C

[2] 罗素《中国到自由之路》，见：沈益洪编《罗素谈中国》，杭州：浙江文艺出版社2001年，第323-326页。

[3] 朱学勤《让人为难的罗素》，《读书》1996年10月第10期。

[4] Ting to Peking Leader Editor, August 5th, 1921, RA1, Class: 710, Document#: 048264, Box#: 5.08, The Bertrand Russell Archives, McMaster Library, UK

文江还向罗素提及他出任北票煤矿总经理一事。[1]其后，罗素还曾向丁文江询问中国人口的增长情况，丁文江予以解答。[2]1924年，英国拟成立中英庚款委员会退还部分庚子赔款给中国。作为筹办委员的罗素推荐丁文江和胡适出任中方委员。两人之后虽无太多交集，正如丁文江一生视罗素为师长，罗素也十分欣赏丁文江并高度珍惜两人之间的友谊。[3]

三、丁文江与外国驻华机构代表

1. 丁文江与莫理循

莫理循（George Ernest Morrison, 1862-1920），出身澳大利亚的苏格兰人，探险家，记者，曾任英国《泰晤士报》驻北京记者近二十年。民国之后出任袁世凯和北洋政府的政治顾问，在清末民初的北京颇有名气，以至于北京有一条以他命名的大街。

丁文江在苏格兰留学期间就常阅读莫理循在《泰晤士报》的报道，获取有关中国的信息。1910年底，丁文江打算毕业回国并沿途做地质考察，格利高里将其介绍给英国《泰晤士报》常驻中国记者莫理循寻求帮助。[4]格利高里（John W. Gregory, 1864-1932）英国地质学家，1904-1929年担任格拉斯哥大学地质系主任。

1911年，丁文江计划毕业回国沿途作地质考察，他拟定了两条路线：一条是从缅甸入云南，至成都再顺江而下到汉口；另一条是从伦敦至俄国，经过塔什干至新疆，然后穿越甘肃、陕西到北京。丁文江向莫理循询问沿途花费、签证、所需设备以及地图等事宜。[5]莫理循在中国游历广泛，而

---

[1] Ting to Russell, January 11, 1922, RA1, Class: 710, Document#: 048265, Box#: 5.08, The Bertrand Russell Archives, McMaster Library, UK

[2] Ting to Russell, July 24, 1922, RA3, Class: 1027, Document#: 250259, Box#: 7.28, The Bertrand Russell Archives, McMaster Library, UK

[3] Russell to Chen, November 2, 1955, RA1, Class:410, Document#:000000, Box#:1.29, The Bertrand Russell Archives, McMaster Library, UK

[4] Gregory to Morrison, 1910/12/14, George Ernest Morrison Papers, 1850-1932, Vol. 56, p.433, Special Collection, State Library of New South Wales, Sydney, Australia

[5] Ting to Morrison, 1910/12/14, George Ernest Morrison Papers, 1850-1932, Vol. 56, pp.433-438, Special Collection, State Library of New South Wales, Sydney, Australia

且多次往返中英两国之间，轻车熟路。他对两条路线都详细提供了建议，并希望在北京见到丁文江。[1]

1913年，丁文江在北京初入职场，供职农工商部。功成名就的莫理循为丁文江提供许多帮助。例如莫理循为丁文江1914年的云南考察提供建议以及英国出版的大比例尺地图。[2]莫理循在北京有座私人图书馆，系统收藏有关中国的书籍。他无偿向丁文江开放。1915年丁文江由于编写中国矿业史，介绍自己的助理前往查阅资料。[3]1917年，莫理循又借给丁文江两本有关北京的俄国书籍。[4]作为回报，丁文江为莫理循获得了斯文·赫定的书籍。[5]1917年，由于维持一座价值三万五千英镑的图书馆是一个很大的负担和风险，莫理循最终将图书馆卖给日本的岩崎久弥男爵。丁文江闻知后非常遗憾，但尊重莫理循的决定。[6]1920年莫理循代表中国参加巴黎和会期间病逝。两人相识十年，莫理循是丁文江早期重要的支持者。[7]

2. 对华基金会

丁文江来往的另一类驻华机构是外国基金会。民国时期，在华的重要基金会有洛克菲勒基金会、中华文化教育基金会以及中英庚款委员会等。丁文江与这些外国基金会联系密切，为中国地质研究获得重要的国际资助。

洛克菲勒基金会（Rockefeller Foundation）是美国石油巨头洛克菲勒家族1913年在纽约成立的著名基金会。民国时期，洛氏基金会对中国的医药卫生和文化教育进行了广泛资助。1921年，洛

---

[1] Morrison to Ting, 1911/2/11, George Ernest Morrison Papers, 1850-1932, Vol. 57, pp.243-249, Special Collection, State Library of New South Wales, Sydney, Australia

[2] Ting to Morrison, 1914/1/2, George Ernest Morrison Papers, 1850-1932, Vol. 78, p.13, Special Collection, State Library of New South Wales, Sydney, Australia

[3] Ting to Morrison, 1915/5/3, George Ernest Morrison Papers, 1850-1932, Vol.83, p.301, Special Collection, State Library of New South Wales, Sydney, Australia

[4] Ting to Morrison, 1917/3/3, George Ernest Morrison Papers, 1850-1932, Vol. 91, p.401, Special Collection, State Library of New South Wales, Sydney, Australia

[5] Ting to Morrison, 1916/11/2, George Ernest Morrison Papers, 1850-1932, Vol. 90, p.9, Special Collection, State Library of New South Wales, Sydney, Australia

[6] Ting to Morrison, 1917/8/14, George Ernest Morrison Papers, 1850-1932, Vol.94, pp.101-103, Special Collection, State Library of New South Wales, Sydney, Australia

[7] Ting to Mrs. Morrison, 1920/6/22, George Ernest Morrison Papers, 1850-1932, Vol.113, p.141, Special Collection, State Library of New South Wales, Sydney, Australia

克菲勒基金会董事长小洛克菲勒访问北京，丁文江被介绍给洛克菲勒基金会长文森特，希望寻求在北京建立自然历史博物馆的资助。[1] 丁文江邀请小洛克菲勒一行参观他们选定在紫禁城的馆址，但后因访问日程安排紧凑，并未成行。[2] 此时洛氏基金会在华主要资助医学，自然科学并非其关注重点。不过，洛克菲勒基金会协助中国地质调查所与它资助的学术机构，如美国自然历史博物馆、哥伦比亚大学等，建立出版物定期交换制度。[3] 1929年随着周口店的发掘，洛克菲勒基金最终决定出资赞助中国地质调查所与北京协和医院解剖系共同建立新生代研究室，重点研究"北京人"。

与洛克菲勒基金会相比，丁文江参与更多是中华教育文化基金董事会。中华教育文化基金董事会（The China Foundation for the Promotion of Education and Culture）是美国为退还第二批庚子赔款在1924年设立的基金会。在中基会成立之前，丁文江曾致美方委员函顾临（Roger S. Greene, 1881-1947）等人，认为退款不能只用于改进科学教育，同时应该补助科学研究，因为补助现有机构比创建新机构更易收立竿见影之效。而中国地质调查所兼顾理论与实际的研究，成绩有目共睹，正是应该补助的对象。[4] 1924-1926年，丁文江被选为中基会董事，并兼任秘书，1934至1935年再次当选董事。1930年，中基会资助中国地质调查所成立土壤研究室。1931-1935年，中基会与北京大学合聘丁文江为北大地质系教授。地质学也成为中基会用力最多的地方之一，这与丁文江的努力分不开的。1936年丁文江去世，中基会通过两项决议：一是中基会对其辞世深表哀思，专门函丁夫人唁电；二捐助设立丁文江纪念奖学金。[5]

四、结语

作为民国重要学者，丁文江构建了一张宽广的海外交游网络，主要包括三类人群：一是在华工作的外国学者，二是来华考察和访问的外国学者，三是海外驻华的机构代表。在交游范围上，丁文

---

[1] Ting to G. R. Vincent, 1921 undated, CMB RF. RG4.1 Box 85, Folder 1982, Rockefeller Archive Center, New York

[2] Vincent to Ting, 1921/9/26, CMB RF. RG4.1 Box 85, Folder 1982, Rockefeller Archive Center, New York

[3] Vincent to Ting, 1922/4/20, CMB RF. RG4.1 Box 85, Folder 1982, Rockefeller Archive Center, New York

[4] Ting to Greene, June 30, 1924, RSG50/2097, Roger S. Greene's papers, Box 50, folder 2097, Houghton Library of Harvard University.

[5] 中国第二历史档案馆藏中基会档案，全宗号四八四（2），案卷号2，转引：宋广波《丁文江年谱》，哈尔滨：黑龙江教育出版社2009年，第495页。

江跨越地质、考古学、人类学等，展示一个民国科学家的学术修养和眼界。在时间阶段上，丁文江的前期交游因留学关系以英国学者为主，后期则以美国学者为主。这也反映了一战之后美国在中国地质学界影响逐渐增加。

丁文江以中国为平台结识在华或来华的学者与机构，从而进行推荐学生，交流学术，获取基金。科学主义是丁文江维系交游的重要纽带。在交往过程中，一生服膺科学主义的丁文江充分体现了科学无国界的原则，与国际学者共享中国的地质研究，互惠互利。这是中国地质学研究获取世界声誉的一个重要途径和模式。但是丁文江也保留了一定的民族主义，例如在美国自然历史博物馆科考中要求充分尊重中国地质调查所的地位和贡献。总之，丁文江庞大的海外交游网络不仅为研究丁氏本人，而且为解读民国地质学乃至民国学术提供了一种珍贵的域外视角。

编著说明

丁文江为民国著名学者，留学英伦，打造具有国际声誉的中国地质调查所，有民国干才之称。丁氏书信通讯遍及欧美，藏诸名山。在本编所集书信之中，丁文江的通讯对象有罗素、莫理循、毕士博、安竹斯、巴尔博等，涉及机构有美国史密斯森研究所、美国自然历史博物馆、美国洛克菲勒基金会等，通讯内容则涵盖中国地质研究、中国考古、美国亚洲科考等。

具体而言，本编书信主题有三个方面：一是 1910-1920 年丁文江与《泰晤士报》驻北京记者莫理循的交往，涉及地质考察、莫理循图书利用等，是研究民国初期丁文江以及中国地质学的重要资料；二是 20 世纪 20 年代，丁文江与美国自然历史博物馆奥斯朋和安竹斯等人的通信，是研究美国第三次亚洲科考的重要史料；三是丁文江与美国史密斯研究所毕士博长达十年有关中国文明与考古的通信，是研究丁文江和中国考古的重要史料。此外，还有丁文江与罗素的通讯，以及与巴尔博关于苏联之行的通讯，则为研究丁氏政治思想的第一手资料。

本编所收丁文江书信分别藏于美国 Smithsonian Institute 档案部、美国自然历史博物馆档案部、美国洛克菲勒档案中心、美国芝加哥 Field 博物馆档案部、美国 Huntington 图书馆特藏部、美国哈佛大学 Houghton 图书馆、美国辛辛那提大学档案馆、英国 McMaster 图书馆特藏部、英国格拉斯哥大学档案馆、澳大利亚南威尔士大学图书馆特藏部。

本编书信多为首次面世，是研究中国地学史和中外学术交流史的珍贵资料，在一定程度上也反映了民国地质学的国际脉络。由于编者财力和眼界有限，此次所集书信主要限于收藏于美国的，部分涉及收藏于英国和澳大利亚的。然而即使在美国，也未敢轻言倾其所有。例如美国哥伦比亚大学孟禄（Paul Monroe）档案不对研究者开放，只能付费由档案馆员查询，难免疏漏。有鉴于此，本编权且抛砖引玉，以待来者。

　　本编所集丁文江书信大多数为未出版的英文书信，编后附有数封已经出版的丁氏书信。本编的书信以时间为顺序编排，涵盖1910年至1955年。丁文江书信既有丁氏的亲笔书信，也包括丁氏友朋的来函。本编书信所涉及的主要通信人，在开篇之前均有简介。每封书信均以影印形式出版，之后附有文字转录。文字转录部分，遇有个别漫灭难辨的文字，在文中均有以（？）标出，以示存疑。

丁文江通讯人物简介
（以通讯时间顺序）

格利高里（John W. Gregory, 1864-1932），英国地质学家，1904-1929年间担任格拉斯哥大学地质系主任，对澳大利亚和东非地质造诣很深的格利高里，对滇藏地区的地质也非常有兴趣。格利高里是丁文江的老师，1922年格利高里自缅甸入云南做地质考察，得到丁文江的多方帮助。

莫理循（George Ernest Morrison, 1862-1920），出身澳大利亚的苏格兰人，1887年毕业于爱丁堡大学。莫理循曾任英国《泰晤士报》驻北京记者近二十年。民国之后出任袁世凯和北洋政府的政治顾问，在清末民初的北京政坛颇有名气，以至北京王府井大街改名为莫理循大街。

维里士（Bailey Willis, 1857-1949），美国地质学家，斯坦福大学教授。1903年9月至1904年6月，在卡内基研究所支持下，维里士一行曾对中国进行地质考察，回美之后出版三卷本《中国的调查研究》(Research in China)。

赫尔德利奇卡（AlešHrdlièka, 1869-1943），美国人类学家，美国国家博物馆体质人类学部主任，他曾提出印第安人源自亚洲说。1920年，曾应北京协和医院解剖系步达生（Davidson Black, 1884-1934）之邀访问中国。

奥斯朋（Henry F. Osborn, 1857-1935），美国地质学家，古生物学家，曾担任美国自然历史博物馆馆长长达二十五年。1923年9月受邀访华，在燕京大学演讲。

安竹斯（Roy Chapman Andrews, 1884-1960），美国著名探险家，曾任美国自然历史博物馆馆长，以20世纪初对中国及蒙古的科考而知名。1922-1930年间，他率领美国自然历史博物馆科考队先后对蒙古进行五次考察，发现大量恐龙和其他大型哺乳动物化石。

文森特（George E. Vincent, 1864-1941），教育家，社会学家，美国芝加哥大学教授，美国洛克菲勒基金会主席。

罗素（Bertrand A. W. Russell, 1872-1970），英国著名哲学家，数学家，1920年10月至1921年7月来华讲学十个月，丁文江作为翻译和总招待随侍左右，深受罗氏思想影响。

毕士博（C. W. Bishop, 1881-1942），美国东亚考古学家，美国史密森学会弗瑞尔美术馆（Freer Gallery of Art, Smithsonian Institute）馆长，1923-1934年间，他主持弗瑞尔美术馆先后与清华大学、中央研究院史语所合作考古发掘。

劳费尔（Berthold Laufer, 1874-1934），美国人类学家，著名东方语言学家，芝加哥菲尔德自然历史博物馆（Field Museum）东方部主任，从1901-1923年间多次在中国考察。

顾临（Roger S. Greene, 1881-1947），美国外交官，东亚事务专家，曾任美国驻汉口总领事，长期担任洛克菲勒基金驻华代表，并代理北京协和医院校长。

格兰杰（Walter Willis Granger, 1872-1941），美国脊椎古生物专家，任职于美国自然历史博物馆，1922至1928年间，全程参与安竹斯主持的美国自然历史博物馆蒙古戈壁考察。

巴尔博（George Brown Barbour, 1890-1977），英国地质学者，曾任燕京大学地学系教授和美国辛辛那提大学教授，对华北地文循环模型以及黄土起源研究都有精湛研究。

书信影印件及文本

1910 年

University of Glasgow

14th December, 1910.

Dear Dr Morrison,

Allow me to introduce to you a distinguished student of this University - Mr V. K. Ting, who is returning to China in the summer and is anxious to travel over land to do some geological work; and he would be very glad for some advice from you as to the route.

For any help you can give him I shall be much obliged.

Yours sincerely,

J C Gregory

Geological Department

University of Glasgow

14th December, 1910.

Dear Dr. Morrison,

Allow me to introduce to you a distinguished student of this University-Mr. V. K. Ting, who is returning to China in the summer and is anxious to travel over land to do some geological work; and he would be very glad for some advice from you as to the route.

For any help you can give him I shall be much obliged.

Yours sincerely,

J.W. Gregory

℅ McIlraith
5, Welton Mansions
Kelvinside N.
Glasgow
14 Dec. '10

Dear Dr Morison

Prof. J. W. Gregory under whom I have been privileged to study geology, is kind enough to give me a letter of introduction to you which I enclose herewith.

I hope to finish up my study next April and to leave for China immediately. After some years of absence in Europe I am naturally eager to see my own country, and it occurs to me that it would be a very interesting journey to get to Peking via Kashgar. My intension is to travel to Kashgar from Russia and thence to Peking by traversing Kansu, Shensi and Shansi. My primary object is merely to wander through this historical region, but without any scientific pretension. I shall endeavour to make some geological observations on the country traversed — even if it merely serves to modify Richthofen's remarks about the Chinese literati, "Zu Fuss zu gehen ist in seinen Augen erniedrigend, und die Beschäftigung des Geologen ein directes Aufgeben aller Menschenwürde."

I shall be very glad if you will give me your advice on the following points:—

① The approximate cost of the whole journey from London, and the time needed under ordinary

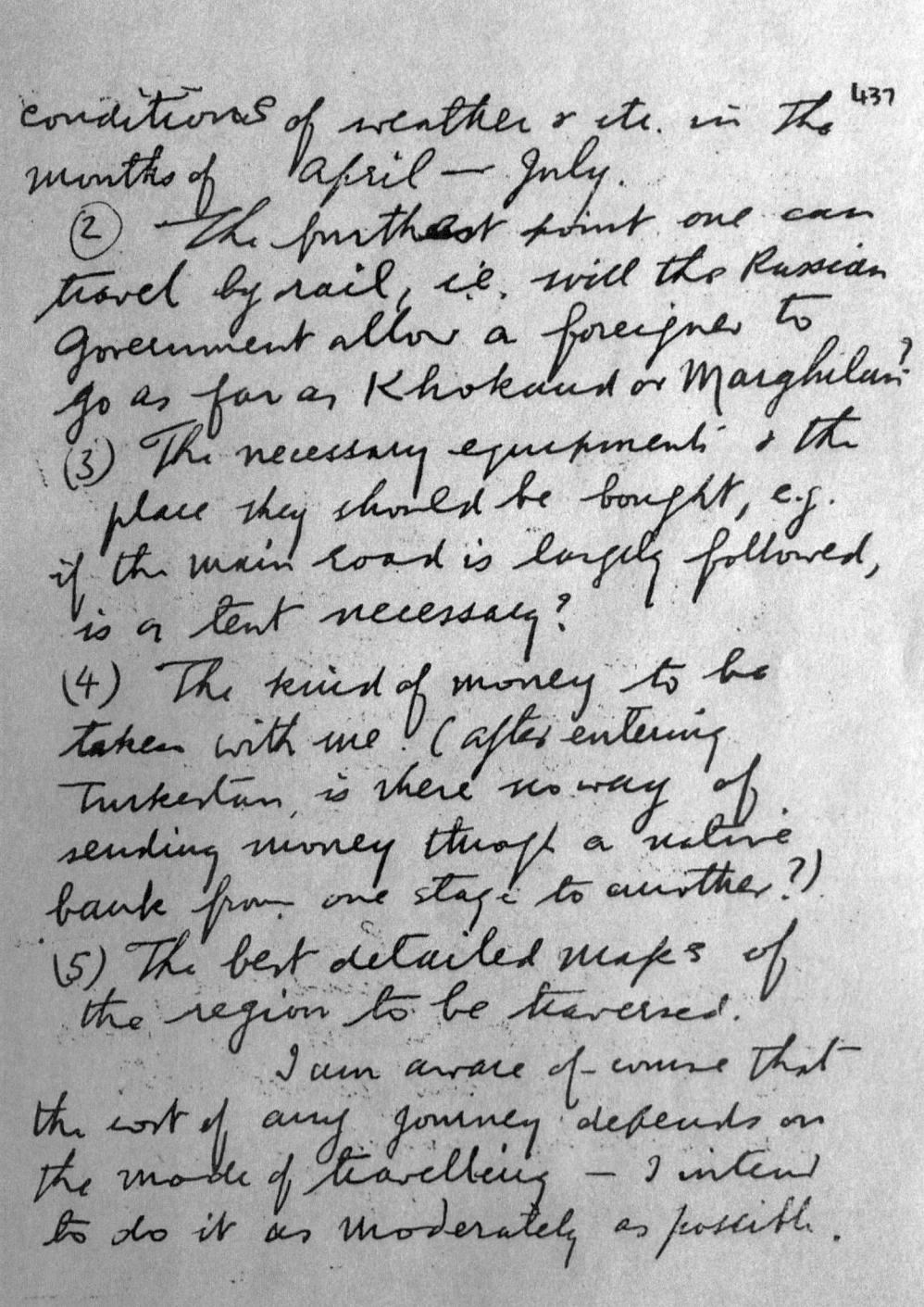

conditions of weather & etc. in the months of April — July.

(2) The furthest point one can travel by rail, i.e., will the Russian Government allow a foreigner to go as far as Khokand or Marghilan?

(3) The necessary equipments & the place they should be bought, e.g. if the main road is largely followed, is a tent necessary?

(4) The kind of money to be taken with me. (After entering Turkestan, is there no way of sending money through a native bank from one stage to another?)

(5) The best detailed maps of the region to be traversed.

I am aware of course that the cost of any journey depends on the mode of travelling — I intend to do it as moderately as possible.

Happily, geological work does not require many expensive and heavy instruments, and extra carriage will only be required for specimens — this will not be so very much if the collection is carefully chosen.

In case the proposed journey turns out to be too much for the pocket of a student, I will go to the S.W. instead, i.e., to get to Chengtufu via Yünnan and then follow the River Yangtse to Hankow. So I shall also be very glad to have your advice on similar things concerning that journey. News from Peking has been rather scarce lately, and all of us are hoping that you will go back soon to fill the "Times" with more inspiring letters.

Apologising for the trouble I am giving you, yours sincerely

V. K. Ting

To Mr. Smith
5 Wilton Mansions
Kelvinside N.
Glasgow
14 Dec. 10

Dear Dr. Morrison,

Prof. J. W. Gregory under whom I have been privileged to study geology is kind enough to give me a letter of introduction to you which I enclosed herewith.

I hope to finish up my study next April and to leave for China immediately after some years of absence in Europe I am actually eager to see my own country and it occurs to me that it would be a very interesting journey to get to Peking via Kashgar, my interest is to travel to Kashgar from Russia and thence to Peking by travelling Kansu, Shensi and Shansi, my previous object is merely to wander through the historical region, but without any scientific exploration, I shall endeavor to make some geological observations in the country traverse—if it merely serves to modify Richthofen's remarks about the Chinese literati, "---"(德语略)

I shall be very glad if you will give me your advice on the following questions:

① The approximate cost of the whole journey from London and the time needed under ordinarily conditions of weather within the month of April to July.

② The furthest point one can travel by rail, will the Russian government allow a foreigner to go as far as Khokaud or Marghilan?

③ The necessary equipment and the place they should be bought, eg. If the main road is largely followed, is a tent necessary?

④ The kind of money to be taken with me, (after entering Turkistan, is there no way of sending money though a native bank from one stay to another?)

⑤ The best detailed maps of the region to be traversed.

I am aware of some that the cost of any journey depends on the mode of travelling. —I intend to do it as modesty as possible. Happily, geological work does not require many expensive and heavy instruments and extra carriage will only be required for specimens. —This will not be so very much if the collection is carefully chosen.

In case the proposed journey turns out to be too much for the pocket of a student, I will go to the S. W instead, to get to Chengtufu via Yunnan and then follow the River Yangtze to Hankow. So I shall also be very glad to have your advice as similar things concerning that journey.

News from Peking has been rather scarce lately and all of us are hoping that you will go back soon to fill the "Times" with more inspiring letters.

Apologizing for the trouble I am giving you.

Yours Sincerely,

V. K. Ting

Artillery Mansions,
Victoria Street, S.W.
30th December 1910.

Dear Mr. Ting,

I have just returned to London and have your letter of the 14th of December.

I will be glad to answer the questions in your letter to the best of my ability.

Professor Gregory has written to me about you, and it has given me much pleasure, admiring as I do the Chinese, to read the Professor's flattering report of the distinguished ability of one of the students from China, a country where I have spent fifteen most interesting years.

With kind regards,

Very sincerely yours,

Artillery Mansions,

Victoria Street, S. W.

30th December 1910.

Dear Mr. Ting,

I have just returned to London and have your letter of the 14th of December.

I will be glad to answer the questions in your letter to the best of my ability.

Professor Gregory had written to me about you, and it has given me much pleasure, admiring as I do the Chinese, to read the Professor's flattering report of the distinguished ability of one of the students from China, a country where I have spent fifteen most interesting years.

With kind regards,

Very sincerely yours,

[G. E. Morrison]

1911 年

C/o Mr Thwaite
5, Wilton Mansions
Kelvinside N.
Glasgow
25, Jan. 1911

Dear Dr Morrison

I hope you received my letter of the 1st of Jan. 1911 written from Redbourne Hotel, London, in which I asked you to give me your advice, sometime this month, on the questions asked in my first letter (Dec. 1910), i.e., the approximate cost of a journey from Kashgar to Peking and the time necessary, the best route to Kashgar (whether it is cheaper to travel by the Caspian sea or via Orenburg), the best detailed maps of the route from Kashgar to Peking, the necessary equipments, and the way in which money may be forwarded.

If you are at the present too busy to give me detailed information that would be useful to me, I shall be grateful if you can tell me which is the better route to Kashgar and what are the best maps.

Apologising for the trouble I am giving you,

Yours faithfully,

V. K. Ting

To Mr. Smith

5 Wilton Mansions

Kelvinside N.

Glasgow

25, Jan, 1911

Dear Mr. Morrison,

I hope you received my letter of the 1st of Jan, 1911 written from Redhorse (?) Hotel, London, in which I asked you to give me your advice, sometimes this month, on the questions asked in my first letter (December, 1910), the approximate cost of a journey from Kashgar to Peking and the time necessary, the route to Kashgar, the best detailed maps of the route from Kashgar to Peking, the necessary equipment and the way in which money may be forwarded.

If you are at the present too busy to give me detailed information that would be useful to me, I shall be grateful if you can tell me which is better route to Kashgar and what are the best maps.

Apologizing for the trouble I am giving to you,

Yours faithfully

V. K. Ting

Artillery Mansions,
Victoria Street,
London, S.W.
11th February 1911.

Dear Mr. Ting,

I am leaving for China next Tuesday, passing through the plague area, and I have had to get ready more quickly than I had expected.

In your letter of the 14th of December you put various questions to me which I will now answer.

It is difficult to say what would be the cost of a journey from London to Peking by the route you suggest taking. My journey, travelling in good style with three servants and two horses from the Chinese Railway to the Russian Railway and thence by railway to London via St. Petersburg, cost me in all £400. You could, by going more modestly, do the whole journey for, I think, considerably less than one half of this. Allowing a margin for detention through sickness, I should say you could cover the six months' journey comfortably for £150.

You could go by railway all the way to Andijan. The exact cost of this railway journey from London by the two routes via Moscow and Samara and by the Transcaspian can be ascertained for you by Thomas Cook & Son's agent in Glasgow. The further you travel in Russia, the cheaper relatively is the

2.

cost.   It is very much cheaper to book from one Russian frontier to the other than to book at different sections on this route.

You will require your Chinese passport to be visé by the Russian Embassy in London. The necessary visé can be obtained for you by Cooks.

No tent is necessary. You travel by railway as light as possible, for the transport of baggage by railway is very expensive.

If you can speak Kuanhua you will have no difficulty. You will find Chinese in Andijan: you will find Chinese further in Osh, and in Osh you will have no difficulty in arranging for your transport across to Kashgar. The only difficulty in the journey is the swelling of the rivers by rain, but this difficulty is not serious until after the 30th of June.

Your money affairs you would arrange through the Russo-Chinese Bank by a letter of credit. The Bank has agents in Kashgar, and of course in all important towns such as Tashkut, Khokand and Andijan. They have an office in London, and if you wrote to them they would give you full instructions. In Kashgar you would have no difficulty in buying a Chinese letter of credit that would take you all the way through to Peking. The best way to manage about money when you get to Kashgar is to arrange with the Imperial Chinese Post Office to

3.

cash your letter of credit at the different chief post offices. You would require enough then to take you from Kashgar to Urumchi, the capital of the Hsin Chiang.

The best detailed maps of the region to be traversed are Russian maps, but they are in Russian, they are very expensive, and I think you would have to get them at St. Petersburg. Elaborate geological maps have been made of all Russian Turkistan and part of Chinese Turkistan. I am sorry I cannot give you the names. My collection is in Peking, and I have not the names here. A useful map which gives you a general idea of the whole country is the China Inland Mission Atlas which you buy at Stanford's, Long Acre, London, or any good bookseller in Glasgow would get if for you. There are excellent French and German maps of Kansu Province, Shensi, and Shansi. As regards maps, I would advise you to communicate with Sifton Praed & Co., 67 St. James Street, London S.W.

All equipment for your journey other than scientific you can very well obtain in Kashgar.

To get to Chengtufu from Yunnan your best way would be to go by the French Mail Steamer to Saigan, thence by another French steamer to Haiphong, and from Haiphong you can reach in one day Laokai on the Yunnan frontier. I should think that it would cost you second class £60 to land you in Laokai from London. From there you can reach Wunnan by the railway in two days, but I cannot say how long it takes to get to Chengtufu, as I have not travelled this route. A detailed account of the

4.

journey has, however, been written by Mr. Archibald Little, called "Between Two Capitals."

I ought to say that my journey from Peking to London took just under six months.

Please forgive me for the delay in writing to you. I gathered from your letter that you were not leaving this country until April. I hope when you do come to Peking you will come and see me and tell me of your journey, which I am sure will be most interesting and instructive.

Very sincerely yours,

P.S. Of course travelling as a passenger in China and not in your own cart you would greatly economise. In that case £100 would cover I believe all expenses from London to Peking via Kashgar the New Dominion and Kansu.

Artillery Mansions,

Victoria Street,

London, S.W.

11th February 1911.

Dear Mr. Ting,

I am leaving for China next Tuesday, passing through the plague area, and I have had to get ready more quickly than I had expected.

In your letter of the 14th of December you put various questions to me which I will now answer.

It is difficult to say what would be the cost of a journey from London to Peking by the route you suggest taking. My journey, traveling in good style with three servants and two horses from the Chinese Railway to the Russian Railway and thence by railway to London via St. Petersburg, cost me in all 400 pounds. You could, by going more modestly, do the whole journey for, I think, considerably less than one half of this. Allowing a margin for detention through sickness, I should say you could cover the six months' journey comfortably for 150 pounds.

You could go by railway all the way to Andijan. The exact cost of this railway journey from London by the two routes via Moscow and Samara and by the Transcaspian can be ascertained for you by Thomas Cook & Son's agent in Glasgow. The further you travel in Russia, the cheaper relatively is the cost. It is very much cheaper to book from one Russian frontier to the other than to book at different sections on this route.

You will require your Chinese passports to the Visa by the Russian Embassy in London. The necessary visa can be obtained for you by Cooks.

No tent is necessary. You travel by railway as light as possible, for the transport of baggage by railway is very expensive.

If you can speak Kuanhua you will have no difficulty. You will find Chinese in Andijan: you will find Chinese further in Osh, and in Osh you will have no difficulty in arranging for your transport across to Kashgar. The only difficulty in the journey is the swelling of the rivers by rain, but this difficulty is not serious until after the 30th of June.

Your money affairs you would arrange through the Russo-Chinese Bank by a letter of credit. The Bank has agents in Kashgar, and of course in all important towns such as Tashkut, Khokand and Andijan. They have an office in London, and if you wrote to them they would give you full instructions. In Kashgar you would have no difficulty in buying a Chinese letter of credit that would take you all the way through to Peking. The best way to manage about money when you get to Kashgar is to arrange with the Imperial Chinese Post Office to cash your letter of credit at the different chief post offices. You would require enough then to take you from Kashgar to Urumchi, the capital of the Hsin Chiang.

The best detailed maps of the region to be traversed are Russian maps, but they are in Russian, they are very expensive, and I think you would have to get them at St. Petersburg. Elaborate geological maps have been made of all Russian Turkistan and part of Chinese Turkistan. I am sorry I cannot give you the names. My collection is in Peking, and I have not the name here. A useful map which gives you a general idea of the whole country is the China Inland Mission Atlas which you buy at Stanford's, Long Acre, London, or any good bookseller in Glasgow would get if for you. There are excellent French and German maps of Kansu Province, Shensi, and Shansi. As regards maps, I would advise you to communicate with Sifton Praed & Co., 67 St. James Streets, London S. W.

All equipment for your journey other than scientific you can very well obtain in Kashgar.

To get to Chentufu from Yunnan your best way would be to go by the French Mail Steamer to Saigan, thence by another French steamer to Haiphong, and from Haiphong you can reach in one day Laokai on the Yunnan frontier. I should think that it would cost you second class 50 pounds to land you in Laokai from London. From there you can reach Yunnan by the railway in two days, but I cannot say how long it takes to get to Chengtufu, as I have not traveled this route. A detailed account of the journey has, however, been written by Mr. Archibald Little, called "Between Two Capitals."

I ought to say that my journey from Peking to London took just under six months.

Please forgive me for the delay in writing to you. I gathered from your letter that you were not leaving this country until April. I hope when you do come to Peking you will come and see me and tell me of your journey, which I am sure will be most interesting and instructive.

                Very sincerely yours,
                [G. E. Morrison]

P.S. Of course traveling as a passenger in China and not in your own cart you would greatly economize. In that case £100 would cover I believe all expenses from London to Peking via Kashgar the New Dominion and Kansu.

5, Wilton Mansions
Glasgow
13. Feb. '11

Dear Dr Morrison

Let me thank you heartily for your long and detailed letter which must have occupied much of your valuable time. I am very glad to hear that you are leaving for China — at last we may hope to get some trustworthy report of the plague. I only wish I did not give up medicine — I was a medical student for a year — for a medical man may indeed do some real service to his country at this disastrous juncture.

I have not yet decided whether I should go to the South or go through Turkestan. I cannot leave Glasgow till the end of April and if possible, I should like to be in Peking by August as that is the time when the colleges are opened after the vacation & very few teaching posts will be open after it. Again, if I fail to obtain a suitable post in our colleges, I intend to enter the civil service for which the examination is held in September. The S.W. is very interesting geologically, but far less attractive from the point of view of historical associations, but from Yunnan one can make one's own arrangement about the time, as several routes are available. Besides, the journey is less expensive and more money may be spent on scientific instruments.

In any case I shall not fail to come to thank you when I get to Peking in the autumn.

Yours gratefully

V. K. Ting

5, Wilton Mansions

Glasgow

13 Feb, 11

Dear Dr. Morrison,

Let me thank you heartily for your long and detailed letter which must have occupied much of your valuable time. I am very glad to hear that you are leaving for China—at last we may hope to get some trustworthy report of the plague. I only wish I did not give up medicine—I was a medical student for a year—for a medical man may do some real service to his country at this disastrous conjuncture.

I have not yet decided whether I should go to the south or go through Turkestan. I cannot leave Glasgow till the end of April and if possible, I should like to be in Peking by August as that is the time when the colleges are opened after the vacation and very few teaching post will be open after it. Again, if I failed to obtain a suitable post in a college, I intend to enter the civil service for which the examination is held in September. The S. W. is very interesting geologically, far from attractive from the point of view of historical association, but from Yunnan, one can make one's own arrangement about the time, as several reports are available. Besides, the journey is too expensive and more money may be spent on scientific instruments.

In any case I shall not fail to come to thank you when I get to Peking in the Autumn.

Yours faithfully

V. K. Ting

1913 年

THE REPUBLIC OF CHINA

IN YOUR REPLY REFER TO FILE

MINISTRY OF INDUSTRY & COMMERCE

PEKING CHINA

No.

17 May 1913.

Dear Dr. Morrison;--

  Mr. Chang, Mr. Cheng (director-general of the commercial department of our ministry) and myself are going to have some friends to dinner in the Chung-hua restaurant on Tuesday at 7. The minister and the vice-minister of our ministry ~~will~~ and several of our foreign friends will be present. We shall be very glad if you and Mr. Collins will give us the pleasure of your company that night. In the Chinese invitation note you will find the exact address of the restaurant.

  Kindly send the note to Mr. Collins for us, for I can not make out the corresponding Chinese characters from the address on his card.

  Hoping that no ohter engagement will prevent you from coming on Tuesday,

    Yours faithfully,

      V. K. Ting

THE REPUBLIC OF CHINA

MINISTRY OF INDUSTRY & COMMERCE

PEKING CHINA

17 May, 1913.

Dear Dr. Morrison:

Mr. Chang, Mr. Cheng (director-general of the commercial department of our ministry) and myself are going to have some friends to dinner in the Chung-hua restaurant on Tuesday at 7. The minister and the vice-minister of our minister and several of our foreign friends will be present. We shall be very glad if you and Mr. Collins will give us the pleasure of your company that night. In the Chinese invitation note you will find the exact address of the restaurant.

Kindly send the note to Mr. Collins for us, for I cannot make out the corresponding Chinese characters from the address on his card.

Hoping that no other engagement will prevent you from coming on Tuesday,

Yours faithfully,

V. K. Ting

THE REPUBLIC OF CHINA

IN REPLY REFER TO FILE   MINISTRY OF INDUSTRY & COMMERCE

No._____   PEKING CHINA

8 Oct. 1913.

Dear Dr. Morrison:---

    I am afraid I am going to do some thing which may not be altogether welcome----for I am going to ask you a favour but my excuse is that I do it on public ground. Here is my case.

    There has always been a geological section in the Board of Commerce ever since the provisional government was established, but they had neither books nor collections. When I came here last February I put forward a scheme for organising a geological survey with a school attached to it. After some persuasion it was approved by the ministry and its expenditure included in the budget for 1914 (beginning on the first of July 1913). In due course this item was sanctioned by the Board of Finance and I was told to carry my scheme into effect. In my original scheme I required $100,000 about half of which was the initial cost for instruments etc., and the other half for the upkeeping of the school, travelling expense, publication of maps and reports, and the salary of 2 European experts. Considering the magnitude and the importance of the work the sum was certainly not too large, for even Japan, with an area 36 times smaller than that of China, after 30 years of geological work, still spend annually $100,000 for the same purpose. Knowing however the sad condition of the treasury, I was very cautious and tried in every way to save money. The Peking University had a geological section but with only 2 students. I succeeded in persuading the authority to hand over to me all their instruments, and books and collections which costed them more than $30,000. They also agrreed to house us, so

THE REPUBLIC OF CHINA

IN YOUR REPLY REFER TO FILE   MINISTRY OF INDUSTRY & COMMERCE

PEKING CHINA

No. _____

so the initial expense was reduced to a minimum. Instead of two European geologists I engaged only one, namely Dr. F. Solger, a distinguished geologist, who accepted my offer of $400 instead of $600 per month (as he used to get) in the hope of having the honour of doing for China, what Dr. Naumann did for Japan. I also held entrance examination for the geological svchool and engaged several teachers. All this was done before July and without touching any public money.

        Just at that time the budget was introduced into the parliament which threw it out on some technical pretext. Then the second revolution came and the Board of Finance issued a circular stating that any institution that had not already been organised before July would not be supplied with money. As my work really started long before that date, I thought I would get the money, but realising the finantial stress I cut down the expense to about one half the original sum ie. about $30,000 a year with practicall no initial cost. But the Board of Finance refused to pay it, contending that my work did not begin before July. In the mean time Dr. Solger demanded his passage money and the students asked the date of the opening of the school and I was in a position of great difficulty. The minister who approved all my schemes gave me no support whatever. Fortunately, owing to the loan scandal, he resigned and the vice-minister came in charge of the ministry and relieved me by giving me a sum of $3000 out of the funds that were under the difrect control of our ministry and I had the pleasure of seeing my geological school actually opened. In the mean time half a dozen letters passed between me and the Board of Finance, but I received a final answer, simply refuse, to pay the money, so my

and earn the gratitude of   Yours faithfully,

V. K. Ting

THE REPUBLIC OF CHINA

IN YOUR REPLY REFER TO FILE

No. _____

MINISTRY OF INDUSTRY & COMMERCE

PEKING CHINA

position is as difficult as evne. I still have the support of the vice-minister but this is of very little use, as he is only acting minister and his words carry little weight outside his own department. My last hope was the new minister Chang-chien but he is ill and will not take up his duties for sometime and money is urgently required.

In this deperate condition I had a letter from Dr. Solger(who will be here by the end of this month), saying that the President is interested in our work and had asked him to begin his work from Chang-teh-fu. He gave no detail of this in--formation, assuming that I know all about it. Now if this is true then there should be little difficulty in getting the small summ of $2600 per month. Will you, Dr. Morrison use your good influence with the President to help us in our endeavour? That is the favour I was going to ask. I decide to do so because I am convinced of the utility of a geological survey which is too well known to you to need any explanation, and I am equally confident that both Solger and I are competant enough for the work. He was privatdocent in the Berlin University and did good work in Central Asia and North China. As for myself I think Prof. Gregory would give me a testimony, as I was twice medalist in his class, and I am going to publish a paper on the geology of Yunnan and Kweichou. If you would induce the President to take the matter up, you will do a service to my country and earn the gratitude of

Yours faithfully,

V. K. Ting

THE REPUBLIC OF CHINA

MINISTRY OF INDUSTRY & COMMERCE

PEKING CHINA

8 Oct. 1913.

Dear Dr. Morrison,

I am afraid I am going to do something which may not be altogether welcome—for I am going to ask you a favor but my excuse is that I do it on public ground. Here is my case.

There has always been a geological section in the Board of Commerce ever since the provisional government was established but they had neither books nor collections. When I came here last February I put forward a scheme for organizing a geological survey with a school attached to it. After some persuasion it was approved by the ministry and its expenditure included in the budget for 1914 (beginning on the first of July 1913). In due course this item was sanctioned by the Board of Finance and I was told to carry my scheme into effect. In my original scheme I required $100,000 about half of which was the initial cost for instruments etc., and the other half for the up keeping of the school, traveling expense, publication of maps and reports, and the salary of 2 European experts. Considering the magnitude and the importance of the work the sum was certainly not too large, for even Japan, with an area 36 times smaller than that of China, after 20 years of geological work, still spend annually $100,000 for the same purpose. Knowing however the sad condition of the treasury, I was very cautious and tried in every way to save money. The Peking University had a geological section but with only 2 students. I succeeded in persuading the authority to hand over to me all their instruments, and books and collection which cost them more than $30,000. They also agreed to house us, so the initial expense was reduced to a minimum. Instead of two European geologists I engaged only one, namely Dr. F. Solger, a distinguished geologist, who accepted my offer of $400 instead of $600 per month (as he used to get) in the hope of having the honor of doing for China what Dr. Naumann did for Japan. I also held entrance examination for the geological school and engaged several teachers. All this was done before July and without touching any public money.

Just at that time the budget was introduced into the parliament which threw it out on some technical pretext. Then the second revolution came and the Board of Finance issued a circular stating that any institution that had not already been agreed before July would not be supplied with money. As my work really started long before that date, I thought I would get the money, but realizing the financial stress I cut down the expense to about one half of the original sum about $30,000 a year with practical no initial cost. But the Board of Finance refused to pay it, contending that my work did not begin before July. In the meantime, Dr. Solger demanded his passage money and the students asked the date of the opening of the school and I was in a position of great difficulty. The minister who approved all my schemes gave me no support whatever. Fortunately, owing to the loan scandal, he resigned and the vice-minister came in charge of the ministry and relieved me by giving me a sum of $3000 out of the funds that were under the direct control of our ministry and I had the pleasure of seeing my geological school actually opened. In the meantime, half a dozen letters passed between me and the Board of Finance, but I received a final answer simply refusing to pay the money, so my position is as difficult as ever. I still have the support of the vice-minister but this is of very little use, as he is only acting minister and his words carry little weight outside his own department. My last hope was the new minister Chang-chien but he is ill and will not take up his duties for some time and money is urgently required.

In this desperate condition I had a letter from Dr. Solger (who will be here by the end of this month), saying that the President is interested in our work and had asked him to begin his work from Chang-teh-fu. He gave no detail of this information, assuming that I know all about it. Now if this is true then there should be little difficulty in getting the small sum of $2600 per month. Will you, Dr. Morrison use your good influence with the President to help us in our endeavor? That is the favor I was going to ask. I decide to do so because I am convinced of the utility of a geological survey which is too well known to you to need any explanation, and I am equally confident that both Solger and I are competent enough for the work. He was privatdocent in the Berlin University and did good work in Central Asia and North China. As for myself I think Prof. Gregory would give me a testimony, as I was twice medalist in his class, and I am going to publish a paper on geology of Yunnan and Kweichou. If you would induce the President to take the matter up, you will do a service to my country and earn the gratitude of the people.

Yours faithfully,

V. K. Ting

14th October 1913.

Dear Mr. Ting,

    I must apologise for not answering earlier your letter of the 8th of October. You write in a very convincing way and I will be glad to do what I can.

    Mr. Chang Chien will be here in a day or so. I hope you will have an early opportunity of discussing the matter with him and perhaps you might then be kind enough to let me know the result. He is an intelligent man and I have little doubt that he will recognise the need of supporting the scheme, the object of which you state so well.

    With best wishes,

        Very sincerely yours,

14th October 1913.

Dear Mr. Ting,

I must apologize for not answering earlier your letter of the 8th of October. You write in a very convincing way and I will be glad to do what I can.

Mr. Chang Chien will be here in a day or so. I hope you will have an early opportunity of discussing the matter with him and perhaps you might then be kind enough to let me know the result. He is an intelligent man and I have little doubt that he will recognize the need of supporting the scheme, the object of which you state so well.

With best wishes,

Very sincerely yours,
[G. E. Morrison]

THE REPUBLIC OF CHINA

IN YOUR REPLY REFER TO FILE　　MINISTRY OF INDUSTRY & COMMERCE

No. _____　　　　　　　　　~~PEKING CHINA~~ Tsingshing mine

15 Nov. 1913

Dear Dr Morrison

Just a word to let you know how I have been getting on. As soon as Chang Chien came I tried to see him but he was so busy that he could not give the time to consider my proposals. The vice-minister (newly appointed) however listened to me attentively and promised me his support. Few days after the interview Dr Solger arrived from Germany and we are sent out to Shansi for six weeks, to study the geology the province so here I am on the Tsingshinghien mine. You can imagine how happy I am since this is the first day since two day year, when I had any opportunity to do geological work.

Yours faithfully
V. K. Ting

THE REPUBLIC OF CHINA

MINISTRY OF INDUSTRY & COMMERCE

Tsingshing mine

13 Nov, 1913

Dear Dr. Morrison,

Just a word to let you know how I have been getting on. As soon as Chang Chien came I turned to see him, but he was so busy that he could not give the time to consider my proposals. The vice-ministry (newly appointed), however listened to me attentively and provided me his support. Few days after the interview, Dr. Solger arrived from Germany and we all sent out to Shensi for six weeks to study the geology of the province, so here I am at the Tsingshing hsien mine. You can imagine how happy I am since this is the first day since two years, when I had any opportunity to do geological work.

Yours faithfully,

V. K. Ting

1914 年

THE REPUBLIC OF CHINA

IN YOUR REPLY REFER TO FILE

No. _____

MINISTRY OF INDUSTRY & COMMERCE

PEKING CHINA

2nd Jan. 1914

Dear Dr Morrison,

I hope my last letter reached you safely. After nearly 2 months' hard work in the very cold weather of Shansi (the lowest temperature was −18°C) I returned to Peking on the 26th last December. For private reasons I have to leave Peking today. During the last week I had to write my report, draw my maps (for I surveyed about 1500 sq. kilometres), get my things ready — for my wife is going with me and I am closing up my house — so you can imagine how busy I must have been. I tried to call but could not manage it.

Now 2 days ago just as I was taking leave of the new minister, I received orders that I should go to Yunnan directly from the south. I am expected to do geological work along the line of the projected railways. Of course I am very happy that I can go there again to continue my previous work. Can you give me some introductions to the people there? I will be in Shanghai till the 17th inst. so please send your letters to Shanghai for which purpose I enclose an addressed envelope.

With best wishes for the new year,

Yours faithfully

V. K. Ting

P.S. Leaving Peking in a great hurry I forgot to post this note. Have brought it with me to Nanking.

THE REPUBLIC OF CHINA

MINISTRY OF INDUSTRY & COMMERCE

PEKING CHINA

2nd Jan , 1914

Dear Dr. Morrison,

I hope my last letter reached you safely. After nearly 2 months' hard work in the very cold weather of Shansi (the lowest temperature was $-18\,℃$), I returned to Peking on the 26th last December. For private reasons, I have to leave Peking today. During the last week, I had to write my report, draw my maps (for I surveyed about 1500 sq kilometers), get my things ready—for my wife is going with me and I am bringing up my home—so you can imagine how busy I must have been. I tried to call, but could not manage it.

Now 2 days ago just as I was taking leave of the new minister, I received orders that I should go to Yunnan directly from the south. I am expected to do geological work along the line of the projected railway, Of course, I am very happy that I can go there again to continue my previous work. Can you give me some introductions to the people there? I will be in Shanghai till the 17th so please send your letter to Shanghai for which purpose I enclose an addressed envelope.

With best wishes for the New Year,

Yours faithfully,

V. K. Ting

P. S. Leaving Peking in a great hurry, I forgot to put this note, I have brought it with me to Nanking.

1915 年

Telepho! 1335 S.

REPUBLIC OF CHINA
MINISTRY OF AGRICULTURE AND COMMERCE

In reply refer to
file No.

Peking, 5·3·15

Dear Dr. Morrison,

I have been extremely busy in studying the material I have collected in Yunnan so I have not been able to take advantage of your kind offer to use your library. I intend however to compile a series of mining guides and have induced my friends Mr T. C. Chang and Mr P. B. Sze to help me. Both of them are members of the ministry and Mr Sze has met you several times before, for he used to work with Mr W. R. Hughes.

As your library will be invaluable for our purpose, I hope you will allow them to come to work in your library. We will call next Monday at 2.30 if it is convenient to you.

By the way I must apologize to Mrs Morrison for not answering her letter of invitation to lunch, but I received her note a day after I had lunched with you.

With best regards
Yours sincerely
V. K. Ting

中 華 民 國 農 商 部
REPUBLIC OF CHINA
MINISTRY OF AGRICULTURE AND COMMERCE

Peking, 5.3.15

Dear Dr. Morrison,

I have been extremely busy in studying the material I have collected in Yunnan so I have not been able to take advantage of your kind offer to use your library. I intend however to compile a series of mining guides and have introduced my friends Mr. J. C. Chang and Mr. P. B. Sze to help me. Both of them are members of the ministry and Mr. Sze has met you several times before, for he used to work with Mr. W. R. Haynes.

As your library will be invaluable for own purpose, I hope you will allow them to come to work in your library. We will call next Monday at 2:30 if it is convenient to you.

By the way, I must apologize to Mrs. Morrison for not answering her letter of invitation to Lunch, but I received her note a day after I had lunch with you.

With best wishes,

Yours sincerely,
V. K. Ting

1916 年

Peking 29.3.'16

Dear Dr Morrison

Many thanks for your kind letter. Please send me the papers as soon as possible for I expect to leave for Shantung in a few days time.

I am compiling with the assistance of some of my colleagues a work on mining enterprise in China which shall be entitled "Guides to Miners". Foreign mining enterprise shall be one of the chapters. But as I have more work in hand than I can finish, the compilation gets on rather slowly. I hope however to get part of it ready in September.

Thank you again for your invitation to call. I will try to drop in whenever I have time.

Yours sincerely

V.K. Ting

Peking 29.3.'16

Dear Dr. Morrison,

Many thanks for your kind letter. Please send me the papers as soon as possible for I expect to leave for Shantung in a few days' time.

I am compiling with the assistance of some of my colleagues, a work on mining enterprise in China which shall be entitle "Guides to Mines". Foreign mining enterprise shall be one of the chapters. But as I have more work I had than I can finish, the compilation gets on rather slowly. I hope however to get parts of it ready in September.

Thank you again for your invitation to call. I will try to drop in whenever I have time.

Yours sincerely

V. K. Ting

Ministry of Agriculture and Commerce

Peking (China). 15 May '16

Dear Dr Morrison

Thank you for your letter. I enclose $27 & please give the bearer of this a receipt.

I think the day of reckoning for us as a nation has come. When one fine day a country hitherto known as China shall have changed its colour in the Atlas, historians may discuss the causes of the ruin and no doubt many hard things will be said against Chinese officialdom old & new. Then please say a kind word or two in their behalve, for some of them at least have tried hard to do their duty.

I will try to call sometime this week & let you know by telephone in advance.

Yours sincerely,
V. K. Ting

農 商 部
Ministry of Agriculture and Commerce

Peking, 15 May' 16

Dear Dr. Morrison,

Thank you for your letter. I enclosed $27 and please give the treasurer of this a receipt.

I think the day of reckoning for us as a nation has come. When one finds day a country hither to known as China shall have changed it color in the atlas, historians may discuss the causes of the ruins and no doubt many hard things will be said against Chinese officialdom, old or new. Then please say a kind word or two on their behalf, for some of them at least have their hands to do their duty.

I will try to call sometime this week and let you know by telephone in advance.

Yours sincerely,

V. K. Ting

Ministry of Agriculture and Commerce

Peking 2nd. Nov. 1916.
(China).

Dr. G. E. Morrison,
    Peking E.

Dear Dr. Morrison,

  Many thanks for your kind letter. I would have been very glad to get your duplicate copy of Hedin's work, but the Swedish Minister who knows Hedin well promised to get him to send us a copy as a gift. Though I have not yet received the promised copy, I think we will received it as soon as I press the matter - I postpone it because of the uncertain postal conditions. I have duplicates of Richthofen's second and third vols., but not the first.

  The published Japanese maps on Yunnan are rather poor, being based on Chinese and British meterial. Your War Office map is certainly the best, as it is based on the large scale (4 miles to an inch) Frontier Survey series.

  I have been very busy organising the survey, and am also writing a book (joinly with my friend Dr. Wang) on Mining in China, and hope to get it ready for print this year. As I do not get away from office till 5 p. m. and usually work a little at night, I have not been able to pay you a visit though I have thought of it many times. I will try to come sometime next weak, perhaps on Wednesday and will telephone beforehand.

    With kind regards,
      Yours sincerely,

農商部
Ministry of Agriculture and Commerce

Peking 2nd, Nov. 1916.

Dr. G. E. Morrison,

    Peking E.

Dear Dr. Morrison,

Many thanks for your kind letter. I would have been very glad to get your duplicate copy of Hedin's work, but the Swedish Minister who knows Hedin well promised to get him to send us a copy as a gift. Though I have not yet received the promised copy, I think we will receive it as soon as I pressed the matter—I postpone it because of the uncertain postal conditions. I have duplicates of Richthofen's second and third vols., but not the first.

The published Japanese maps on Yunnan are rather poor, being based on Chinese and British material. Your War Office map is certainly the best, as it is based on the large scale (4 miles to an inch) Frontier Survey series.

I have been very busy organizing the survey and am also writing a book (jointly with my friend Dr. Wang) on Mining in China, and hope to get it ready for print this year. As I do not get away from office till 5 p.m. and usually work a little at night, I have not been able to pay you a visit though I have thought of it many times. I will try to come sometimes next week, perhaps on Wednesday and will telephone beforehand.

                                          With kind regards,

                                          Yours sincerely,

                                          V. K. Ting

1917 年

19 Feb. 1917
Peking

335

Dear Dr Morrison,

I have just received your letter this morning. I am very sorry that I have kept the 2 Russian books so long. Originally I intended only to have the figures copied, but finding them unintelligible afterwards, I have been obliged to make translations of certain chapters. This has proved a matter of great difficulty as several men who pretended to know Russian were found to be incompetent and much time has thus been wasted. I shall be very grateful if you would allow me to keep the books a week longer as there are only a few pages left undone.

I think the minister is quite ready to receive such a distinguished foreigner as Père Licent. If you let me have his address in Peking I may be able to arrange a meeting.

I am quite well, but rather busy as I expect to leave for Kiangsu next month to do field work and to arrange with the

Commercial Press the publication of my book.

With best regards,
yours sincerely,
V. K. Ting

19 Feb, 1917

Peking

Dear Dr. Morrison,

I have just received your letter this morning. I am very sorry that I have kept the 2 Russian books so long. Originally I intended only to have the figures copied, but finding them intelligible afterwards, I have been obliged to make translation of certain chapters. This has proved a matter of great difficulty as several men who pretended to know Russian were found to be incompetent and much time has thus been wasted. I shall be very grateful if you would allow me to keep the books a week longer as these are only a few pages left undone.

I think the minister is quite ready to receive such a distinguished foreigner as Peir Licent. If you let me have his address in Peking, I may be able to arrange a meeting.

I am quite well, but rather busy as I expect to leave for Kiangsu next month to do field work and to arrange with the Commercial Press the publication of my book.

With best regards,

Yours sincerely,

V. K. Ting

部 商 農
Ministry of Agriculture and Commerce

Peking 3 March 1917
(China).

Dear Dr. Morrison,

    I enclose the 2 Russian books which you lent me. I begin to be afraid that I have been abusing your kindness as I have not been able to return them within a week as promissed through I have been hurrying the translator almost daily. I hope you will excuse my delay in returning, for the task of translating several chapters has been a very difficult one.

    After this experience I think I will give up the idea of digesting Russian literature in Peking. I have written to M. Bogdanowitch, the president of the Russian "Comité Géologique" who wrote me a charming letter in answer to my previous letter, asking him to find a Russian geologist to made a summary of all Russian literature on the geology of China and let me pay the expense. I think this will prove much more satisfactory.

    With kind regards,

    Yours sincerely,

    V. K. Ting

農 商 部
Ministry of Agriculture and Commerce

Peking, 3 March 1917

Dear Dr. Morrison,

I enclose the 2 Russian books which you lent me. I begin to be afraid that I have been abusing your kindness as I have not been able to return them within a week as promised though I have been hurrying the translator almost daily. I hope you will excuse my delay in returning, for the task of translating several chapters has been a very difficult one.

After this experience I think I will give up the idea of digesting Russian literature in Peking. I have written to M. Bodanowitch, the president of the Russian "Comite Geologique" who wrote me a charming letter in answer to my previous letter, asking him to find a Russian geologist to make a summary of all Russian literature on the geology of China and let me pay the expense. I think this will prove much more satisfactory.

With kind regards,

Yours sincerely,
V. K. Ting

14 August 1917
Peitaiho

Dear Dr Morrison,

Thank you very much for your letter of 8th August which has just been forwarded.

I am sure every one who has had the privilege of seeing — not to say using — your library will be very sorry to hear that it is not to remain in Peking, but of course we understand perfectly your reasons. All the same we shall all miss it and regret that it has not been possible to come to some arrangement with the Government. May I ask when the transfer to Tokyo shall take place?

I had apendicitis on the 8th of July and went through an operation on the 9th. So I had the pleasure of listening to the firing on the 12th in bed. I am practically recovered, but the doctor said that I had better come down here for some time before I resume active work.

I expect to get back by the end of this month.

With kind regards,
Yours sincerely
V. K. Ting

14 August 1917

Pei tai ho

Dear Dr. Morrison,

Thank you very much for your letter of 8th August which has just been forwarded.

I am sure everyone who has had the privilege of seeing—not to say using—your library will be very sorry to hear that it is not to remain in Peking, but of course we understand perfectly from reasons. All the same we shall all miss it and expect that it has not been to some arrangement with the government. May I ask when the transfer to Tokyo shall take place?

I had appendicitis on the 8th of July and went through an operation on the 9th. So I had the pleasure of listening to the firing on the 12th in bed, I am practically recovered, but the doctor said that I had better come down here for some time before I assume active work.

I expect to get back by the end of this month.

With kind regards,

Your sincerely,
V. K. Ting

部 商 農
Ministry of Agriculture and Commerce

Peking September, 17, 1917.
(China).

To:

B. Willis Esquire,

Dear Sir,

Dr. Bain will tell you that we have begun in a modest way to do some geological work out here and a number of young men have been trained for the purpose. They had three years ~~years~~ training and since 1916 have been in the service of the Geological Survey. In order to be thoroughly competent, however, they require some experience outside China, and it seems to me that no country in the world is better suited for the purpose than America.

Through the kindness of Dr. Bain, Mr. Black Welder has already offered us substantial aid in providing an opportunity, as well as a part of the necessary fund, for one of our men to study paleontology, and it has been arranged that he shall sail for Illinois this december.

I have decided however to send two more men to the United States; one to study topography, physiography and methods of exploration, the other to study the practical side of economic geology. We may either send them to your National Survey, or to a university or to let them work with some private company. After discussing with Dr. Bain, we have agreed that there are advantages and disadvantages in each case, and that, as we cannot afford to let them stay abroad for more than two years, we must have some one to look after them on the spot so that no time shall be wasted. May I hope that your interest in Chinese geology

Ministry of Agriculture and Commerce

2. Peking 17/9/17.
(China).

will persuade you to lend us your valuable help? If you will kindly take an interest in the matter, we will leave our men entirely in your hands.

As I have already said, the two men we intend to send, went through a three years training in a Chinese college, two of which were devoted to geology. They had courses in general geology, elementary mineralogy, petrography, ore deposit, physiography and elementary paleontology. After they had left college, they worked for two seasons in the field and are acquainted with the use of the plantable and the commoner methods of geological mapping. Some of their courses were delivered in English so they understand English fairly well when spoken, but they speak it rather badly and write worse. They have however a working knowledge of German and can read more or less easily German books. Our idea is that as soon as they arrive in America they should be at once put into actual work under some-body who will take a personal interest in their training. The one who intends to study methods of exploration, ought to, I think, have a chance to work in the topographical service of your National Survey for at least one season, and he may also learn something about cartography and map printing. The other man is expected to study economic geology and it is necessary that he should have some experience in prospecting work for the more important metals such as iron, copper etc. We do not think that your Survey is the best place for him. These are of course only suggestions on our part and we are very eager to have your opinion on the matter.

Ministry of Agriculture and Commerce

部　商　農

3.　　　　　　　　　Peking 17/9/17.
　　　　　　　　　　(China).

　　We are prepared to pay them a sufficient allowance as well as their passage to America and back, but we cannot pay the travelling expenses when they are working in the field as it will be difficult to make estimates and it will depend entirely on the kind of work they have to do.

　　Hoping that we are not imposing on you too difficult a task and thanking you in advance,

　　　　　　　　　　　　　　　　I remain,
　　　　　　　　　　　　　　　　　yours faithfully,
　　　　　　　　　　　　　　　　　V. K. Ting
　　　　　　　　　　Director of the Geological Survey of China.

農 商 部
Ministry of Agriculture and Commerce

Peking, September, 17, 1917.
(China).

To:

B. Willis Esquire,

Dear Sir,

Dr. Bain will tell you that we have begun in a modest way to do some geological work out here and a number of young men have been trained for the purpose. They had three years training and since 1916 have been in the service of the Geological Survey. In order to be thoroughly competent, however, they require some experience outside China, and it seems to me that no country in the world is better suited for the purpose than America.

Through the kindness of Dr. Bain, Mr. Black Welder has already offered us substantial aid in providing an opportunity, as well as a part of the necessary fund, for one of our men to study paleontology, and it has been arranged that he shall said for Illinois this December.

I have decided however to send two more men to the United States; one to study topography, physiography and methods of exploration, the other to study the practical side of economic geology. We may either send them to your National Survey, or to a university or to let them work with some private company. After discussing with Dr. Bain, we have agreed that there are advantages and disadvantages in each case, and that, as we cannot afford to let them stay abroad for more than two years, we must have someone to look after them on the spot so that on time shall be wasted. May I hope that your interest in Chinese geology will persuade you to lend your valuable help? If you will kindly take an interest in the matter, we will leave our men entirely in your hands.

As I have already said, the two men we intend to send, went through a three years training in a Chinese college, two of which were devoted to geology. They had courses in general geology, elementary mineralogy, petrography, ore deposit, physiography and elementary paleontology. After they had left college, they worked for two seasons in the field and are acquainted with the use of the plane table and the common methods of geological mapping. Some of their courses were delivered in English so they understand English fairly well when spoken, but they speak it rather badly and write worse. They have however a working knowledge of German and can read more or less easily German books. Our idea is that as soon as they arrive in America they should be at once put into actual work under somebody who will take a personal interest in their training. The one who intends to study methods of exploration, ought, I think, to have a chance to work in the topographical service of your National Survey for at least one season, and he may also learn something about cartography and map printing. The other man is expected to study economic geology and it is necessary that he should have some experience in prospecting work for the more important metals such as iron, copper etc. We do not think that your Survey is the best place for him. These are of course only suggestions on our part and we are very eager to have your opinion on the matter.

We are prepared to pay them a sufficient allowance as well as their passage to America and back, but we cannot pay the travelling expenses when they are working in the field as it will be difficult to make estimates and it will depend entirely on the kind of work they have to do.

Hoping that we are not imposing on you too difficult a task and thanking you in advance,

I remain,

Yours faithfully,
V. K. Ting
Director of the Geological Survey of China

October 19, 1917

The Honorable V. K. King,
Director, The Geological Survey of China,
Peking, China.

My Dear Sir:

I am in receipt of your letter of September 17th, inclosed with one from my friend Dr. Bain, in which you make inquiry concerning the conditions at Stanford which may be favorable to two students, one to study topography and physiography and methods of exploration, the other to study the practical side of economic geology.

I have written Dr. Bain somewhat at length in answer to his questions, but I beg to assure you also that I believe we can give the two students the desired opportunity for education and experience both in the University and in practical work in the field, and that I shall be glad to receive them. It would be desirable that they should report here for the beginning of our winter quarter, January 2d, and should bring with them all their credentials, showing what courses they have studied, how long they pursued them, and what grades they received, together with any diplomas or other documents showing their progress.

After having seen these documents, we shall be in a position to judge where they can take up our work to best advantage, and whether they should be admitted as regular or special students.

I am sending you by separate mail a copy of the Announcement of Courses for this year, 1917-18, and also an Announcement for last year, 1916-17. With reference to the latter I would call your attention to the schecule of courses on pages 116 and 117, which show what the curriculum covers. There are some modifications in the present course, since we now have the four-quarter year, but there are no material ones.

It will be a matter of great gratification to me to do anything in my power which can promote the study of geology

D. K. K-10/19/17-2

in China and the investigation of the resources in the country. My brief experiences in China gave me a most profound interest in the people, as well as in the country itself. I understand, in part at least, the difficulties with which you have to contend in organizing your work, and I assure you of my hearty sympathy in your effort. I shall be glad, therefore, to take a personal interest in the training of the men whom you may send me, in order that they may be fully prepared and do justice to yourselves, to China, and to the American education and science.

With much respect, I remain,

Very sincerely yours,

W/RK

October 19, 1917

The Honorable V. K. Ting,
Director, The Geological Survey of China,
Peking, China.

My Dear Sir:

I am in receipt of your letter of September 17th, in close with one from my friend Dr. Bain, in which you make inquiry concerning the conditions at Stanford which may be favorable to two students, one to study topography and physiography and methods of exploration, the other to study the practical side of economic geology.

I have written Dr. Bain somewhat at length in answer to his questions, but I beg to assure you also that I believe we can give the two students the desired opportunity for education and experience both in the University and in practical work in the field, and that I shall be glad to receive them. It would be desirable that they should report here for the beginning of our winter quarter. January 2d, and should bring with them all their credentials, showing what courses they have studied, how long they pursued them, and what grades they received, together with any diplomas or other documents showing their progress.

After having seen these documents, we shall be in a position to judge where they can take up our work to best advantage, and whether they should be admitted as regular or special students.

I am sending you by separate mail a copy of the Announcement of Courses for this year, 1917-18, and also an Announcement for last year, 1916-17. With reference to the latter I would call your attention to the schedule of courses on page 116 and 117, which show what the curriculum covers. There are some modifications in the present course, since we now have the four-quarter year, but there are no material ones.

It will be a matter of great gratification to me to do anything in my power which can promote the study of geology in China and the investigation of the resources in the country. My brief experience in China gave me a most profound interest in the people, as well as in the country itself. I understand, in part at least, the difficulties with which you have to contend in organizing your work, and I assure you of my hearty sympathy in your effort. I shall be glad therefore to take a personal interest in the training of the men whom you may send me, in order that they may be fully prepared and do justice to yourselves, to China, and to the American education and science.

With much respect, I remain

Very sincerely yours,
[Bailey Willis]

1919 年

FURNESS ABBEY HOTEL,
FURNESS ABBEY,
LANCASHIRE.

14 July 1919

Dear Dr Morrison,

I came to England about a month ago and I was very sorry to hear that you had to undergo an operation. As Mr Liang intended to get back to Paris before the 14th July, we all had to work hard to complete his program, so at first I could not find time to call. Later on I went to 3 Devonshire Terrace, but I was told that you had gone away to Sussex and were getting well. Let us hope that you are having a rapid recovery and will soon be able to go back to China again.

I left London a week ago to make a tour in the iron districts. I am going to sail for Sweden from Newcastle on the 18th and I did not want to leave this country without writing to you.

Please remember me to Mrs Morrison,

Yours sincerely,

V. K. Ting

FURNESS ABBEY HOTEL

FURNESS ABBEY

LANCASHIRE

14 July 1919

Dear Dr. Morrison,

I came to England about a month ago and I was very sorry to hear that you had to undergo an operation. As Mr. Liang intended to get back to Paris before the 14 July, we all had to work hard to complete his program, so at first I cannot find time to call. Later on, I went to 3 Devonshire Terrace, but I was told that you had gone away to Sussex and were getting well. Let us hope that you are having a rapid recovery and will soon be able to go back to China again.

I left London a month ago to make a tour in the nine districts, I am going to sail for Sweden from Newcastle on the 18th and I did not want to leave this country without writing to you.

Please remember me to Mrs. Morrison.

Your sincerely,

V. K. Ting

1920 年

Geological Survey
3 Fengshen Hutung
Peking
22 June 1920

Dear Mrs Morrison,

Allow me to offer my sincere condolence on the death of Dr Morrison of which I have only just heard, having been away from Peking. Although I knew him only since 1911 I enjoyed the privilege of exceptional intimacy ever since. During the 10 years I spent at the Capital he showed me great kindness on innumerable occasions, and always allowed me to have access to his library. When I was in Paris last year, I visited him frequently, and even during his illness he never refused to see me. I feel it therefore a great personal loss. All of my countrymen who knew him regard his death as a serious loss to our country.

I remain,
Yours faithfully
V. K. Ting

Geological Survey

3 Fengshen Hutung, Peking

22 June 1920

Dear Mrs. Morrison,

Allow me to offer my sincere condolence on the death of Dr. Morrison of which I have only just heard, having been away from Peking.

Although I knew him only since 1911, I enjoyed the friendship of exceptional intimacy ever since. During the 10 years I spent at the capital, he showed me great kindness on innumerous occasions and always allowed me to have access to his library. When I was in Paris last year, I visited him frequently, and even during his illness he never refused to see me. I feel it therefore a great personal loss. All of my countrymen who knew him regard his death as a serious loss to our country.

I remain,

Yours faithfully,

V. K. Ting

農商部地質調查所
The Geological Survey
Ministry of Agriculture and Commerce

Peking October 26th, 1920.
(China).

Dr. A. Hrdlicka,
Smithsonian Institution,
Washington D. C.

Dear Dr. H

    Dr. Black has handed over to our library a number of bulletins of the American Bureau of Ethnology which you so kindly sent to him for distribution. Please accept my best thanks for your courtesy. Your short stay here has been a great stimulus to anthropological studies, and we are hoping that great things with come out of the association.

    You will remember that I spoke to you about the establishment of international exchange for this Survey. I am still waiting for some of our memoirs in the press, but I hope to approach you in this matter within three weeks time.

                        Yours Sincerely,

                          V. K. Ting

農 商 部 地 質 調 查 所

The Geological Survey
Ministry of Agriculture and Commerce

Peking, October 26th, 1920.

Dr. A. Hrdlicka,

Smithsonian Institution,

Washington D. C.

Dear Dr. H

Dr. Black has handed over to our library a number of bulletins of the American Bureau of Ethnology which you so kindly sent to him for distribution. Please accept my best thanks for your courtesy. Your short stay here has been a great stimulus to anthropological studies, and we are hoping that great things will come out of the association.

You will remember that I spoke to you about the establishment of international exchange for this Survey. I am still waiting for some of our memoirs in the press, but I hope to approach you in this matter within three weeks time.

Yours Sincerely,

V. K. Ting

Copy of letter from Mr. V. K. Ting, Director of the Geological Survey to Professor H. F. Osborn

December 9th, 1920.

Dr. H. F. Osborn,
President of the American
Natural History Museum,
New York, U. S. A.

Dear Dr. Osborn:

My attention has just been drawn to an article written by Mr. Andrews in the current number of the "Asia Magazine" in which the following passage occurs:

"China has no national institution where natural history objects can be studied and exhibited by modern methods and where the scientific work of her own people can be encouraged and directed".

As the director of a Chinese national institution in which natural history objects have been exhibited and studied during the last four years and whose primary object is to encourage and direct scientific study, I cannot allow such public statement to go unchallenged. My first inpulse is to write to "Asia" protesting against the article, but on second reflection I realize that Mr. Andrews made the statement without malice -- though I hope I will succeed in convincing you that such carelessness on his part is not altogether justifiable -- and above all you yourself whose generosity and fair dealing in all scientific matters are well known, cannot

- 2 -

be aware of the effect of Mr. Andrews' article. I am
convinced that if I point out to you the unfairness
of the statement in question, you will be the first
person to deplore it and to give it public contradiction.
I allow myself therefore the liberty in bringing this
matter to your notice by this rather lengthy letter.

  First of all allow me to bring forward evidence
to substantiate my claim that natural history objects
have been exhibited. I am enclosing several photographs
of our museum, both of the exterior and of the interior.
In enclose also blue prints of the plan of our museum as
it exists, and that of an extention which we have decided
to make early next spring. This museum is situated in
the compound of the Geological Survey which is located
in the heart of the city of Peking. It was first organized
in 1916 when the Geological Survey was officially established
as a separate institution. Constant additions have been
made during the last four years until now we have <u>on exhibition</u> 2850 labelled specimens in 87 glass casses and 17 tables.

  Have these natural history objects been studied?
I enclose several prints from the plates we have already
made for illustrating fossil plants and microscopic rock
sections. I further enclose some photographs of drawings
which are going to be heliotyped for illustrating a series
of palaeontological monographs which we hsall call <u>Palaeontologia Sinica</u>. I hope you will see from these sufficient

evidence to prove that we have not only exhibited but also studied our specimens. I need hardly add that such studies as we have begun to make presuppose some encouragement as well as direction.

I read also with interest that ethnology is included in the program of the coming expedition. This is a subject in which many of the members of the Geological Survey have been deeply interested. There is at this moment a collection of stone implement on exhibition in our museum, and much more material can be put up if the claims of the purely geological subjects have not been so pressing.

Of course you may tell me that it is our own fault that we have not made it known to the people at large what we have been doing, That I would readily admit because, apart from my own personal aversion to anything like vulgar advertisement, all our energy has been so much absorbed in organization and administration in addition to original research that none is left to do the work of propaganda. But that is no excuse for Mr. Andrews who has been in Peking and is acquainted with some of the members of our Survey including myself. He was invited several times to pay a visit to our museum but did not to do so although he spent several months in the city.

There is another matter which I should like to bring to your attention. Dr. J. G. Andersson, formerly

- 4 -

Director of the Swedish Geological Survey, has been in the service of the Chinese Government for the last six years. Although he is nominally our mining adviser, his connection with the Geological Survey has been from the beginning intimate and important. In 1917 he became specially interested in the fossil mammals. You will perhaps remember that soon afterwards I approached you for some of your publications which you so generously sent us free of cost. In order to get sufficient funds to do the work on a proper scale Dr. Andersson appealed to his friends in Sweden with considerable success. It was understood from the beginning that the Chinese Geological Survey will take an active part in the collecting, and, also at the recommendation of the Survey, the Swedish gentlemen who provided for the funds, were given Chinese decorations. The men who donated the funds naturally wanted to leave the specimens to the Swedish museum, but Dr. Andersson agreed to divide all his collections between the latter and the Geological Survey. For the last two years some 250 (3' x 1 1/2' x 1') boxes containing thousands of fragments and complete skulls of fossil mammals have been collected and despatched to Prof. Wiman of Upsala who has kindly undertaken the study. Soon afterwards the question of publication of the results came up and I pointed out to Dr. Andersson that the Geological Survey of China had a legitimate claim to have all such material collected in China described and printed in its own publications. Dr. Andersson at once agreed to this proposal, and since

- 5 -

then Prof. Wiman has consented to write a monograph in our Palaeontologia Sinica which I have already had occasion to mention. Furthermore Dr. Andersson has given me a large personal contribution to the publication fund which I have been endeavouring to form for the Palaeontologia Sinica. This last series is going to contain not only mammals but also plants and invertebrate fossils. The former are in the hands of Prof. Halle of the Riksmuseum of Stockholm who kindly allows also one junior member of the Geological Survey of China to study with him. The invertebrate fossils are now in the hands of Dr. Graban, formerly of Columbia but now Prof. of Palaeontology in the Peking University and Palaeontologist to the Chinese Survey. Much of the work is now well advanced and some of the plates I send you are intended for the particular publication in question.

When Mr. Andrews was in Peking, he was always on very friendly terms with Dr. Andersson who not only told him of his plans but also showed him many of his find specimens. Mr. Andrews talked of organizing an expedition to Central Asia or Turkestan, a scheme which both Dr. Andersson and myself enthusiastically supported, but he said not a word about collecting fossil mammals in northern China to which region our collecting has been largely restricted because of the political cleavage between the North and the South which has made many of the interesting southern provinces inaccessible. Imagine my surprise to find in Mr. Andrews' article in "Asia" a detailed plan mapped out by Mr. Andrews for Dr. Granger to work in northern China, going over precisely the same ground that Dr. Andersson and other members of the Survey have been working! I have it to you to judge whether Mr. Andrews' action is fair and justifiable. Indeed it is rather strange for Mr. Andrews to ignore all the work done by the official Chinese institution when the professed object of his expedition is to encourage native development of scientific study.

Please don't misunderstand me. The Geological Survey of China claims no monopoly of any kind. Nothing is more welcome, to me than that the scientific abroad begin to be more alive to the immense possibilities of scientific discovery in China, and it has been the settled policy of the Survey to do all that is in its power to help foreigners coming over here to work. Many Americans including Mr. Andrews himself will be able to substantiate this statement. We realize most clearly that China is practically an unknown continent and the more people work at it the better known it will become. But apart from the fact that Dr. Andersson and the Geological Survey have been working at the very same problems for the last two years, and that therefore in justice and fairness to them, their priority should be taken into consderation, it is certainly in the interest of everybody as well as that of science to arrange coöperation and division of labour instead of undesirable competition. I may suggest a concrete example to show what I mean. It is known that in northern China the Hipparion fauna dominates to a large extent but the country on the southern side of the Yangtse river, especially the southwestern provinces, Yunnan and Szechuan, seems to have a different history. For polotical reasons we have not been able to reach these provinces which are nominally at war with the Centreal Government. But nothing will prevent Dr. Granger to go and work there. Again, Mr. Andrews' original suggestion about Turkestan and Thibet indicates another vast area. If it is the desire of your museum to have a representative collection of fossil mammals from China rather than to work out any special problem, I will be only too glad to supply you with dupilcate material of all the faunas in northern China including the Hipparion fauna provided that you will consent to an arrangement similar to that which was agreed between the Chinese Geological Survey and the Natural History Museum of Stockholm. It seems to me that it will be a great pity to let Dr. Granger describe and print in New York the same fossils which Professor Wiman is going to describe and print in the Palaeontologia Sinica. Surely science is already burdened with such unhappy competitions as that of Marsh and Cope to require any additional example from Eastern Asia.

I hope I am giving no annoyance. Had I not been sure of your well-known reputation for fairness and of your sympathy for new institutions struggling to gain their recognition, I would not have written in such a frank and unreserved manner. I sincerely hope that yoy will think out some scheme that will be fair to all concerned and will do away with any possible compatition that may cloud over the success of Dr. Granger's expedition.

     I remain,

       Yours faithfully,

    (Signed) V. K. Ting

     Director, Geological Survey of China

December 9th, 1920.

Dr. H. F. Osborn
President of the American
Natural History Museum,
New York, U. S. A.

Dear Dr. Osborn,

My attention has just been drawn to an article written by Mr. Andrews in the current number of the "Asia Magazine" in which he following passage occurs:

"China has no national institution where natural history objects can be studied and exhibited by modern methods and where the scientific work of her own people can be encouraged and directed".

As the director of a Chinese national institution in which natural history objects have been exhibited and studies during the last four years and whose primary object is to encourage and direct scientific study, I cannot allow such public statement to go unchallenged. My first impulse is to write to "Asia" protesting against the article, but on second reflection I realize that Mr. Andrews made the statement without malice---though I hope I will succeed in convincing you that such carelessness on his part is not altogether justifiable---and above all you yourself whose generosity and fair dealing in all scientific matters are well known, cannot be aware of the effect of Mr. Andrews' article. I am convinced that if I point out to you the unfairness of the statement in question, you will be the first person to deplore it and to give it public contradiction. I allow myself therefore the liberty in bringing this matter to your notice by this rather lengthy letter.

First of all, allow me to bring forward evidence to substantiate my claim that natural history objects have been exhibited. I am enclosing several photographs of our museum, both of the exterior and of the interior. In enclose also blue prints of the plan of our museum as it exists, and that of an extension which we have decided to make early next spring. This museum is situated in the compound of the Geological Survey which is located in the heart of the city of Peking. It was first organized in 1916 when the Geological Survey was officially established as a separate institution. Constant additions have been made during the last four years until now we have on exhibition 2850 labeled specimens in 87 glass cases and 17 tables.

Have these natural history objects been studies? I enclose several prints from the plates we have already made for illustrating fossil plants and microscopic rock sections. I further enclose some photographs of drawing which are going to be heliotyped for illustrating a series of paleontological monographs which we will call Paleontologia Sinica. I hope you will see from these sufficient evidence to prove that we have not only exhibited but also studies our specimens. I need hardly add that such studies as we have begun to make presuppose some encouragement as well as direction.

I read also with interest that ethnology is included in the program of the coming expedition. This is a subject in which many of the member of the Geological Survey have been deeply interested. There is at this moment a collection of stone implement on exhibition in our museum, and much more material can be put up if the claims of the purely geological subjects have not been so pressing.

Of course you may tell me that it is our own fault that we have not made it known to the people at large what we have been doing. That I would readily admit because, apart from my own personal aversion to anything like vulgar advertisement, all our energy has been so much absorbed in organization and administration in addition to original research that none is left to do the work of propaganda. But that is no excuse for Mr. Andrews who has been in Peking and is acquainted with some of the members of our Survey including myself. He was invited several times to pay a visit to our museum but did not to do so although he spent several months in the city.

There is another matter which I should like to bring to your attention. Dr. J. G. Andersson, formerly Director of the Swedish Geological Survey, has been in the service of Chinese Government for the last six years. Although he is nominally our mining adviser, his connection with the Geological Survey has been from the beginning intimate and important. In 1917 he became specially interested in the fossil mammals. You will perhaps remember that soon afterwards I approached you for some of your publications which you so generously sent us free of cost. In order to get sufficient funds to do the work on a proper scale Dr. Andersson appealed to his friends in Sweden with considerable success. It was understood from the beginning that the Chinese Geological Survey will take an active part in the collecting, and also at the recommendation of the Survey, the Swedish gentlemen who provide for the funds, were given Chinese decorations. The men who donated the funds naturally wanted to leave the specimens to the Swedish museum, but Dr. Andersson agreed to divide all his connections between the latter and the Geological Survey. For the last two years some 250 boxes containing thousands of fragments and complete skulls of fossil mammals have been collected and dispatched to Prof. Wiman of Uppsala who has kindly undertaken the study. Soon afterwards the question of publication of the results came up and I pointed out to Dr. Andersson that the Geological Survey of China had a legitimate claim to have all such material collected in China described and printed in its own publications. Dr. Andersson at once agreed to this proposal, and since then Prof. Wiman has consented to write a monograph in our Palaeontologia Sinica which I have already had occasion to mention. Furthermore Dr. Andersson has given me a large personal contribution to the publication fund which I have been endeavoring to form for the Paleontologia Sinica. This last series is going to contain not only mammals but also plants and invertebrate fossils. The former are in the hands of Prof. Halle of the Riksmuseum of Stockholm who kindly allows also one junior member of the Geological Survey of China to study with him. The invertebrate fossils are now in the hands of Dr. Grabau, formerly of Columbia but now Prof. of Paleontology in the Peking University and Paleontologist to the Chinese Survey. Much of the work is now well advanced and some of the plated I send you are intended for the particular publication in question.

　　When Mr. Andrews was in Peking, he was always on very friendly term with Dr. Andersson who not only told him of his plans but also showed him many of his find specimens. Mr. Andrews talked of organizing an expedition to Central Asia or Turkestan, a scheme which both Dr. Andersson and myself enthusiastically supported, but he said not a word about collecting fossil mammals in northern China to which region our collecting has been largely restricted because of the political cleavage between the North and the South which has made many of the interesting southern provinces inaccessible. Imagine my surprise to find in Mr. Andrews' article in "Asia" a detailed plan mapped out by Mr. Andrews for Dr. Granger to work in northern China, going over precisely the same ground that Dr. Andersson and other members of the Survey have been working! I have it to you to judge whether Mr. Andrews' action is fair and justifiable. Indeed, it is rather strange for Mr. Andrews to ignore all the work done by the official Chinese Institution when the professed object of this expedition is to encourage native development of scientific study.

Please don't misunderstand me. The Geological Survey of China claims no monopoly of any kind. Nothing is more welcome, to me than that the scientific abroad begin to be more alive to the immense possibilities of scientific discovery in China, and it has been the settle policy of the Survey to do all that is in its power to help foreigners coming over here to work. Many Americans including Mr. Andrews himself will be able to substantiate this statement. We realize most clearly that China is practically an unknown continent and the more people work at it the better known it will become. But apart from the fact that Dr. Andersson and the Geological Survey have been working at the very same problems for the last two years, and that therefore in justice and fairness to them, their priority should be taken into consideration, it is certainly in the interest of everybody as well as that of science to arrange cooperation and division of labor instead of undesirable competition. I may suggest a concrete example to show what I mean. It is known that in northern China the Hipparion fauna dominates to a large extent but the country on the southern side of the Yangtze river, especially the southwestern provinces, Yuanan and Szechuan, seems to have a different history. For political reasons we have not been able to reach these provinces which are nominally at war with the Central Government. But nothing will prevent Dr. Granger to go and work there. Again, Mr. Andrew's original suggestion about Turkestan and Tibet indicates another vast area. If it is the desire of your museum to have a representative collection of fossil mammals from China rather than to work out any special problem, I will be only too glad to supply you with duplicate material of all the faunas in northern China including the Hipparion fauna provided that you will consent to an arrangement similar to that which was agreed between the Chinese Geological Survey and the Natural History Museum of Stockholm. It seems to me that it will be a great pity to let Dr. Granger describe and print in New York the same fossils which Professor Wiman is going to describe and print in the Paleontologia Sinica. Surely science is already burdened with such unhappy competitions as that of Marsh and Cope to require any additional example from Eastern Asia.

    I hope I am giving no annoyance. Had I not been sure of your well-known reputation for fairness and of your sympathy for new institutions struggling to gain their recognition, I would not have written in such a frank and unreserved manner. I sincerely hope that you will think out some scheme that will be fair to all concerned and will do away with any possible competition that may cloud over the success of Dr. Granger's expedition.

    I remain,

    Yours faithfully,
V. K. Ting
Director, Geological Survey of China

C O P Y

(Letter head omitted)

Peking, March 25, 1921

Dear President Osborn:

Your letter of the 10th Feb. reached me a few days ago, and I hasten to thank you heartily for your extreme courtesy. Mr. Andrews' letter came to hand sometime ago, but as he will leave America before my answer can possibly reach him, I have not written. I need hardly tell you that we are looking forward with intense interest to the arrival of your expedition and I have been trying to think out a general plan which will be satisfactory to all concerned.

Your interest in the Far East is most encouraging to those of us who have been struggling out here for the last few years. It does one good to hear that such an eminent scientist as yourself is paying great attention to our problems. I was unfortunate enough to have missed you both times when I called at the museum, but your letter gives me the hope that I will very soon have the chance of entertaining you in my own country. Such a visit can not fail to rouse interest in scientific researches in China, and I am already authorized by the National University of Peking to invite you to give a few lectures on any subject you choose, and I sincerely hope that you may find it possible to accept such an invitation.

Your kind promise to hand to us a duplicate set of your collection is of course welcome, for it has always been my ambition to help to establish a real natural history museum in China, as I was deeply interested in zoology before I turned to geology. It reminds me however that we still lack the publications of the American Museum, for except the books you yourself personally sent us in 1919, we have not yet received any of the publications of the American Museum - we have not applied for them in fact, because we have been waiting to have some publications of our own before asking for outside help. Now we have ready a number of bulletins and memoirs of which I enclose a few copies. Will you kindly send us a complete set of the various publications of the Museum as well as putting us on your permanent exchange list?

Thanking you once more,

Yours sincerely,

(Signed) V. K. Ting

Director of the Geological Survey
of China.

Peking, March 25, 1921

Dear President Osborn:

Your letter of the 10th Feb. reached me a few days ago, and I hasten to thank you heartily for your extreme courtesy. Mr. Andrews' letter came to hand some time ago, but as he will leave America before my answer can possibly reach him, I have not written. I need hardly tell you that we are looking forward with intensive interest to the arrival of your expedition and I have been trying to think out a general plan which will be satisfactory to all concerned.

Your interest in the Far East is most encouraging to those of us who have been struggling out here for the last few years. It does one good to hear that such an eminent scientist as yourself is paying great attention to our problems. I was unfortunate enough to have missed you both time when I called at the museum, but your letter gives me the hope that that I will very soon have the chance of entertaining you in my own country. Such a visit cannot fail to rouse interest in scientific research in China, and I am already authorized by the National University of Peking to invite you to give a few lectures on any subject you choose, and I sincerely hope that you may find it possible to accept such an invitation.

Your kind promise to hand to us a duplicate set of your collection is of course welcome, for it has always been my ambition to help to establish a real natural history museum in China, as I was deeply interested in zoology before I turned to geology. It reminds me however that we still lack the publications of the American Museum, for except the books you yourself personally sent us in 1919, we have not yet received any of the publications of the American Museum-we have not applied for them in fact, because we have been waiting to have some publications of our own before asking for outside help. Now we have ready a number of bulletins and memoirs of which I encloses a few copies. Will you kindly send us a complete set of the various publications of the Museum as well as putting us on your permanent exchange list?

Thanking you once more,

                              Yours sincerely,

                              V. K. Ting

                              Director of the Geological Survey of China

The Geological Survey
Ministry of Agriculture and Commerce

Peking **April 18th, 1921.**
(China).

Roy Chapman Andrews Esq.,
    Peking.

Dear Mr. Andrews,

    With reference to our conversation this morning about the best plan of coöperation and division of labour, I should like to let you know that we are already interested in the following areas and want to preserve them for the Survey and Dr. Andersson to work in exclusively.

    Provinces: Chihli,
               Shantung,
               Shansi,
               Honan,
               Shensi,
               Kansu,
               Manchuria;

Small area round Hallong Osso as shown by map,
    District of Kueichoufu and Wanhsien(Szechuan).

    We shall be delighted to put at Dr. Granger's disposal all our material and information and if possible, to show him some of our best localities provided that he will not make any collections of fossil mammals in, or write any paper on the areas mentioned above. You are perfectly welcome to work in any other place not thus preserved, and we will try to give you all

農商部地質調查所
The Geological Survey
Ministry of Agriculture and Commerce

(2).

Peking
(China).

the help we can and provide such duplicates as we are able to share for your Museum in return for this courtesy.

Hoping that you will approve of the proposal,

Yours sincerely,

V. K. Ting

農 商 部 地 質 調 查 所
The Geological Survey
Ministry of Agriculture and Commerce

Peking, April 18th, 1921.

Roy Chapman Andrews Esq.,

    Peking.

Dear Mr. Andrews,

With reference to our conversation this morning about the best plan of cooperation and division of labor, I should like to let you know that we are already interested in the following areas and want to preserve them for the Survey and Dr. Andersson to work in exclusively.

Provinces: Chihli,

    Shantung,

    Shansi,

    Honan,

    Shensi,

    Kansu,

    Manchuria;

Small area round Hallong Osso as shown by map,

District of Kueichoufu and Wanhsien (Szechuan).

We shall be delighted to put at Dr. Granger's disposal all our material and information and if possible, to show him some of our best localities provided that he will not make any collections of fossil mammals in, or write any paper on the areas mentioned above. You are perfectly welcome to work in any other place not thus preserved, and we will try to give you all the help we can and provide such duplicates as we are able to share for your Museum in return for this courtesy.

Hoping that you will approve of the proposal,

Yours sincerely,

V. K. Ting

農商部地質調查所
The Geological Survey
Ministry of Agriculture and Commerce

Peking 17 May 1921
(China).

Roy Chapman Andrews Esq.,
10, Tzui Hua Hutung,
Peking E.

Dear Mr. Andrews,

Herewith I enclose the map and a letter from Dr. Andersson. The latter was dated 3rd May but did not reach me until this morning!

As soon as he is back we will discuss our plan in detail, and I hope to be able to put Dr. Granger on to some good locality so that he can make a good collection straightway.

I have heard that the Chinese student Mr. Yuan is still in America. Do you want me to hurry him back?

With kind regards,

Yours sincerely,

農商部地質調查所
The Geological Survey
Ministry of Agriculture and Commerce

Peking, 17 May 1921

Roy Chapman Andrews Esq.,

10, Tsui Hua Hutung,

Peking E.

My Dear Mr. Andrews,

Herewith I enclose the map and a letter from Dr. Andersson. The latter was dated 3rd May but did not reach me until this morning!

As soon as he is back we will discuss our plan in detail, and I hope to be able to put Dr. Granger on to some good locality so that he can make a good collection straightway.

I have heard that the Chinese student Mr. Yuan is still in America. Do you want me to hurry him back?

With kind regards,

Yours sincerely,

V. K. Ting

The Geological Survey
Ministry of Agriculture and Commerce
Peking 23 May 1921
(China).

Roy Chapman Andrews Esq.,
Tsui Hua Hutung,
Peking.

My Dear Mr. Andrews,

You will remember the letter I handed to you in my office on the 18th of April in which I stated the areas which we wanted to be reserved, namely, the provinces Chihl, Shantung, Shansi, Honan, Shensi, Kansu, Manchuria, small area round Hallong Osso, and the district of Kueichoufu and Wanhsien. You have already kindly promised that the above areas should be excluded from your program, but after thinking over the possible ways of giving Mr. Granger some locality from which he could obtain a good collection straight away, I thought that we we might hand over to him the district of Kueichou and Wanhsien which we have discovered to produce fossil mammals. Dr. Andersson has just returned from his field trip, and after I have told you courteous attitude towards our work, he not only agrees to my proposal that we should let Dr. Granger to go to Wanhsien, but he is also willing to hand over to him the Hallong Osso locality for collection. The latter locality is of considerable importance as it contain a f fauna which is quite distinct from that of China proper.

Please let me know if you have received my last letter and the map. I may add that Dr. Andersson is leaving for Manchuria in a weeks time and is very eager to have a talk with you.

Yours sincerely

V. K. Ting

P. S. Many thanks for the generous remarks you made about our work the other night.

農商部地質調查所
The Geological Survey
Ministry of Agriculture and Commerce

Peking, 23 May, 1921

Roy Chapman Andrews Esq.,

Tsui Hua Hutung,

Peking.

My Dear Mr. Andrews,

You will remember the letter I handed to you in my office on the 13th of April in which I stated the areas which we wanted to be reserved, namely, the provinces Chihli, Shantung, Shansi, Honan, Shensi, Kansu, Manchuria, small area round Hallong Osso, and the district of Kueichoufu and Wanhsien. You have already kindly promised that the above areas should be excluded from your program, but after thinking over the possible ways of giving Mr. Granger some locality from which he could obtain a good collection straight away, I thought that we might hand over to him the district of Kueichou and Wanhsien which we have discovered to produce fossil mammals. Dr. Andersson he just returned from his field trip, and after I have told you courteous attitude towards our work, he not only agrees to my proposal that we should let Dr. Granger go to Wanhsien, but he is also willing to hand over to him the Hallong Osso locality for collection. The latter locality is of considerable importance as it contains a fauna which is quite distinct from that of China proper.

Please let me know if you have received my last letter and the map. I may add that Dr. Andersson is leaving for Manchuria in a works time and is very eager to have a talk with you.

              Yours sincerely

              V. K. Ting

P.S. Many thanks for the generous remarks you made about our work the other night.

27 May 1921
Peking

Dear Mr Andersson,

Thank you very much for your kind invitation to dine with you on Monday. I shall be delighted to come.

Yours sincerely,
V. K. Ting

P.S. I hear from Dr Andersson that you are going to have Mr Kunghao King that night. I shall much prefer that you will say nothing about our plans for the Museum that night.

27 May 1921

Peking

Dear Mr. Andrews,

Thank you very much for your kind invitation to dine with you on Monday. I will be delighted to come.

Yours sincerely,

V. K. Ting

P. S. I hear from Dr. Andersson that you are going to have Mr. Kung and Mrs. Kung that night. I shall much prefer that you will say nothing about our plan for the museum that night.

To the Editor of the Peking Leader.

Dear Sir,

In your editorial of yesterday's date on Mr. Russel in Japan, there appeared the astounding statement that "it must be admitted that he (Mr. Russel) did not make a very profound and deep-going (sic) impression here in China". As a member of the Society which invited Mr. Russel to lecture and as one of those who were fortunate enough to come into close personal contact with Mr. Russel during his stay in Peking, I must protest most strongly against this misstatement of fact.

Instead of posing as the Second Confucius and formulating dogmas for our salvation without being acquainted with the country and its people, Mr. Russel from the very beginning wisely reserved his opinion on Chinese affaires, an attitude entirely in keeping with his scientific habit of mind. He then went on straightway to lecture on psychology and mathematical physics which form the foundation of his philosophy. No doubt to the superficial journalist who is accustomed to express an opinion on all subjects under the sun at a moment's notice and has never tried to analyse either mind or matter, this was a great disappointment. But the impression made on those who heard his lectures was both profound and "deep-going" (what ever that may mean), for they realised for the first time that philosophy is nothing but the synthetic results of all the sciences and Mr. Russel's ideas of social reconstruction were based the outcome of mature thinking and profound knowledge. His admirable style and masterly delivery won for him enthusiastic admiration even from such a so great a master as Prof. Dewey. The formation of the Russel Society, the wide circulation enjoyed by his published lectures and the universal anxiety shown by the student during his severe illness all testify that young China did not grudge him for the stiff diet he provided, and completely refute the statement contained in your editorial.

Although his last unfortunate illness cut short his lectures on ˄social reconstruction, his last address nearly made up for the deficit. Still weak from his illness and hardly able to 跷 stand on his legs, he delivered his farewell speach to an overflowing audience with so much warmth and sincerity as well as wisdom that every word sank deep into the heart of his hearers. His clear conception of the responsibility of the intellectual minority has certainly awakened many of us from our uncomfortable slumber and will not fail to bear fruit in the near future.

Had such a statement appeared in any other English newspaper in China, it would be hardly worthwhile to make a denial as the real facts are too well-known to require reaffirmation. But the Peking Leader, being a Chinese paper so closely associated with the very people who extended ˄to Mr. Russel their invitation and hospitality, cannot be ignored without producing misleading impressions abroad. I venture to suggest that the Editor owes a clear duty to his associates as well as to the public to make a complete retraction of the editorial in question.

I may be doing the Editor an injustice. Perhaps the editorial was written by some hired foreign scribe who cares nothing for ˄about either Mr. Russel or the Peking Leader and smuggled the article into print without the consent of the responsible Editor, in which case I humbly offer him my sincerest sympathy.

Yours faithfully,

V. K. T. [V. K. Ting]

5th August 1921, Tientsin.

To the Editor of the Peking Leader

Dear Sir,

In your editorial of yesterday's date on Mr. Russell in Japan, there appeared the astounding statement that "it must be admitted that he (Mr. Russel) did not make a very profound and deep-going (sic) impression here in China." As a member of the Society which invited Mr. Russell to the lecture and as one of those who were fortunate enough to come into close personal contract with Mr. Russell during his stay in Peking, I must protest most strongly against this misstatement of fact.

Instead of posing as the Second Confucius and formulating dogmas for our salvation without being acquainted with the country and its people, Mr. Russell form the very beginning wisely reserved his opinion on Chinese affairs, an attitude entirely in keeping with his scientific habit of mind. He then went on straightway to lecture on psychology and mathematical physics which from the foundation of his philosophy. No doubt to the superficial journalist who is accustomed to express an opinion on all subjects under the sun at a moment's notice and has never tried to analyze either mind or matter, this was a great disappointment. But the impression made on those who heard his lectures was both profound and "deep-going" (whatever that may mean), for they realized for the first time that philosophy is nothing but the synthetic results of all the sciences and Mr. Russell's ideas of social reconstruction were the outcome of mature thinking and profound knowledge. His admirable style and masterly delivery won for him enthusiastic admiration even from so great a master as Prof. Dewey. The formation of the Russell society, the wide circulation enjoyed by his published lectures and the universal anxiety shown by the student during his severe illness all testify that young China did not grudge him for the stiff diet he provided, and completely refute the statement contained in your editorial.

Although his last unfortunate illness cut short his lectures on social reconstruction, his last address nearly made up for the deficit. Still weak from his illness and hardly able to stand on his legs, he delivered his farewell speech to an overflowing audience with so much warmth and sincerity as well as wisdom that every word sank deep into the heart of his hearers. His clear conception of the responsibility of the intellectual minority has certainly awakened many of us from our uncomfortable slumber and will not fail to bear fruit in the near future.

Had such a statement appeared in any other English newspaper in China, it would be hardly worthwhile to make a denial as the real facts are too well-known to require reaffirmation. But the Peking Leader, being a Chinese paper so closely associated with the very people who extended Mr. Russell their invitation and hospitality, cannot be ignored without producing misleading impressions abroad. I venture to suggest that the Editor owes a clear duty to his associates as well as to the public to make a complete retraction of the editorial in question.

I may be doing the Editor an injustice. Perhaps the editorial was written by some hired foreign scribe who cares nothing about either Mr. Russell or the Peking Leader and smuggled the article into print without the consent of the responsible Editor, in which case I humbly offer him my sincerest sympathy.

Yours faithfully

V. K. Ting

5th August 1921, Tientsin

29 August 1921
Geological Survey
Peking

R. Andrews Esq.

Dear Mr Andrews,

I was so busy that I did not manage to telephone to you until 4 this afternoon when you had gone to Kung Hsien Hutung. I was going to ask you to come over at 5, but as it is too late now, please come here anytime between 9 & 12 on Wednesday.

With kind regards,
Yours sincerely
V. K. Ting

29 August 1921

Geological Survey

Peking

R. Andrews Esq.

Dear Mr. Andrews,

I was so sorry that I did not manage to telephone to you until 4 this afternoon when you had gone to Kung Hsien Hutung. I was going to ask you to come over at 5, but as it is too late now. Please come here anytime between 9 to 12, on Wednesday.

With kind regards

Yours sincerely,

V. K. Ting

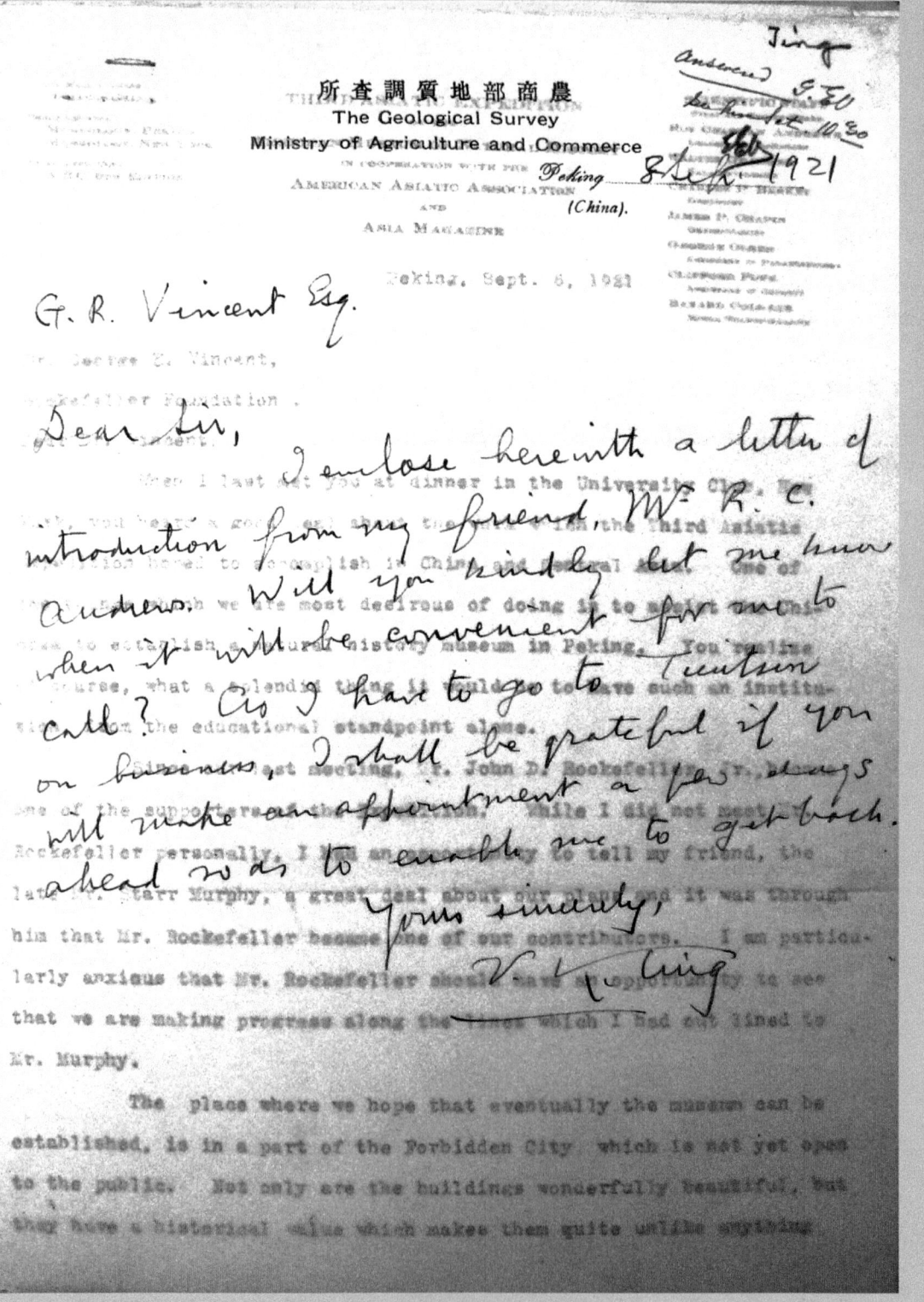

農商部地質調查所
The Geological Survey
Ministry of Agriculture and Commerce
Peking (China).

Peking, Sept. 6, 1921

G. R. Vincent Esq.

Dear Sir,

I enclose herewith a letter of introduction from my friend, Mr. R. C. Andrews. Will you kindly let me know when it will be convenient for me to call? As I have to go to Tientsin on business, I shall be grateful if you will make an appointment a few days ahead so as to enable me to get back.

Yours sincerely,

V. K. Ting

農 商 部 地 質 調 查 所

The Geological Survey

Ministry of Agriculture and Commerce

Peking, 1921

G. E. Vincent Esq.,

Dear Sir,

I enclose here with a letter of introduction from my friend, Mr. R. C. Andrews. Will you kindly let me know when it will be convenient for me to call? Since I have to go to Tientsin on business, I shall be grateful if you will make an appointment a few days ahead so as to enable me to get back.

Yours sincerely,
V. K. Ting

Dr. V. K. TING
Directeur du Service Géologique Chinois

Pékin (Chine)

Sept. 26, 1921.

Dr. V. K. Ting,
Directeur du Service Geologique Chinois,
Peking.

My dear Dr. Ting:

I am sorry it was not possible for Mr. Rockefeller to visit the site which you have in mind for the new museum. I spoke to him about it, as I promised, and gave him a brief idea of what you were hoping to accomplish.

It was a pleasure to meet you again the other day in the Western Hills. We were much impressed with the institutions which are being built up there.

With best wishes, I am

Yours sincerely,

G E Vincent

GEV:Mc.

Sept, 26, 1921

Dr. V. K. Ting,
Directeur du Service Geologique Chinois,
      Peking.

My dear Dr. Ting:

I am sorry it was not possible for Mr. Rockefeller to visit the site which you have in mind for the new museum. I spoke to him about it, as I promised, and gave him a brief idea of what you were hoping to accomplish.

It was a pleasure to meet you again the other day in the Western Hills. We were much impressed with the institutions which are being built up there.

With best wishes, I am

Yours sincerely
G. E. Vincent

In re Third Asiatic Expedition

September the twenty-eighth
Nineteen hundred twenty-one

My dear Sir:

I have just returned from an important archaeological and scientific tour in western Europe and find excellent reports from Messrs. Andrews and Granger of our Third Asiatic Expedition.

I hasten to express our appreciation of the cordial manner in which you are planning for our coöperation, and of the generous spirit of scientific interest which you are displaying. Chief Andrews writes that both yourself and Messrs. Andersson and Grabau have done everything in your power to make our share in the great undertaking of geological, palaeontological, and archaeological exploration in China a success. I feel sure that you will never have any reason to regret this spirit of coöperation, but, on the other hand, that we shall be able to strengthen you as you have strengthened us.

I am especially interested in the report of the discovery of Neolithic man in China by your Survey. This in itself marks a distinct step forward which will be followed, I am confident, by further archaeological discoveries, possibly reaching back to Palaeolithic time.

Believe me,

Cordially yours,

President.

Dr. V. K. Ting,
Director, Geological Survey of China
Peking, China.

September the twenty-eighth,

Nineteen Hundred twenty-one

My dear Sir:

I have just returned from an important archaeological and scientific tour in Western Europe and find excellent reports from Messrs. Andrews and Granger of our Third Asiatic Expedition.

I hasten to express our appreciation of the cordial manner in which you are planning for our cooperation and of the generous spirit of scientific interest which you are displaying. Chief Andrews writes that both yourself and Messrs. Andersson and Grabau have done everything in your power to make our share in the great undertaking of geological, paleontological, and archaeological exploration in China success. I feel sure that you will never have any reason to regret this spirit of cooperation, but, on the other hand, that we shall be able to strengthen you as you have strengthened us.

I am especially interested in the report of the discovery of Neolithic man in China by your Survey. This in itself marks a distinct step forward which will be followed, I am confident, by further archaeological discoveries, possibly reaching back to Paleolithic time.

Believe me,

Cordially yours,

President

Dr. V. K. Ting,
Director, Geological Survey of China
Peking, China.

1922 年

The Peipiao Coal Mining Co., Ltd.,
HEAD OFFICE.

Telegraphic Address: 4384.
Telephone 3055.

41 Via Marco Polo,
Italian Concession.

Tientsin, 11 Jan. 1922.

Dear Mr. Russel,

I am sending you two pamphlets of somewhat different nature with the idea that they may remind you that some of us have not entirely forgotten your recent visit.

I have no news to give beyond what you have no doubt read in the London newspapers. All the people you have met are still more or less alive, at least physically. As for myself, I am resigning from civil service to become manager of a coal mining company, deserting the deep sea for the devil, I am afraid.

With the compliments of the season and congratulations to Mrs. Russel,

Yours sincerely,

V. K. Ting

北票煤礦有限公司
The Peipiao Coal Mining Co., Ltd.

TELGRAPHIC ADDRESS 4384	HEAD OFFICE.	38 VIA PRINCIPE DI UDINE
TELEPHONE 3055.		ITALIAN CONCESSION

Tientsin, 11 Jan., 1922

Dear Mr. Russell,

I am sending you two pamphlets of somewhat different nature with the idea that they may remind you that some of us have not entirely forgotten your recent visit.

I have no news to give beyond what you have no doubt read in the London newspaper. All the people you have met are still more or less alive, at least physically. As for myself, I am resigning from civil service to become manager of a coal mining company, deserting the deep sea for the devil, I am afraid.

With the compliments of the season and congratulations to Mrs. Russell,

Yours sincerely
V. K. Ting

農商部地質調查所
The Geological Survey
3, Feng-Sheng Hutung,
W. Peking, China

Peking (China). 15th April 1922

Roy Chapman Andrews Esq.,
Kung Hsien Hutung,
Peking.

Dear Mr. Andrews,

I am glad to hear from Dr. Wong that the summary of Russian literature compiled by Leuchs has safely arrived. In his letter he explains that it was impossible to get the maps ready as the Russians never published any and to compile from the topographical maps would take far too much time.

Please kindly send me a draft (payable to Dr. Leuchs Munich) of 10,000 marks as agreed.

Yours sincerely;

V. K. Ting

農 商 部 地 質 調 查 所
The Geological Survey
3, Feng-Sheng Hutung,
W. Peking, China

Peking, 15th April, 1922

Roy Chapman Andrews Esq.,

Kung Hsien Hutung,

Peking.

My Dear Mr. Andrews,

I am glad to hear from Dr. Wong that the summary of Russian literature complied by Leuch has safely arrived. In his letter he explains that it was impossible to get the maps ready as the Russians never published any and to compile from the topographical maps would take far too much time.

Please kindly send me a draft (payable to Dr. Leuchs Munich) of 10,000 marks as agreed.

Yours sincerely,

V. K. Ting

My dear Doctor Ting:

A number of responses have been received to requests for publications for the Geological Survey. I think you may be interested and am, therefore, appending a list of those received to date. We shall be glad to write you from time to time as we have information of further responses.

I hope that ample and valuable material may reach you promptly.

With best wishes,

Sincerely yours,

GEORGE E. VINCENT

Doctor V. K. Ting
Director, The Geological Survey
Ministry of Agriculture and Commerce
Peking, China

NFS:MJS:E

April 20, 1922

My dear Doctor Ting:

A number of responses have been received to requests for publications for the Geological Survey. I think you may be interested and am, therefore, appending a list of those received to date. We shall be glad to write you from time to time as we have information of further responses.

I hope that ample and valuable material may reach you promptly.

With best wishes,

Sincerely yours,
George E. Vincent

Doctor V. K. Ting

Director, The Geological Survey

Ministry of Agriculture Commerce

Peking, China

April 20, 1922

American Museum of Natural History
President, Doctor Henry Fairfield Osborn

*** We are sending immediately a very fine series of Geological and Paleontological volumes to the Survey. April 7, 1922

New York Academy of Sciences
President Robert A. Harper

*** Personally the project appeals to me strongly and I shall be very glad to lay the matter before the council of the Academy at its next meeting, Wednesday, April 12.   April 7, 1922

New York Botanical Garden
Mr. N. L. Britton, Director-in-Chief

*** I am taking pleasure in sending to Dr. Ting a complete set of Bulletins, New York Botanical Garden, 10 volumes and part of the 11th volume, and have put his name upon our exchange list for this bulletin.
   Our other publications are disposed of by sale. I am sending Dr. Ting a printed list of them.
   As regards the publications of the Torrey Botanical Club, these are only disposed of by sale or subscriptions, or exchange with botanical organizations.   April 15, 1922

Columbia University
Amy L. Hepburn, Librarian Natural Sciences

*** We regret that volume I is entirely out of stock. We should be glad to send current volume and place the Geological Survey, Ministry of Agriculture and Commerce, Peking, China, upon our mailing list for future publications. Our supply of previous volumes is so incomplete that we prefer not to send them.   April 10, 1922.

Buffalo Society of Natural Sciences
Mr. Henry R. Howland, Corresponding Secretary

*** It will give us great pleasure to send to Dr. Ting a set of our Bulletins so far as they are now on hand. Naturally, in the course of so many years, the supply of some of them has been exhausted, but enough remain to be of service, I think to the Survey in China."   Apr 7, 1922

April 20, 1922

American Museum of Natural History

President, Doctor Henry Fairfield Osborn

We are sending immediately a very fine series of Geological and Paleontological volumes to the Survey. April 7, 1922

New York Academy of Sciences

President Robert A. Harper

Personally the project appeals to me strongly and I shall be very glad to lay the matter before the council of the Academy at its next meeting, Wednesday, April 12. April 7, 1922

New York Botanical Garden

Mr. N. L. Britton, Director-in-Chief

I am taking pleasure in sending to Dr. Ting a complete set of Bulletins, New York Botanical Garden, 10 volumes and part of the 11th volume, and have put his name upon our exchange list for this bulletin.

Our other publications are disposed of by sale. I am sending Dr. Ting a printed list of them.

As regards the publications of the Torrey Botanical Club, these are only disposed of by sale or subscriptions, or exchange with botanical organizations. April 15, 1922

Columbia University

Amy L. Hepburn, Librarian Natural Sciences

We regret that volume I is entirely out of stock. We should be glad to send current volume and place the Geological Survey, Ministry of Agriculture and Commerce, Peking, China, upon our mailing list for future publications. Our supply of previous volumes is so incomplete that we prefer not to send them. April 10, 1922

Buffalo Society of Natural Sciences

Mr. Henry R. Howland, Corresponding Secretary

It will give us great pleasure to send to Dr. Ting a set of our Bulletins so far as they are now on hand. Naturally, in the course of so many years, the supply of some of them has been exhausted, but enough remain to be of service, I think to the Survey in China. April 7, 1922

The Peipiao Coal Mining Co., Ltd.,

HEAD OFFICE.

TELEGRAPHIC ADDRESS: 4384.
TELEPHONE: 3055.

41 VIA MARCO POLO,
ITALIAN CONCESSION.

Tientsin, 24 July 1922.

Dear Mr. Russell,

    I must apologise for not answering your kind letter of 20th Feb. before now. My excuse is that I have been unusually busy and have not been in the best of health. For, although I became general manager of a coal mining company, my old friends in the Geological Survey persuaded me to accept the position of a Hon. Director which entails a good deal of work. I have also been trying to help my friend, Dr. Hu, by contributing regularly to his newly published political weekly, "the Endeavour".

    I am sorry to say that I never received the photograph of your child. This is no surprise to me because I have no official connection with the University and the man who is in charge of the postal matters may not know my name in English. Thank you all the same for your kindness in thinking of me. In fact I should be very grateful if you can send me a photograph of yourself and Mrs. ~~Black~~ Russell. I will send you one of mine as soon as I have one taken.

    The facts I gave about birth-rate in China are based on very limited data therefore by no means conclusive. But there is no doubt that our increase of population has been grossly exaggerated. On this subject I have collected a good deal of material which seems to indicate that in the cities at least the population 300 years ago was as great as it is to-day. For example the city of Kiang-Ying (near the mouth of the Yangtse) suffered a terrible

massacre in the hands of the envading Manchus. After the departure
of the latter a monk undertook to bury the dead and the exact
number of corpses was then recorded in a tablet. This number is
practical the same as the actual population of Kiang-Ying. When
I have a little more time I hope to carry on some serious research
work on this line as it may throw a great deal of light upon some
of the fundamental questions of civilisation.

The rsult of the recent fighting near Peking has been
again disappointing. But we are by no means so disheartened. Time
is necessary to settle these things, and, unfortunately, the serious
financial situation hardly allows us any breathing space.

My heartest congratulation on your marriage. Whilst
it may not give you any moral satisfaction, it will no doubt
help to do away with the social annoyance which invariably awaits
the pioneer.

I hear quite often from Chao who claims to have solved
the problem of denoting the tones. I think he is going to publish
a book on the subject.

With best regards to Mrs. Russell and yourself,
Yours sincerely,

(V. K. Ting)

北票煤礦有限公司
The Peipiao Coal Mining Co., Ltd.

TELGRAPHIC ADDRESS 4384	HEAD OFFICE.	38 VIA PRINCIPE DI UDINE
TELEPHONE 3055.		ITALIAN CONCESSION

Tientsin, 24 July, 1922.

Dear Mr. Russell,

I must apologize for not answering your kind letter of 20th Feb. before now. My excuse is that I have been unusually busy and have not been in the best of health. For, although I became general manager of a coal mining company, my old friends in the Geological Survey persuaded me to accept the position of a Hon. Director which entails a good deal of work. I have also been trying to help my friend, Dr. Hu, by contributing regularly to his newly published political weekly, "the Endeavour".

I am sorry to say that I never received the photography of your child. This is no surprise to me because I have no official connection with the University and the man who is in charge of the postal matters may not know my name in English. Thank you all the same for your kindness in thinking of me. In fact, I should be very grateful if you can send me a photography of yourself and Mrs. Russell. I will send you one of mines as soon as I have one taken.

The facts I gave birth-rate in China are based on very limited data therefore by no means conclusive. But there is no doubt that our increase of population has been grossly exaggerated. On this subject I have collected a good deal of material which seems to indicate that in the cities at least the population 300 years ago was as great as it is today. For example, the city of Kinag-Ying (near the mouth of the Yangtze) suffered a terrible massacre in the hands of the invading Manchus. After the departure of the latter a monk undertook to bury the dead and the exact number of corpses was then recorded in a tablet. This number is practical the same as the actual population of Kiang-Ying. When I have a little more time I hope to carry on some serious research work on this line as it may throw a great deal of light upon some of the fundamental questions of civilization.

The result of the recent fighting near Peking has been again disappointing. But we are by no means so disheartened. Time is necessary to settle these things and unfortunately, the serious financial situation hardly allow us any breathing space.

My heartiest congratulation on your marriage. Whilst it may not give you any moral satisfaction, it will no doubt help to do away with the social annoyance which invariably awaits the pioneer.

I hear quite often from Chao who claims to have solved the problem of denoting the tone. I think he is going to publish a book on the subject.

With best regards to Mrs. Russell and yourself.

Yours sincerely
V. K. Ting

1923 年

農商部地質調查所
The Geological Survey
3, Feng-Sheng Hutung,
W. Peking, China

Peking, Jan. 6, 1923.
(China).

Roy Chapman Andrews Esq.,
The Third Asiatic Expedition,
American Museum of Natural History,
Kung Hsien Hutung, Peking.

Dear Mr. Andrews,

I have just returned from a trip to Jehol and have heard with delight that your plan for establishing a Natural History Museum here in Peking is being pushed a step further. You have my best wishes for success.

Allow me however to make a suggestion. The term "Natural History" includes in its usual meaning not only zoology and botany, but also geology, mineralogy and palaeontology. There is in Peking no real museum exhibiting zoological and botanical specimens which is urgently needed, but the Geological Survey has been since 1914, even before its official inauguration, deeply interested in, not only collecting, but also exhibiting objects illustrating the geology and palaeontology of this country in all their branches. In fact two new halls have just been built for housing the plant and vertebrate fossils collected by the Survey. It has been and, I think, will always be the policy of the Geological Survey not to neglect this educational side of its activities. It seems to me therefore a duplication of effort to represent these branches of science in a separate museum in the same city and that it is highly desirable to arrange some division of labour in order to avoid unnecessary competition.

2

I am well aware that in some countries the representation of both geology and palaeontology is left entirely in the hands of the natural history museum, and the geological survey confines itself to the making of geological maps, but this arrangement is by no means universal, and it is largely a matter of historical tradition where the museum had existed before the geological survey was organised, or again the survey and the museum are not in the same city. Of late there is more and more cooperation between these related institutions even in such countries. For example the English Geological Survey is moving from its historical home in Jermyn Street to South Kensington in order to be near to the British Museum, and the close relation between the U. S. Geological Survey and the Smithsonian Institution is no doubt well known to you. In China the Geological Survey has already organised a geological and palaeontological museum before any scheme of forming a general natural history museum was thought of. It seems to me therefore not unnatural that it should claim to be the official representative of the sciences of geology, mineralogy and palaeontology including prehistoric archaeology in which it has been deeply interested, on which it has done a considerable amount of work, and for which it has spent not a little money to house and exhibit the collections. I think this will in no way interfere with the original scheme of the Third Asiatic Expedition which has every right to leave its collections---even the geological and palaeontological collections---in any museum or institution it may consider best suitable. I am only

3

hoping that the natural history museum you are trying to organise will recognise the priority of the Chinese Geological Survey in collecting, describing and exhibiting geological and palaeontological objects, and come to some arrangement or understanding to avoid competition and duplication of effort in the interest of science.

I have been hesitating a great deal in writing this letter as it may seem that I am trying to interfere with your plans, but I have finally decided to do so in rereading Dr. Osborn's letter of 10th Feb. 1921 in which he said as follows:

"We conceived the plan of presenting to the Chinese Government a duplicate set as far as possible of all the collections.----This we hope will prove a stimulation for a general natural history museum in China. It may be that the plans for the future of the Geological Survey are so broad that they would include the exhibition of objects of general natural history interest; our collection would be best presented to the Survey. This is a matter which I will be glad to discuss with you when I visit China."

Remembering also your willingness of accepting my suggestion for collecting vertebrate fossils, I am encouraged to think that you will receive this in the same spirit in which it is written. To avoid misunderstandings, I may add that the Geological Survey has no plan to include zoology or botany in its museum which exhibits only geological, palaeontological and archaeological specimens.

4

  To the best of my knowledge you have never yet gone through our museum. Perhaps you may have the idea that we are confining our attention to practical geology which is by far not the case. Dr. Wong is in fact organising a special exhibition of our palaeontological material. I think he will take care to invite you. Even if the particular day is unsuitable, you are welcome to come any other time if you will only let Dr. Wong know a few hours in advance. I think an inspection of our collections will give you a far better idea of our plans than any letters I can write.

  As I understand that you will probably refer all such matters to President Osborn, I have taken the liberty to send him a copy of this letter.

  With kind regards,

      Yours sincerely,

      V. K. Ting

      Director of the Geological Survey

農 商 部 地 質 調 查 所
The Geological Survey
3, Feng-Sheng Hutung,
W. Peking, China

Peking, Jan. 6, 1923.

Roy Chapman Andrews Esq.,
The Third Asiatic Expedition,
American Museum of Natural History,
Kung Hsien Hutung, Peking.

My Dear Mr. Andrews,

I have just returned from a trip to Jehol and have heard with delight that your plan for establishing a Natural History Museum here in Peking is being pushed a step further. You have my best wishes for success.

Allow me however to make a suggestion. The term "Natural History" includes in its usual meaning not only zoology and botany, but also geology, mineralogy and paleontology. There is in Peking no real museum exhibiting zoological and botanical specimens which is urgently needed, but the Geological Survey has been since 1914, even before its official inauguration, deeply interested in, not only collecting, but also exhibiting objects illustrating the geology and paleontology of this country in all their branches. In fact, two new halls have just been built for housing the plant and vertebrate fossils collected by the Survey. It has been and, I think, will always be the policy of the Geological Survey not to neglect this educational side of its activities. It seems to me therefore a duplication of effort to represent these branches of science in a separate museum in the same city and that it is highly desirable to arrange some division of labor in order to avoid unnecessary competition.

I am well aware that in some countries the representation of both geology and paleontology is left entirely in the hands of the natural history museum, and the geological survey confines itself to the making of geological maps, but this arrangement is by no means universal, and it is largely a matter of historical tradition where the museum had existed before the geological survey was organized, or again the survey and the museum are not in the same city. Of late there is more and more cooperation between these related institutions even in such countries. For example, the English Geological Survey is moving from its historical home in Jermyn Street to South Kensington in order to be near to the British Museum, and the close relation between the U.S Geological Survey and the Smithsonian Institution is no doubt well known to you. In China the Geological Survey has already organized a geological and paleontological museum before any scheme of forming a general natural history museum was thought of. It seems to me therefore not unnatural that it should claim to be the official representative of the sciences of geology, mineralogy and paleontology including prehistoric archaeology in which it has been deeply interested, on which it has done a considerable amount of work, and for which it has spent not a little money to house and exhibit the collections. I think this will in no way interfere with the original scheme of the Third Asiatic Expedition which has every right to leave its collections—even the geological and paleontological collections-in any museum or institution it may consider best suitable. I am only hoping that the natural history museum you are trying to organize will recognize the priority of the Chinese Geological Survey in collecting, describing and exhibiting geological and paleontological objects, and come to some arrangement or understanding to avoid competition and duplication of effort in the interest of science.

I have been hesitating a great deal in writing this letter as it may seem that I am trying to interfere with your plans, but I have finally decided to do so in rereading Dr. Osborn's letter of 10th Feb.1921 in which he said as follows:

"We conceived the plan of presenting to the Chinese Government a duplicate set as far as possible of all the collections. —This we hope will prove a stimulation for a general natural history museum in China. It may be that the plans for the future of the Geological Survey are so broad that they would include the exhibition of objects of general natural history interest; our collection would be best presented to the Survey. This is a matter which I will be glad to discuss with you when I visit China."

Remembering also your willingness of accepting my suggestion for collecting vertebrate fossils, I am encouraged to think that you will receive this in the same spirit in which it is written. To avoid misunderstandings, I may add that the Geological Survey has no plan to include zoology or botany in its museum which exhibits only geological, paleontological and archaeological specimens.

To the best of my knowledge you have never yet gone through our museum. Perhaps you may have the idea that we are confining our attention to practical geology which is by far not the case. Dr. Wong is in fact organizing a special exhibition of our paleontological material. I think he will take care to invite you. Even if the particular day is unsuitable, you are welcome to come any other time if you will only let Dr. Wong know a few hours in advance. I think an inspection of our collections will give you a far better idea of our plans than any letters I can write.

As I understand that you will probably refer all such matters to President Osborn, I have taken the liberty to send him a copy of this letter.

With kind regards,

Yours sincerely,
V. K. Ting
Director of the Geological Survey

The Peipiao Coal Mining Co., Ltd.,

TELEGRAPHIC ADDRESS: 4384.
TELEPHONE: 3055.

HEAD OFFICE.

38 VIA PRINCIPE DI UDINE
ITALIAN CONCESSION.

Tientsin, 15 November '23 192 .

C. W. Bishop Esq.,
℅ American Legation,
Peking.

Dear Mr. Bishop,

Many thanks for your interesting letter of the 7th inst. I was in Peking on the 7th, but was unable to attend Hedin's lecture at the Geological Society because I had to deliver a lecture myself on the same day at Tsinghua. On the 9th however I had a long talk with him after dinner at the Swedish Legation where we set up till 2 o'clock in the morning.

I have never met Mr. Karlbeck but have heard much of him from Dr. Andersson. You are quite right in thinking that the art of forging swords was discovered fairly early in the Yangtse Valley. In both the Wu Yueh Chun Chiu (吳越春秋) and the Yueh Chueh Shu (越紀書), mentions are made of the wonderful swords. In the latter the ore is said to come from 茨山 Tzu Shan. It is not possible to identify it positively, but very probably it is one of the small deposits near Wuchou on the Taihu Lake. Again the numerous iron deposits on the border of Kiangsu and Anhuei on the southern bank of the Yangtse must have been worked in very early times. The fact that these deposits could be mined by open cuts and that they were near proximity to forests to the south which must have supplied the fuel, are important factors in helping to develop an early iron industry in the lower Yangtse. Nowhere in northern China could a primitive people obtain iron with the same facility.

    Of course the forging of these swords means the discovery of making steel rather than of iron, which was known much earlier. You are no doubt aware of the fact that the bronze arrow-heads had always iron cores inside. Even iron was probably a southern discovery, for we have in Shun Tsu 荀子 and Han Fei Tsu 韓非子 mentions of iron articles made by the people of Chu 楚. Such evidence is even more reliable than Wu Yueh Chun Chiu and Yueh Chueh Shu which were written by Han people. Besides the very character "iron" consists of originally the two characters Chin 金 and yih 夷, suggesting that iron was a metal of the barbarians 夷. Recent investigation on the origin of the mythical emperor Yu seems to suggest that Yu was really one of the legendary emperors of the Yangtse tribes and was only incoporated into the northern legends when the Wu and Yueh tribes became important states in the feudal system. All these indicate that the early civilisation in the Lower Yangtse Valley was probably just as important, if not more so, than that in the region of the Yellow River.

    I shall be extremely interested in reading your report on the Hsin Cheng find. I sent down one of my men there as soon as I heard of the discovery and he was able to make a map of the region and to partly reconstruct the excavation. Later on we re-excavated the human remains said to be found together with the bronze. Dr. Li Chi, an anthrpologist, is making a study of them.

       I expect to be in Peking on the 20th inst, and will try to look you up.

       With kind regards,

          Yours sincerely,

            (V.K.TING)

北票煤礦有限公司
The Peipiao Coal Mining Co., Ltd.

TELGRAPHIC ADDRESS 4384	HEAD OFFICE.	38 VIA PRINCIPE DI UDINE
TELEPHONE 3055.		ITALIAN CONCESSION

Tientsin, 15 November, 1923

C. W. Bishop Esq.,

% American Legation,

Peking.

Dear Mr. Bishop,

  Many thanks for your interesting letter of the 7th inst. I am in Peking on the 7th, but was unable to attend Hedin's lecture at the Geological Society because I had to deliver a lecture myself on the same day at Tsinghua. On the 9th however I had a long talk with him after dinner at the Swedish Legation where we set up till 2 o'clock in the morning.

  I have never met Mr. Karlbeck but have heard much of him from Dr. Andersson. You are quite right in thinking that the art of forging swords was discovered fairly early in the Yangtse Valley. In both the Wu Yueh Chun Chiu（吳越春秋）and the Yueh Chueh Shu（越絕書）, mentions are made of the wonderful swords. In the latter the ore is said to come from Tzu Shan（茨山）. It is not possible to identify it positively, but very probably it is one of the small deposits near Wuchou on the Tiahu Lake. Again the numerous iron deposits on the border of Kiangsu and Anhuei on the southern bank of the Yangtse must have been worked in very early times. The fact that these deposits could be mined by open cuts and that they were to near to forests to the south which must have supplied the fuel, are important factors in helping to develop an early iron industry in the lower Yangtse. Nowhere in northern China could a primitive people obtain iron with the same facility.

Of course the forging of these swords means the discovery of making steel rather than of iron, which was known much earlier. You are no doubt aware of the fact that the bronze arrow-heads had always iron cores inside. Even iron was probably a southern discovery, for we have in Shun Tsu（荀子）and Han Fei（韓非子）mentions of iron articles made by the people of Chu（楚）. Such evidence is even more reliable than Wu Yueh Chun Chiu and Yueh Chueh Shu which were written by Han people. Besides the very character "iron" consists of originally the two characters Chin（金）and yin（夷）, suggesting that iron was a metal of the barbarians. Recent investigation on the origin of the mythical emperor Yu（禹）seems to suggest that Yu was really one of the legendary emperors of the Yangtze tribes and was only incorporated into the northern legends when the Wu and Yueh tribes became important states in the feudal system. All these indicate that the early civilization in the Lower Yangtse Valley was probably just as important, if not more so, than that in the region of the Yellow River.

I shall be extremely interested in reading your report on the Hsin Cheng find. I sent down one of my men there as soon as I heard of the discovery and he was able to make a map of the region and to reconstruct partly the excavation. Later on we re-excavated the human remains said to be found together with the bronze. Dr. Li Chi, an anthropologist, is making a study of them.

I expect to be in Peking on the 20th inst, and will try to look you up.

With kind regards

Yours sincerely

V. K. Ting

The Peipiao Coal Mining Co., Ltd.,

HEAD OFFICE.

TELEGRAPHIC ADDRESS: 4384.
TELEPHONE: 3055.

41 VIA MARCO POLO.
ITALIAN CONCESSION.

Tientsin, 18 December 1923.

Mr. C. W. Bishop,
℅ American Legation,
Peking.

Dear Mr. Bishop,

    Your friend Mr. Tangier-Smith came in to see me the other day and told me his plans for scientific work. He wished to have a man from the Geological Survey to do some geological and geographical work and I promised to let him know definitely next January whether we will be able to get a man. It so happens that one of our men who was sent to America for further training will be back by the end of the month and I hope that he will be willing to undertake the work, but I must wait for his arrival before I write to Mr. Tangier-Smith.

    I told Dr. Wong about your desire to have a man to translate something for you and he says that Dr. Grabau has a pupil of his who is quite good for this kind of work. Please communicate with Dr. Wong if you still require assistance.

    Dr. Li Chi who will undertake the study of the human remains from Hsincheng will be in Peking in the beginning of next year. Will you kindly hand over to Dr. Stevenson of the P.U.M.C. the bones in your position as he is going to give Dr. Li a room there? You will be glad to hear that the Honan authorities have formally invited Mr. Lo Cheng Yü to study the bronze collection and he will leave for Kaifeng in a few days. I think you have made some photographs. Is it possible to get copies of them at my expense? I shall be also grateful if you can let me see your report which may be of help to Dr. Li in his studies. I will supply you with copies of his and Mr. Tan's report as soon as they are ready. The preparation of these has been delayed owing to Mr. Tan's absence from Peking.

  With kindest regards,

   Yours sincerely,

    V. K. Ting (V.K.TING)

P.S. Have you seen Prof. Ma's report on the Hsincheng find? It was published in the Peking paper called Ch'eng Pao or "Morning Post" about 2 months ago.

北票煤礦有限公司
The Peipiao Coal Mining Co., Ltd.

TELGRAPHIC ADDRESS 4384	HEAD OFFICE.	38 VIA PRINCIPE DI UDINE
TELEPHONE 3055.		ITALIAN CONCESSION

Tientsin, 18 December, 1923

C. W. Bishop Esq.,

℅ American Legation,

Peking.

Dear Mr. Bishop,

  Your friend Mr. Tangier-Smith came in to see me the other day and told me his plans for scientific work. He wished to have a man from the Geological Society to do some geological and geographical work and I promised to let him know definitely next January whether we will be able to get a man. It so happens that one of our men who was sent to America for further training will be back by the end of the month and I hope that he will be willing to undertake the work, but I must wait for his arrival before I write to Mr. Tangier-Smith.

  I told Dr. Wong about your desire to have a man to translate something for you and he says that Dr. Grabau has a pupil of his who is quite good for this kind of work. Please communicate with Dr. Wong if you still require assistance.

  Dr. Li Chi who will undertake the study of the human remains from Hsincheng will be in Peking in the beginning of next year. Will you kindly hand over to Dr. Stevenson of the PUMC the bones in your position as he is going to give Dr. Li a room there? You will be glad to hear that the Honan authorities have formally invited Mr. Lo Cheng Yu to study the bronze collection and he will leave for Kaifeng in a few days. I think you have made some photographs. Is it possible to get copies of them at my expense? I shall be also grateful if you can let me see your report which may be of help to Dr. Li in his studies. I will supply you with copies of his and Mr. Tan's report as soon as they are ready. The preparation of these has been delayed owing to Mr. Tan's absence from Peking.

With kindest regards

Yours sincerely
V. K. Ting

P.S. Have you seen Prof. Ma's report on the Hsingcheng find? It was published in the Peking Paper called Ch'eng Pao or "Morning Post" about 2 months ago.

1924 年

Peking, 2 January, 1924.

Dr. V. K. Ting, Director,
The Geological Survey,
41 Via Marco Polo, Tientsin.

Dear Dr. Ting:-

Let me, to begin with, extend to you my heartiest good wishes for the New Year; may it bring to you all the accomplishment and prosperity and success that you can possibly cram into it!

I wish I might have been able to attend the meetings now going on. But I have just shifted my quarters from the Peking Hotel to a house of my own, and am in the throes of getting my things straightened out, besides attending to a lot of work that I don't dare allow to get too far ahead of me. And I presume, besides, that abstracts, at least, of most of the papers will appear later.

I shall try to lay my hands this afternoon on the films of the photographs which I took down at Chêng Chow and Hsin-chêng Hsien (and which, if I do say it myself, turned out very well), and will get a set of prints made for you in the morning. The pictures are of course the property of the Smithsonian Institution; so in case you wished to publish any of them, I should appreciate it if you made mention of the fact. I shall be anxious to have your opinion of them; I will write on the back of each the particulars concerning it.

My own very brief and sketchy preliminary report of what I saw

Dr VKT-2.

of this find is already in the hands of Dr. Tyau, and will, I presume, appear in the next issue of the "Review". I hope that later on I may be enabled to draw up a complete report in English, with maps, plans, and illustrations, and with a brief historical sketch of the region in which the discovery was made. I trust that I may be permitted, in this connection, to make use (of course giving the fullest credit) of the conclusions of Dr. Li Chi and Mr. Tan; and I shall be pleased, in return, to place my material at their disposal.

I have already spoken to Dr. Stevenson about the human material I secured, and shall be pleased to turn it over to Dr. Li Chi whenever he is ready for it.

What you have to say regarding the superior culture of the early Yangtse Valley is extremely interesting, and falls in with what I have long maintained---that there were at least three culture foci along that river: Wu, Ch'u, and, above the Gorges, Shuh-Pa, which attained a degree of culture at least comparable to that of the Ho Valley, altho' having for its basis a totally different system of food economy, viz., the cultivation of irrigated rice with the water-buffalo instead of that of millet and wheat with the aid of plow oxen.

This southern system of agriculture seems by most authorities to be derived from the region about the head of the Bay of Bengal; and inasmuch as the knowledge of iron appears very early in India, I wonder whether that too maynot have formed part of this culture drift along the very ancient trade-route between Burma and western China, and so

DrVKT-3.

eventually down the Yangtse and, laterally, up the affluents of the latter. The fact that Wu appears as an important power only some centuries later than Ch'u would seem to suggest that the drift of this rice-buffalo-iron culture complex was from west to east and not the reverse. There is of course always the possibility that the knowledge of iron was acquired independently in the Yangtse Valley; but I believe that the tendency among modern anthropologists is to favor for most of the more important discoveries a single rather than a multiple origin. The question can only, of course, if ever, be settled by archaeological investigation along the two or three routes by which the knowledge of iron may have reached China.

About the locality from which the iron used by the early smiths of the Yangtse region was obtained, if my recollection serves, it is the people of Wu and Yüeh who are represented as anxious to possess themselves of the iron of Ch'u for the purpose of making arms. But the Wu-chou region, about the T'ai-hu, was in the territory of Wu, was it not? My impression is that Ch'u only rarely extended its influence this far east.

There is also, I recall, a passage in the Yü Kung or "Tribute of Yü" which states that in addition to gold, silver, and copper, iron also is obtained from a region usually regarded as corresponding in a general way to the modern eastern Szechuan---or in other words, to the Shuh-Pa culture focus. If my memory serves me rightly, this is the only one of the Nine Chow mentioned in the Yü Kung to which iron is

DrVKT-4.

ascribed. I am nearly certain that it is not given as among the products of either Ching Chow or Yang Chow, corresponding somewhat to the later Ch'u and Wu. This again suggests a movement of the iron culture west to east, down the Yangtse.

I have, unfortunately, no books of reference at hand; but I believe that iron was an object of taxation in Ch'i (Shantung) as early as the eighth century; but that at that time only domestic utensils and tools of various sorts were made of it, bronze still being used in war, exactly as the case in western Asia and in Europe long after iron was perfectly well known.

It would be interesting to know whether there attached, in ancient China, any such body of superstitions to the bronze worker's craft as there undoubtedly did to that of the iron worker, in ancient China as elsewhere, from Japan to Iceland and West Africa.

The question of the beginnings of steel, of course, is an entirely different one; but I think it significant that so many of the old iron working processes in China have resembled those used in working bronze; in other words, so much of the ancient Chinese iron is cast where in contemporary Europe it would have been wrought.

I also recall a passage somewhere in the Early Han History giving a letter from the king of Nan-Yüeh to the Chinese court, complaining that an embargo had been placed upon the exportation to his dominions of iron farming implements and water buffaloes. This would seem to tend to confirm my idea that both wet rice culture with the

DrVKT-5.

use of the buffalo and the use of iron worked down the Yangtse and spread up its affluents---at least to the south. The history of these culture elements to the north of the river may well have been more complex.

Your analysis of the character for iron as composed of the two elements "metal" and "barbarian" seems to me very pertinent. Of course, to the peoples of the Ho valley, no doubt the word here used for "barbarian" might have connoted equally well either the people of Wu, or Ch'u, or Shuh-Pa, or perhaps even other non-Chinese tribes. I wonder whether, in still earlier times the word was restricted to any particular group of barbarians? If this could be shown to be the case it would have some bearing upon the origin of iron.

But I have bored you long enough with these lucubrations, for which I have had to rely entirely upon my memory, and which are, in consequence, painfully hazy and inexact. Such as they are, however, I should greatly enjoy having your opinion of them.

My present permanent address is still the American Legation; but I am living at 3ª Hsiang Ri-tzŭ Hou Hêng (East City); and Mr. Tung, my helper, whom you have met, and who lives next door, has a telephone, East 3944. Thanks again for your good letters, and believe me, with kindest regards,

          Very sincerely yours,

Peking, January 6, 1924

Dr. V. K. Ting, Director
The Geological Survey,
41 Via Marco Fold, Tientsin

Dear Dr. Ting:

Let me to begin with, extend to you my heartiest good wishes for the New Year; may it bring to you all the accomplishment and prosperity and success that you can possibly craw into it!

I wish I might have been able to attend the meetings now going on. But I have just shifted my quarters from the Peking Hotel to a house of my own, and am in the threes of getting my things straightened cut, besides attending to a lot of work that I don't dare allow to get too far ahead of me. And I presume, besides, that abstracts, at least, of most of the paper will appear later.

I shall try to lay my hands this afternoon on the films of the photographs which I took down at Cheng Chow and Hsin-cheng Hsien (and which, if I do say it myself, turned out very well), and will get a set of prints made for you in the morning. The pictures are of course the property of the Smithsonian Institution; so in case you wished to publish any of them, I should appreciate it if you made mention of the fact. I shall be anxious to have your opinion of them; I will write on the back of each the particulars concerning it.

My own very brief and sketchy preliminary report of what I saw of this find is already in the hands of Dr. Tyau, and will, I presume, appear in the next issue of the "Review". I hope that later on I may be enabled to draw up a complete report in English, with maps, plans, and illustrations, and with a brief historical sketch of the region in which the discovery was made. I trust that I may be permitted, in this connection, to make use (of course giving the fullest credit) of the conclusion of Dr. Li Chi and Mr.

Tan; and I shall be pleased, in return, to place my material at their disposal.

I have already spoken to Dr. Stevenson about the human material I secured, and shall be pleased to turn it over to Dr. Li Chi whenever he is ready for it.

What you have to say regarding the superior culture of the early Yangtse Valley is extremely interesting, and falls in with what I have long maintained—that there were at least three culture foci along the river: Wu, Ch'u, and above the Gorges, Shu-Pa, which attained a degree of culture at least comparable to that of the Ho Valley, although having for its basis a totally different system of food economy, viz., the cultivation of irrigated rice with the water-buffalo instead of that the millet and wheat with the aid of plow oxen.

This southern system of agriculture seems by most authorities to be derived from the region about the head of the Bay of Bengal; and in as much as the knowledge of iron appears very early in India, I wonder whether that too magnet (?) have formed part of this culture drift along the very ancient trade route between Burma and western China, and so eventually down the Yangtse and, laterally, up the affluent of the latter. The fact that Wu appears as an important power only some centuries later than Ch'u would seem to suggest that the drift of this rice-buffalo culture complex was from west to east and not the reverse. There is of course always the possibility that the knowledge of iron was acquired independently in the Yangtse Valley; but I believe that the tendency among modern anthropologists is to favor for most of the more important discoveries a single rather than a multiple origin. The question can only, of course, if ever, be settled by archaeological investigation along the two or three routes by which the knowledge of iron may have reached China.

About the locality from which the iron used by the early smiths of the Yangtse region was obtained, if my recollection serves, it is the people of Wu and Yueh who are represented as anxious to possess themselves of the iron of Ch'u for the purpose of making arms. But the Wu-chu region, about the T'ai-hu, was in the territory of Wu, was it not? My impression is that Ch'u only rarely extended its influence this far east.

There is also, I recall, a passage in the Yu Gong on "Tribute of Yu" which state that in addition to gold, silvers, and copper, iron also is obtained from a region usually regarded as corresponding in a general way to the modern eastern Szechuan---or in other words, to the Shuh-Pa culture focus. If my memory serves me rightly, this is the only one of the Nine Chow mentioned in the Yu Gong to which iron is attributed. I am nearly certain that it is not given as among the products of either Ching Chow or Yang Chow, corresponding somewhat to the later Ch'u and Wu. This again suggests a movement of the iron culture west to east, down the Yangtse.

I have, unfortunately, no books of reference at hand; but I believe that iron was an object of taxation in Ch'i (Shantung) as early as the eighth century; but that at that time only domestic utensils and tools of various sorts were made of it, bronze still being used in war, exactly as the case in western Asian and in Europe long after iron was perfectly well known.

It would be interesting to know whether attached, in ancient China, any such body of superstition to the bronze worker's craft as there undoubtedly did to that of the iron worker, in ancient China as elsewhere, form Japan to Iceland and West Africa.

The question of the beginnings of steel, of course, is an entirely different one; but I think it significant that so many of the old iron working processes in China have resembled those used in working bronze; in other words, so much of the ancient Chinese iron is cast where in contemporary Europe it would have been wrought.

I also recall a passage somewhere in the Early Han History giving a letter from the king of Nan-Yueh to the Chinese court, complaining that an embargo had been placed upon the exportation to his dominions of iron farming implements and water buffaloes. This would seem to tend to confirm my idea that both wet rice culture with the use of buffalo and the use of iron worked down the Yangtse and spread up its affluent—at least to the south. The history of these culture elements to the north of the river may well have been more complex.

Your analysis of the character for iron as composed of the two elements "mental" and "barbarian" seems to me very pertinent. Of course, to the peoples of the Ho valley, no doubt the word here used for "barbarian" might have connected equally well either the people of Wu or Ch'u, or Shuh-Pa, or perhaps even other non-Chinese tribes. I wonder whether, in still earlier times the word was restricted to any particular group of barbarians? If this could be shown to the case it would have some bearing upon the origin of iron.

But I have bored you long enough with these lucubration, for which I have had to rely entirely upon my memory, and which are, in consequence, painfully hazy and inexact. Such as they are, however, I should greatly enjoy having your opinion of them.

My present permanent address is still the American Legation; but I am living at 26 Fsiang Pi-tzu Hou Keng (East City); and Mr. Tung, my helper, whom you have met, and who lives next door, has a telephone East 3944. Thanks again for your good letters, and believe me, with kindest regards,

            Very sincerely yours,
            [C. W. Bishop]

The Peipiao Coal Mining Co., Ltd.,

TELEGRAPHIC ADDRESS: 4384.
TELEPHONE: 3055.

HEAD OFFICE.

38 VIA PRINCIPE DI UDINE
ITALIAN CONCESSION.

Tientsin, 14 January 1924.

C. W. Bishop Esq.,
26, Hsiang Pi Tzu Hou Kung,
Peking E.

My dear Mr. Bishop,

Many thanks for your long and interesting letter. I was in fact in Peking for the meeting and 'phoned you up, but you were out riding.

First of all let me thank you heartily for your kind promise to let me have a set of your photographs. I have no intention of publishing them. In any case I will first get your permission before doing so. Is it possible to let me see a copy of the paper you wrote for Dr. Tyau since I do not see the "Review" regularly and may miss it?

I think Dr. Li Chi and Mr. Tan will get the report ready sometime before the end of February and I will send you a copy as soon I receive it. I think also the only inscription deciphered by Mr. Wang Kuo Wei will be interesting to you. In addition Mr. Lo has brought back quite a lot of information and material which he is unwilling to diverge publicly for fear of getting somebody into trouble. His statement about the disposition of the bronze is a direct contradiction to the story given out officially---that is one of the reasons why I wanted to hear from you, as Mr. Tan was there later than you, and cannot give direct evidence. I am also getting some of the so-called cinnabar analysed to see if it is not only haematite as often is the case.

Your suggestion about the origin of the southern culture is most interesting. I am very ignorant about things Indian. Can you give me a list of literature on the older culture of India? My own impression has been that there is still no very reliable chronology either historic or prehistoric since even the date of the birth of Buddha is not known with absolute certainty.

You are quite right in your quotation of Yü Kung, but I beg to remind you of two things. Firstly, Liang Chou includes that part of Shensi south of the Tsingling range. "Between Heisui and Huayang" is the original definition, but Heisui has never been located with certainty. Now southern Shensi and northern Hupeh are famous for the primitive iron industry based on magnatic sands. The last is commonly believed to be the first iron ore worked by man. May the reference to iron in Liangchou not be merely an indication of the existence of the working of the magnatic sands? Secondly, Yü Kung is now admitted to be a comparative late production---perhaps during or a little before the time of Confucius. Among the metals mentioned together with iron is the metal Lou (镂), commonly interpreted as steel. If such interpretation is correct, Yü Kung must even be later.

Your reference to the taxation on iron in Ch'i must have come from Kuan Tzu which is unfortunately a forgery, made not earlier than the third century B. C. So its evidence is not of much value. It is interesting however to note that the word Yi can only mean "the eastern barbarian" when it is used in the sense of a people particular, and not as a general term. By the way, Yi is practically the only word applied to non-Chinese people without any contempt in the original ~~sense~~ sense in contrast to such terms as Ti, Jung and Man.

I think you are wrong in saying that the people of Wu and Yüeh were anxious to get iron from Chu. On the contrary, Chu obtained the iron masters from the two latter states. Chu was said to be rich in bronze, for in Tso Ch'uan it was recorded that Chu gave a lot of that metal to Cheng, but made the latter swear not to use it for making weapons.

To sum up I think iron was known in the time of Confucius, but its general use, especially in the manufacture of arms, began only towards the end of the Chou dynasty.

Have you any data on Pa and Shu? My impression is that they were Lolos, because a transliteration of a poem written in the Han turns out to be of Lolo language, and because to this very day the chieftains in southern Hupeh are all Lolos.

Yes, there was a great deal of superstition attached to the arm manufactureers as you can read in the Yü Chü Shu and elsewhere.

I have not yet had time to look up your reference to the letter from the king of Nan Yüeh, But I presume that it is the famous letter of King Chao Tô to Han Wen TI. If that is the case, then it has no value in proving anything, for Nan Yüeh is Canton to which the trade route was via Kiangsi. Besides it is of such a late date (beginning of Han). It would prove, if anything, that the Nan Yüeh people did not have iron.

Can you favour me with some of your publications as I understand you have written a number of papers on such questions?

Yours sincerely,

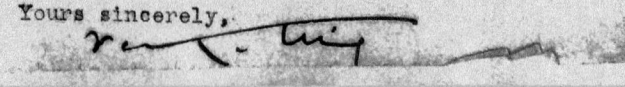

北票煤礦有限公司
The Peipiao Coal Mining Co., Ltd.

TELGRAPHIC ADDRESS 4384	HEAD OFFICE.	38 VIA PRINCIPE DI UDINE
TELEPHONE 3055.		ITALIAN CONCESSION

Tientsin, 14 January, 1924

C. W. Bishop Esq.,

26, Hsiang Pi Tzu Hou Keng,

Peking E.

My dear Mr. Bishop,

Many thanks for your long and interesting letter. I was in fact in Peking for the meeting and phoned you up, but you were out riding.

First of all, let me thank you heartily for your kind promise to let me have a set of your photographs. I have on intention of publishing them. In any case I will first get your permission before doing so. Is it possible to let me see a copy of the paper you wrote for Dr. Tyau since I do not see the "Review" recently and may miss it?

I think Dr. Li Chi and Mr. Tan will get report ready sometime before the end of February and I will send you a copy as soon as I receive it. I think also the only inscription deciphered by Mr. Wang Kuo Wei will be interesting to you. In addition, Mr. Lo has brought back quite a lot of information and material which he is unwilling to diverge publicly for fear of getting somebody into trouble. His statement about the position of the bronze is a direct contradiction to the story given out officially—that is one of the reasons why I wanted to hear from you, as Mr. Tan was there later than you, and cannot give direct evidence. I am also getting some of the so-called cinnabar analyzed to see if it is not only hematite as often is the case.

Your suggestion about the origin of the southern culture is most interesting. I am very ignorant about things Indian. Can you give me a list of literature on the older culture of India? My own impression has been that there is still no very reliable chronology either historic or prehistoric, since even the date of the birth of Buddha is not known with absolute certainty.

You are quite right in your quotation of Yu Kung, but I beg to remind you of two things. Firstly, Liang Chou includes that part of Shensi south of Tsingling range. Between Heisui and Huayang, is the original definition, but Heisui has never been located with certainty. Now southern Shensi and northern Hupeh are famous for the primitive iron industry based on magnetic sands. The last is commonly believed to be the first iron ore worked by man. May the reference to iron in Liangchou not be merely an indication of the existence of the working of the magnetic of the existence of the working of the magnetic sands? Secondly, Yu Kung is now admitted to be a comparative late production—perhaps during, or a little before, the time of Confucius. Among the metals mentioned together with iron is the metal Lou（鏤）, commonly interpreted as steel. If such interpretation is correct, Yu Kung must even be later.

Your reference to the taxation on iron in Ch'i must have come from Kuan Tzu which is unfortunately a forgery, made not earlier than the third century B. C. So its evidence is not of much value. It is interesting however to note that the word Yi can only mean "the eastern barbarian" when it is used in the sense of a particular people, and not as a general term. By the way, Yi is practically the only word applied to non-Chinese people without any contempt in the original sense in contract to such terms as Ti, Jung and Man.

I think you are wrong in saying that the people of Wu and Yu were anxious to get iron from Chu. On the contrary, Chu obtained the iron masters from the two latter states. Chu was said to be rich in bronze, for in Tso Chuan it was recorded that Chu gave a lot of that metal to Cheng, but made the latter swear not to use it for making weapons.

To sum up I think iron was known in the time of Confucius, but its general use, especially in the manufacture of arms, began only towards the end of the Chou dynasty.

Have you any data on Pa and Shu? My impression is that they were Lolos, because a transliteration of a poem written in the Han turns out to be of Lolo language, and because to this very day the chieftains in southern Hupeh are all Lolos.

Yes, there was a great deal of superstition attached to the arm manufacturers as you can read in the Yue Chu Shu and elsewhere.

I have not yet had time to look up your reference to the letter from the king of Nan Yueh, but I presume that it is the famous letter of King Chao To to Han Wen Ti. If that is the case, then it has no value in proving anything, for Nan Yue is Canton to which the trade route was via Kiangsi. Besides it is of such a late date (beginning of Han). It would prove, if anything, that the Nan Yueh people did not have iron.

Can you favor me with some of your publications as I understand you have written a number of papers on such questions?

Yours sincerely

V. K. Ting

The Peipiao Coal Mining Co., Ltd.,
HEAD OFFICE.

Tientsin, January 20, 1924.

Dr. B. Lanfer,
Chicago Field Museum,
Chicago, U. S. A.

Dear Dr. Lanfer,

A friend of mine has just pointed out to me a passage in the Shuo Yuan (說苑) which gives a transliteration of a Yueh (越) song together with a translation. As one of the most interesting problems in Chinese history is the nature and origin of the ancient culture in the Yangtze delta, this unique piece of linguistic evidence is obviously important. I take the liberty therefore to send you the transliteration with its translation (on another sheet of paper), hoping that your extensive knowledge of asiatic languages will enable you to tell us something about the language used.

With kindest regards,

Yours sincerely,

(V. K. Ting)

Enc. A passage in Chinese.

说苑旧说篇，所载越女櫂歌。说是楚国的王子鄂君子晳泛舟在越溪游耍，船家女子于"拥楫而歌"，歌的是越音，其词如下："滥兮抃草滥予昌枑泽予昌州州鍖乎秦胥胥缦予乎昭澶秦踰渗堤随河湖"鄂君听着，自然一字不懂，於是叫人译成楚国话如下：：

今夕何夕兮，搴舟中流；今日何日兮，得与王子同舟。
蒙羞被好兮，不訾诟耻，心几顽而不绝兮，知得王子。山有木兮木有枝，心说君兮君不知。

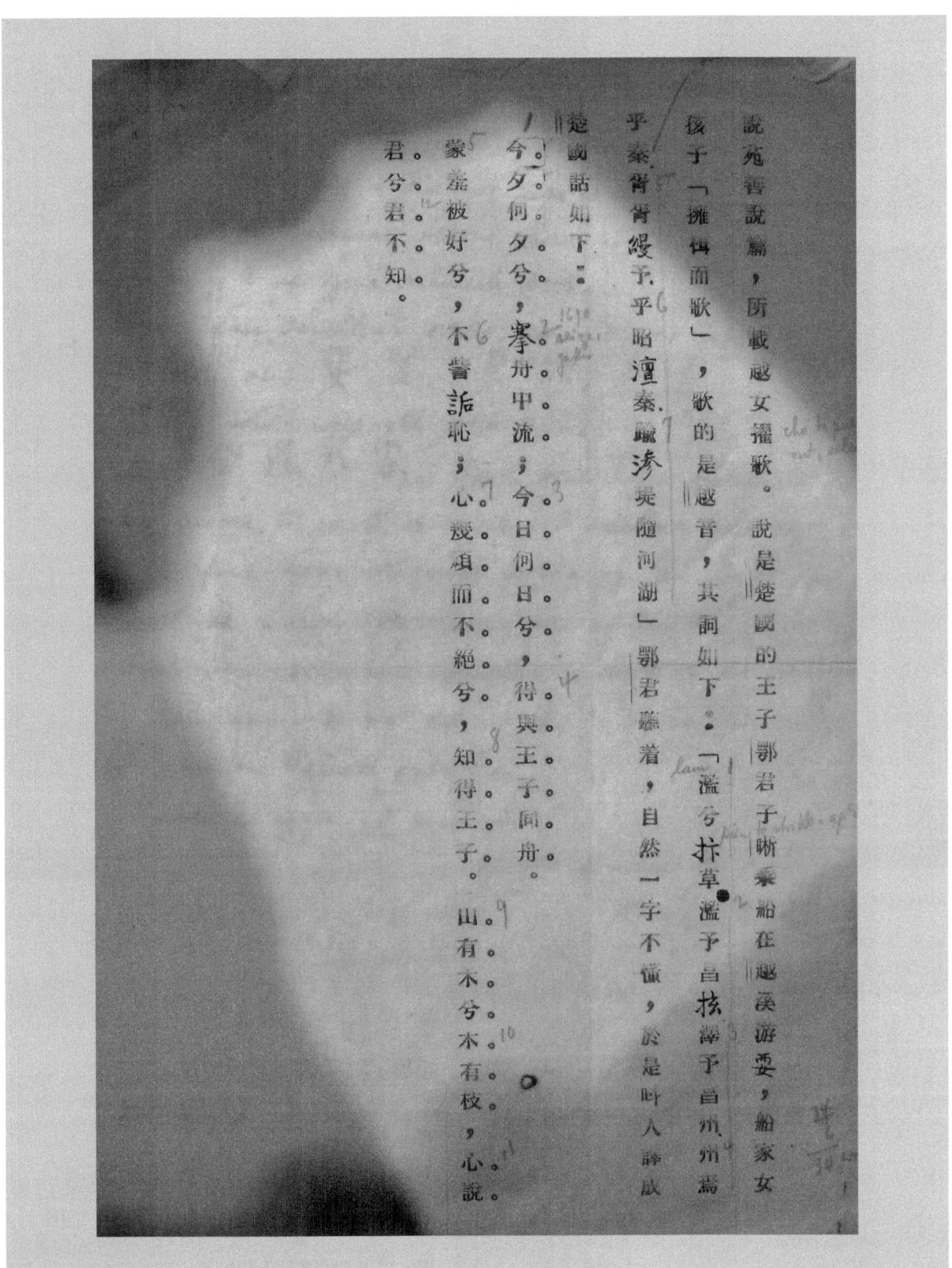

北票煤礦有限公司
The Peipiao Coal Mining Co., Ltd.

TELGRAPHIC ADDRESS 4384	HEAD OFFICE.	38 VIA PRINCIPE DI UDINE
TELEPHONE 3055.		ITALIAN CONCESSION

Tientsin, January 20, 1924

Dr. B. Laufer,

Chicago Field Museum,

Chicago, U. S. A.

Dear Dr. Laufer,

  A friend of mine has just pointed out to me a passage in the Shuo Yuan (說苑) which gives a transliteration of a Yueh (越) song together with a translation. As one of the most interesting problems in Chinese history is the nature and origin of the ancient culture in the Yangtze delta, this unique piece of linguistic evidence is obviously important. I take the liberty therefore to send you the transliteration with its translation (on another sheet of paper), hoping that your extensive knowledge of Asiatic languages will enable you to tell us something about the language used.

               With kindest regards,

               Yours sincerely

               V. K. Ting

               Enc. A passage in Chinese

說苑善說篇，所載越女擢歌。說是楚國的王子鄂君子晳乘船在越溪遊耍，船家女孩子"擁楫而歌"，歌的是越音，其詞如下："濫兮抃草，濫予昌枑，澤予昌州，州𩛩乎秦，胥胥縵予，乎昭澶秦，逾滲惿隨河湖。"鄂君聽著，自然一字不懂，於是叫人譯成楚國話如下："今夕何夕兮，搴舟中流；今日何日兮，得與王子同舟。蒙羞被好兮，不訾詬恥；心幾頑而不絕兮，知得王子。山有木兮木有枝，心說君兮君不知。"

COPY

WOODS HOLE, MASS.

August 28, 1924.

V. K. Ting, Esq.
Director
The Geological Survey
3 Feng-Sheng Hutung
W. Peking
China

My dear Mr. Ting:

    Your letter of June 30th, enclosing a memorandum from the Geological Survey suggesting the use of a portion of the indemnity fund made available by the recent decision of the United States Government to remit the balance of the Boxer Indemnity to China reached me upon my recent return to this country from Europe.

    You have no doubt seen in the papers my letter to Secretary of State Hughes in which it was stated that the funds made available by the remitted indemnity would be administered by a Board. I would suggest, therefore, that you address the memorandum to the Board when it has been formed.

                                    Sincerely yours,

WOODS HOLE, MASS

August 28, 1924

V. K. Ting, Esq.

Director

The Geological Survey

3 Feng-Sheng Hutung

W. Peking

China

My dear Mr. Ting:

Your letter of June 30th, enclosing a memorandum from the Geological Survey suggesting the use of a portion of the indemnity fund made available by the recent decision of the United States Government to remit the balance of the Boxer Indemnity to China reached me upon my recent return to this country from Europe.

You have no doubt seen in the papers my letter to Secretary of State Hughes in which it was stated that the funds made available by the remitted indemnity would be administered by a Board. I would suggest, therefore, that you address the memorandum to the Board when it has been formed.

Sincerely yours,

[Roger S. Greene]

THE GEOLOGICAL SURVEY
3, Feng-Sheng Hutung,
W. Peking, China.

MEMORANDUM

The generosity of the American people in returning to China the remaining portion of the Boxer Indemnity imposes upon the Chinese a duty to devise ways and means to utilise the fund to the best advantage so that such generosity may not be wasted. It seems to the undersigned that before putting forth any particular scheme or claim, the following principles must be recognized.

1. The money should be used to subsidise existing institutions rather than establishing new ones, since this is obviously the best policy from the point of view of economy.

2. It has already been decided to employ the money for educational and cultural purposes. Now this should be interpreted in the most comprehensive sense so as to include those institutions which are doing scientific research. For education and culture cannot be improved by teaching alone --- most of the institutions of higher learning abroad fulfil the double function of teaching and research, the latter being necessary even to make the teaching effective. In China there are a few organisations which have been doing a good deal of research work under difficult conditions, and any help from the new fund will enormously increase their usefulness and efficiency.

3. In making any appropriation to such institutions <u>first consideration should be given to their past record</u> which is after all the only just standard.

- 2 -

If the above principles are admitted, then the undersigned wish to submit the claims of the Geological Survey to those in charge of the said fund. The importance of such an institution needs not be enlarged upon, as similar organisations exist in all the civilized countries. The Chinese Geological Survey can perhaps put forth a greater claim than usual. For ever since its organisation in 1916, it has not only undertaken the work of making geological maps and the surveying of mineral resources, both of which are the primary functions of the Geological Survey in all countries, but it has also striven to carry on purely scientific researches such as palaeontology and archaeology. So apart from practical utility, it has become a centre of intellectual activity. The following is a summary of the work already done by the Survey during the last 8 years of its existence:

1. <u>Geological mapping</u> --- The provinces of Shantung, Shansi, and Kiangsu have been already surveyed on the scale of 1:200,000. two sheets on the scale of 1:1,000,000 are in the press. The latter covers a large part of North-eastern China and are made according to the rules adopted by the International Geographical Congress. Two more sheets will be ready in a short time. In addition reconnaissance surveys on various scales have been made all over China including such distant provinces as Yunnan, and Kansu.

2. <u>Surveying of mineral resources:</u>---- Every mineral region has been visited by the members of the Survey and the results of such work have been published in a memoir,"The Mineral Resources of China". Special attention has been paid to the coal and the iron fields. A very detailed monograph on the iron resources has already been published with a profusely illustrated atlas, and a monograph on the coal resources on similar lines is in preparation.

— 3 —

3. <u>Palaeontology and Archaeology</u> --- Extensive work has been done in the above mentioned subjects and the results have partly been published in a series of monographs entitled Palaeontologia Sinica. Dr. J. G. Andersson, sometimes Director of the Geological Survey of Sweden, and Professor A. W. Grabau, formerly Professor of Palaeontology in Columbia University, have contributed largely to this branch of scientific work, but famous scientific workers all over the world, such as Schlosser of Germany, Boule of Paris are also among our co-workers.

4. <u>Museum and Library</u> --- The Geological Survey has organized a museum consisting of 7 rooms exhibiting not only the mineral deposits, but also, stratigraphy, dynamic geology, pataeontology and archaeology. The library contains nearly 20,000 volumes and is in exchange with scientific institutions all over the world.

5. <u>Other Scientific work</u> includes stratigraphy, tectonic geology, earthquake investigations, physiography and change of climate. Many important papers dealing with such subjects are to be found in the various publications of the Survey.

6. <u>Publications</u> --- The following publications have already appeared.

    Bulletins 1 - 5.
    Memoirs Ser. A. 1 - 3, Ser. B. 1 - 2, Ser. C.1.
    Palaeontologia Sinica 4 monographs.

All this have been accomplished in the space of 8 years with an annual budget of $50,000, and a staff of 20 geologists and palaeontologists including two foreigners already mentioned and 10 returned students. That the work has been appreciated both by the foreign scientific institutions and the Chinese public is

— 4 —

by the fact that numerous articles of appreciation have appeared in the scientific papers in Europe and America and that the library and the museum have been built by private donation.

    Money however is urgently needed in order to extend the museum and to defray the current expenses, for in common with the other government institutions, the appropriation of the Geological Survey has not been reguarly paid for many months. If nothing is done to improve its financial status, the institutions must in time suffer disintegration and many of its most active members will be obliged to resign. It is estmiated that an annual budget of 60,000 to 100,000 dollars is needed to put the institution on a proper basis. Any help given either in the form of an endowment fund or an annual grant will save the Institution from decay:

                                              V.K.Ting
                      Director of the Geological Survey

                                         Wongwenhai
                  Acting Director of the Geological Survey

Henry J. Noughton
Paul H. Stevenson
C.W. Bishop
Monlin Chiang
Hu Shih (Suh Hu)

THE GEOLOGICAL SURVEY
3 Feng-Sheng Hutung,
W. Peking, China.

MEMORANDUM

The generosity of the American people in returning to China the remaining portion of the Boxer Indemnity imposes upon the Chinese a duty to devise ways and means to utilize the fund to the best advantage so that such generosity may not be wasted. It seems to the undersigned that before putting forth any particular scheme or claim, the following principle must be recognized.

1. The money should be used to subsidize existing institutions rather than establishing new ones, since this is obviously the best policy from the point of view of economy.

2. It has already been decided to employ the money for educational and cultural purposes. Now this should be interpreted in the most comprehensive sense so as to include those institutions which are doing scientific research. For education and culture cannot be improved by teaching alone—most of the institutions of higher learning abroad fulfil the double function of teaching and research, the latter being necessary even to make the teaching effective. In China there are a few organizations which have been doing a good deal of research work under difficult conditions, and any help from the new fund will enormously their usefulness and efficiency.

3. In making any appropriation to such institutions first consideration should be given to their past record which is after all the only just standard.

If the above principles are admitted, then the undersigned wish to submit the claims of the Geological Survey to those in charge of the said fund. The importance of such an institution needs not be enlarged upon, as similar organizations exist in all the civilized countries. The Chinese Geological Survey can perhaps put forth a greater claim than usual. For ever since its organization in 1916, it has not only undertaken the work of making geological maps and the surveying of mineral resources, both of which are the primary functions of the Geological Survey in all countries, but it has also striven to carry on purely scientific researches such as paleontology and archaeology. So apart from practical utility, it has become a center of intellectual activity. The following is a summary of the work already done by the Survey during the last 8 years of its existence:

1. <u>Geological mapping</u>----The province of Shantung, Shansi, and Kiangsu have been already surveyed on the scale of 1: 200,000, two sheets on the scale of 1: 1,000,000 are in the press. The latter covers a large part of the north-eastern China and are made according to the rules adopted by the International Geographical Congress. Two more sheets will be ready in a short time. In addition, reconnaissance surveys on various scales have been made all over China including such distant provinces as Yunnan, and Kangsu.

2. <u>Surveying of mineral resources:</u> ---Every mineral region has been visited by the members of the Survey and the results of such work have been published in a memoir, "The Mineral Resources of China". Special attention has been paid to the coal and the iron fields. A very detailed monograph on the iron resources has been already been published with a profusely illustrated atlas, and a monograph on the coal resources on similar lines is in preparation.

3. <u>Paleontology and Archaeology</u>---Extensive work has been done in the above mentioned subjects and the results have partly been published in a series of monographs entitled Palaeontologia Sinica. Dr. J. G. Andersson, sometimes Director of the Geological Survey of Sweden, and Professor A. W. Grabau; formerly Professor of Paleontology in Columbia University, have contributed largely to this branch of scientific work, but famous scientific workers all over the world, such as Schlosser of Germany, Boule of Paris are also among our co-workers.

4. <u>Museum and Library</u>---The Geological Survey has organized a museum consisting of 7 rooms exhibiting not only the mineral deposits, but also, stratigraphy, dynamic geology, pataeonotology and archaeology. The library contains nearly 20,000 volumes and is in exchange with scientific institutions all over the world.

5. <u>Other Scientific work</u> includes stratigraphy, tectonic geology, earthquake investigations, physiography and change of climate. Many important papers dealing with such subjects are to be

found in the various publications of the Survey.

6.Publications---The following publications have already appeared.

Bulletin 1-5

Memoirs Ser. A. 1-3, Ser. B. 1-2, Ser. C. 1

Palaeontologia Sinica 4 monographs.

All this have been accomplished in the space of 8 years with an annual budget of $ 50,000 and a staff of 20 geologists and paleontologists including two foreigners already mentioned and 10 returned students. That the work has been appreciated both by the foreign scientific institutions and the Chinese public is by the fact that numerous articles of appreciation have appeared in the scientific papers in Europe and America and that the library and the museum have been built by private donation.

Money however is urgently needed in order to extend the museum and to defray the current expenses, for in common with the other government institutions, the appropriation of the Geological Survey has not been regularly paid for many months. If nothing is done to improve its financial status, the institution must in time suffer disintegration and many of its most active members will be obliged to resign. It is estimated that an annual budget of 60, 000 to 100,000 dollars is needed to put the institution on a proper basis. Any help given either in the form of an endowment fund or an annual grant will save the Institution from decay:

V. K. Ting

Director of the Geological Survey

Wong Wenhao

Acting Director of the Geological Survey

Henry J. Noughton

Paul H. Stevenson

C. W. Bishop

Molin Chiang

Hu Shih

1925 年

Tung, V. K.

The Peipiao Coal Mining Co., Ltd.,

TELEGRAPHIC ADDRESS: 4384.
TELEPHONE: 3055.

HEAD OFFICE.

38 VIA PRINCIPE DI UDINE
ITALIAN CONCESSION.

Tientsin, 4 May 1925.

Dear Mr. Bishop,

Many thanks for your letter of the I inst. I am not sure at all whether I can stay at Peitaiho for any length of time, but I can always come down for a week end.

Mr. Tung's supposition about the Tat'ung cave is however quite incorrect. Whilst there are plenty of igneous rocks there, no occurence of volcanic rocks (not to say volcanoes) is to be found. That has been well-surveyed already by one of our men, and a geological map has been published in one of bulletins. (Title: Tat'ung Coal Field, by C. C. Wang).

I expect to be in Peking on the I4th and I5th May, but all my time has been booked up. I will telephone to you on my arrival in order to arrange a meeting.

Yours sincerely,

北票煤礦有限公司
The Peipiao Coal Mining Co., Ltd.

TELGRAPHIC ADDRESS 4384	HEAD OFFICE.	38 VIA PRINCIPE DI UDINE
TELEPHONE 3055.		ITALIAN CONCESSION

Tientsin, 4 May, 1925

Dear Mr. Bishop,

Many thanks for your letter of the I inst. I am not sure at all whether I can stay at Peitaiho for any length of time, but I can always come down for a week end.

Mr. Tung's supposition about the Tat'ung cave is however quite incorrect. Whilst there are plenty of igneous rocks there, no occurrence of volcanic rocks (not to say volcanoes) is to be found. That has been well-surveyed already by one of our men, and a geological map has been published in one of the bulletins. (Title: Tat'ung Coal Field, by C. C. Wang)

I expect to be in Peking on the 14th and 15th May, but all my time has been booked up. I will telephone to you on my arrival in order to arrange a meeting.

Yours sincerely
V. K. Ting

Tsing, V. K

The Peipiao Coal Mining Co., Ltd.,

HEAD OFFICE.

TELEGRAPHIC ADDRESS: 4384.
TELEPHONE: 3066.

38 VIA PRINCIPE DI UDINE,
ITALIAN CONCESSION.

Tientsin, June 29, 1925.

C. W. Bishop,
Light House Point,
Peitaiho.

Dear Mr. Bishop,

Many thanks for your letter of the 26th inst. I will send Mr. Karlbeck's book to your Peitaiho address in a few days. But as Dr. Li Chi is going their, will you kindly ask him to let me know the train he is leaving by so that I can see him at the Tientsin station and give him the book is question? Tell him also that I may also get the things he wants to have ready.

With kind regards,

Yours sincerely,

V. Tsing

北票煤礦有限公司
The Peipiao Coal Mining Co., Ltd.

TELGRAPHIC ADDRESS 4384　　　　HEAD OFFICE.　　　　38 VIA PRINCIPE DI UDINE

TELEPHONE 3055.　　　　　　　　　　　　　　　　　　　　ITALIAN CONCESSION

Tientsin, June 29, 1925.

C. W. Bishop,

Light House Point,

Peitaiho,

Dear Mr. Bishop,

Many thanks for your letter of the 26th inst. I will send Mr. Karlbeck's book to your Peitaiho address in a few days. But as Dr. Li Chi is going their, will you kindly ask him to let me know the train he is leaving by so that I can see him at the Tientsin station and give him the book is question? Tell him also that I may also get the things he wants to have ready.

With kind regards

Yours sincerely,

V. K. Ting

The Peipiao Coal Mining Co., Ltd.,

HEAD OFFICE.

TELEGRAPHIC ADDRESS: 4384.
TELEPHONE: 3055.

38 VIA PRINCIPE DI UDINE,
ITALIAN CONCESSION.

Tientsin, July 17, 1925.

Dear Mr. Bishop,

Many thanks for your kind letter of the 16th July. Evidently you have not received my last letter addressed to Peitaiho just about the time you arrived there. I asked you in that letter to tell Li Chi to let me know the train he was going to travel by, so that I ~~may~~ send Karlbeck's book to the train as I am afraid that the beautiful book may get damaged if I send it by post. However I am going to write to Li myself.

I do not know the Kung Yi Hwei people, but will try to get in touch with them for you.

Yours sincerely,

V. K. Ting

C. W. Bishop, Esq.,
Light House Point,
Peitaiho.

北票煤礦有限公司
The Peipiao Coal Mining Co., Ltd.

TELGRAPHIC ADDRESS 4384　　　　　　HEAD OFFICE.　　　　　　38 VIA PRINCIPE DI UDINE

TELEPHONE 3055.　　　　　　　　　　　　　　　　　　　　　　　ITALIAN CONCESSION

Tientsin, July 17, 1925.

Dear Mr. Bishop,

Many thanks for your kind letter of the 16th July. Evidently you have not received my last letter addressed to Peitaiho just about the time you arrived there. I asked you in that letter to tell Li Chi to let me know the train he was going to travel by, so that I may send Karlbeck's book to the train as I am afraid that the beautiful book may get damaged if I send it by post. However, I am going to write to Li myself.

I do not know the Kung Yi Hwei people, but will try to get in touch with them for you.

Yours sincerely

V. K. Ting

C. W. Bishop, Esq.,

Light House Point,

Peitaiho.

Ting, V.K

The Peipiao Coal Mining Co., Ltd.,

司 公 限 有 礦 煤 票 北

TELEGRAPHIC ADDRESS: 4384.
TELEPHONE: 3055.

HEAD OFFICE.

38 VIA PRINCIPE DI UDINE,
ITALIAN CONCESSION.

Tientsin, July 21, 1925.

C. W. Bishop, Esq.,
Light House Point,
Peitaiho.

Dear Mr. Bishop,

Many thanks for your kind letter of yesterday. As far as I know no really good historical atlas of recent date has appeared. The older ones are very rough and on a very small scale. I will show you what I have got when we meet again.

An archaeological survey would of course be very important. But under the present conditions it would be difficult to get the necessary funds even if we can get over the political difficulties.

I have made inquiries about the Kung Yi Hwei. The directors and the chairman are all absent from Peitaiho. Fortunately however its former chairman, Mr. Chu Ch'i-chien 朱啟鈐, has just gone down. He was responsible for 99% of the improvement of Peitaiho, and although he has resigned, he practically still dominates the organisation. Besides he is deeply interested in Archaeology is a collector of old textiles. I wrote to him just before he left Tientsin and he responded in the most cordial manner. So please call on him and put the whole case before him. If he cannot help him, nobody else can. He lives near the house I stayed in last year, and everybody in the neighbourhood will show you the way, if you will mention Mr. Chu's name. He does not speak English

2.

so you must bring an interpreter with you.
With kind regards,
Yours sincerely,

[signature]

P.S. I enclose a letter of introduction
to Chiviene.

北票煤礦有限公司
The Peipiao Coal Mining Co., Ltd.

TELGRAPHIC ADDRESS 4384　　　　HEAD OFFICE.　　　　38 VIA PRINCIPE DI UDINE

TELEPHONE 3055.　　　　　　　　　　　　　　　　　　　ITALIAN CONCESSION

Tientsin, July 21, 1925

C. W. Bishop, Esq.,

Light House Point,

Peitaiho.

Dear Mr. Bishop,

Many thanks for your kind letter of yesterday. As far as I know no really good historical atlas of recent date has appeared. The older ones are very rough and on a very small scale. I will show you what I have got when we meet again.

An archaeological survey would of course be very important. But under the present conditions it would be difficult to get the necessary funds even if we can get over the political difficulties.

I have made inquiries about the Kung Yi Hwei. The directors and the chairman are all absent from Peitaiho. Fortunately, however its former chairman, Mr. Chu Ch'i-chien 朱啟鈐, has just gone down. He was possible for 99% of the improvement of Peitaiho, and although he was resigned, he practically still dominates the organization. Besides he is deeply interested in Archaeology is a collector of old textiles. I wrote to him just before he left Tientsin and he responded in the most cordial manner. So please call on him and put the whole case before him. If he cannot help him, nobody else can. He lives near the house I stayed in last year, and everybody in the neighborhood will show you the way, if you will mention Mr. Chu's name. He does not speak English so you must bring an interpreter with you.

With kind regards

Yours sincerely
V. K. Ting

P.S. I enclose a letter of introduction in Chinese.

Ting, V. K.

The Peipiao Coal Mining Co., Ltd.,

HEAD OFFICE.

TELEGRAPHIC ADDRESS: 4384.
TELEPHONE: 3055.

88 VIA PRINCIPE DI UDINE,
ITALIAN CONCESSION.

Tientsin, Sept. 1, 1925.

C. W. Bishop, Esq.,
19, Ta Yang Yi Ping Huting,
P e k i n g.

Dear Mr. Bishop,

     Many thanks for your letter of the 26th August. I am glad to hear that you have begun to write something at last. I am deeply interested in both of your subjects. Is it possible to have a look at your manuscript? We say in Chinese: "Hsien Tu Wei K'uai", or "eager to be the first reader".

     With best regards,

     Yours sincerely,

V. K. Ting

P. S. I have forgotten the exact title of Karlbeck's book which I sent to your Peitaiho address. Please drop me a note when you write next.

北票煤礦有限公司
The Peipiao Coal Mining Co., Ltd.

TELGRAPHIC ADDRESS 4384　　　HEAD OFFICE.　　　38 VIA PRINCIPE DI UDINE

TELEPHONE 3055.　　　　　　　　　　　　　　　　ITALIAN CONCESSION

Tientsin, Sept. 1, 1925

C. W. Bishop, Esq.,

19, Ta Yang Yi Ping Huting,

Peking.

Dear Mr. Bishop,

　　Many thanks for your letter of the 26th August. I am glad to hear that you have begun to write something at last. I am deeply interested in both of your subjects. Is it possible to have a look at your manuscript? We say in Chinese: "Hsien Tu Wei K'uai", or "egger to be the first reader".

　　　　　　　　　　　　　　　　With best regards

　　　　　　　　　　　　　　　　Yours sincerely

　　　　　　　　　　　　　　　　V. K. Ting

　　P. S. I have forgotten the exact title of Karlbeck's book which I sent to your Peitaiho address. Please drop me a note when you write next.

1926 年

Ting, V. K.

19, Ta Yang I-pin Hutung, Peking.
26 June, 1926.

Dear Dr. Ting:-

When I saw Mr. Karlbeck recently he told me that you had a book of his which he was anxious to have me see, and so he authorized me to ask you to turn it over to me when you are done with it. Inasmuch as we are just on the eve of leaving for Peitaiho and expect to close up this place for the summer, with only a caretaker, perhaps it would be best for you to mail me the book at the American Legation; or possibly you might find it more convenient to let me have it in Peitaiho, where I look forward to having the pleasure of seeing as much as possible of you.

Dr. Andersson and Dr. Li were here for luncheon yesterday, and the former very kindly promised to make out, upon his return home, a list of suggestions regarding books and periodicals for our reference library which we are in course of building up. I trust we shall soon have something worth while in this line.

We expect to leave Tuesday evening, the 30th, for Peitaiho, and our address there will be Lighthouse Point (the cottage belonging to Dr. Houghton; I do not know the number). I expect Dr. Li will join us shortly, and I look forward to

2.

getting some real work accomplished, more particularly in the direction of writing a number of long promised papers on topics having to do with Chinese archaeology.

Do let me hear from you at any time, and believe me, with all good wishes, as always,

Sincerely yours,

19, Ta Yang I-pin Hutung, Peking,

26 June, 1926.

Dear Dr. Ting:

When I saw Mr. Karlbeck recently he told me that you had a book of his which he was anxious to have me see, and so he authorized me to ask you to turn it over to me when you are done with it. Inasmuch as we are just on the eve of leaving for Peitaiho and expect to close up this place for the summer, with only a caretaker, perhaps it would be best for you to mail me the book at eh American Legation; or possibly you might find it more convenient to let me have it in Peitaiho, where I look forward to having the pleasure of seeing as much as possible of you.

Dr. Andersson and Dr. Li were here for luncheon yesterday, and the former very kindly promised to make out, upon his return home, a list of suggestions regarding books and periodicals for our reference library which we are in course of building up. I trust we shall soon have something worth while in this line.

We expect to leave Tuesday evening, the 30th, for Peiptaiho, and our address there will be lighthouse Point (the cottage belonging to Dr. Houghton; I do not know the number). I expect Dr. Li will join us shortly, and I look forward to getting some real work accomplished, more particularly in the direction of writing a number of long promised papers on topics having to do with Chinese archaeology.

Do let me hear from you at any time, and believe me, with all good wishes, as always.

Sincerely yours

[C. W. Bishop]

1927 年

INITIALED FILE COPY

COPY SENT TO PEKING 1/21/27
(two letters) January 17, 1927

Dear Dr. Ting:

I am much distressed to learn from the Shanghai papers of the serious injuries which you suffered last month in an automobile accident. I hope very much that the encouraging reports which the newspapers gave as to the prospect for your early recovery were actually justified.

You must know with what keen and sympathetic interest your friends are watching the important work that you are doing in Shanghai. We believe that you have a very important contribution to make to the welfare of your country and to the establishment of better relations with foreign powers based on the recognition of the right of China to the equal treatment which she deserves as a great nation.

I am expecting to leave for China early in May and hope to see you either in Shanghai or Peking early in June.

With kindest regards and best wishes, I am

Yours sincerely,

ROGER S. GREENE

Dr. V. K. Ting, Director
Shanghai-Woosung Special Municipality
Shanghai, China.

RSG:EE

January 17, 1927

Dear Dr. Ting:

I am much distressed to learn from the Shanghai papers of the serious injuries which you suffered last month in an automobile accident. I hope very much that the encouraging reports which the newspapers gave as to the prospect for your early recovery were actually justified.

You must know with what keen and sympathetic interest your friends are watching the important work that you are doing in Shanghai. We believe that you have a very important contribution to make to the welfare of your country and to the establishment of better relations with foreign powers based on the recognition of the right of China to the equal treatment which she deserves as a great nation.

I am expecting to leave for China early in May and hope to see you either in Shanghai or Peking early in June.

With kindest regards and best wishes, I am

Yours sincerely
Roger S. Greene

Dr. V. K. Ting, Director
Shanghai-Woosung Special Municipality
Shanghai, China

DIRECTORATE OF THE PORT OF SHANGHAI AND WOOSUNG
LUNGHUA, SHANGHAI

MARSHAL SUN CHUAN-FANG — DIRECTOR-GENERAL
V. K. TING — DIRECTOR
GENERAL Y. H. WEN — DEPT. OF GENERAL AFFAIRS
Y. HSU — DEPT. OF FOREIGN AFFAIRS
C. FU — DEPT. OF POLITICAL AFFAIRS
T. Y. YEN — DEPT. OF PUBLIC PEACE
W. H. CHEN — DEPT. OF PUBLIC WORKS
T. Y. TSUI — DEPT. OF FINANCE

TELEPHONE:
PRIVATE EXCHANGE 1590
DEPT. OF GENERAL AFFAIRS { 1591 / 1592

Mar. 2, 1927.

Roger S. Greene, Esq.,
 Room 2701, 61 Broadway,
  New York,
   U. S. A.

Dear Sir,

   Your letter to Dr. V. K. Ting dated Jan. 17 has been duly received. I am glad to inform you that he has fully recovered from the accident. But the doctor advised him to have a change of climate, so he is now on leave in North China. I shall forward your letter to him in time.

   Yours truly,

   Secretary.
   M. C. Chu.

淞滬商埠督辦公署
DIRECTORATE OF THE PORT OF SHANGHAI AND WOOSUNG
LUNCHUA, SHANGHAI

Mar., 2, 1927.

Roger S. Greene, Esq.,
Room 2701, 61 Broadway,
New York,
U. S. A.

Dear Sir,

Your letter to Dr. V. K. Ting date Jan. 17 has been duly received, I am glad to inform you that he has fully recovered from the accident. But the doctor advised him to have a change of climate, so he is now on leave in north China. I shall forward your letter to him in time.

Yours truly,

Secretary,
M. C. Chu

Hotel du Nord
京北德國飯店
PEKING, 10 March 1927
Ha-ta-men

Ting, V. K.

Dear Mr Bishop,

Many thanks for your kind note and invitation. I am not free until next Tuesday (15th) when I shall be glad to come to dine with you. If you can get hold of Li Chi, please do so as I have not yet seen him this time.

Yours sincerely,
V. K. Ting

Memorandum

北京德國飯店

Hotel du Nord

Peking, 10 March, 1927

Ha-ta-men

Telephone. E. 720

A. B. C. Code 5th ed

Tel. Address Nord Hotel

Dear Mr. Bishop,

Many thanks for your kind note and invitation. I am not free until next Tuesday (15th) when I shall be glad to come to dine with you. If you can get hold of Li Chi, please do so as I have not yet seen him this time.

Your sincerely,

V. K. Ting

March 21, 1927

Dear Dr. Ting:

This will introduce to you Mr. Vincent Sheean, an American writer who is going to China partly to execute a commission for "Asia", an American magazine published in New York City which has taken a very liberal and, I think, far-sighted view of the policy which the United States ought to adopt in China. I shall greatly appreciate any help that you can give Mr. Sheean in his task of trying to get a right idea about what is actually going on in China.

Yours sincerely,

ROGER S. GREE
Director

Dr. V. K. Ting

RSG:KE

March 21, 1927

Dear Dr. Ting:

This will introduce to you Mr. Vincent Sheean, Esq., an American writer who is going to China partly to execute a commission for "Asia", an American magazine published in New York City which has taken a very liberal and, I think far-sighted view of the policy which the United States ought to adopt in China. I shall greatly appreciate any help that you can give Mr. Sheean in his task of trying to get a right idea about what is actually going on in China.

Yours sincerely,

Roger S. Greene
Director

Dr. V. K. Ting

The Geological Survey,
3, Feng-Sheng Hutung,
W. Peking, China.

13th April 1927

Dear Granger,

Herewith I enclose a map showing the Lake Deposits containing molluscs near Chiutsing. If in any near future you find yourself in Yunnan, the place will be worth visiting as mammalia fossils may also be found.

Yours sincerely,
V. K. Ting

農 商 部 地 質 調 查 所
The Geological Survey
3, Feng-Sheng Hutung,
W. Peking, China

13th, April, 1927

Dear Granger,

Herewith I enclose a map showing the Lake deposit containing mallucs (?) near Chintsing. If in any near future, you find yourself in Yunnan, the place will be worth visiting as mammalian fossils may also be found.

Yours sincerely,
V. K. Ting

Ting, V. K.

6 North Compound, P.U.M.C., Peking,
21 April, 1927.

Dear Dr. Ting:-

You are so elusive around the hotel, that I have despaired of ever seeing much of you there. So I am taking this method of getting in touch with you.

On account of the unsettled state of affairs arising from the sudden death of Dr. Walcott and the resignation of the head of the Freer Gallery, I have been instructed to return to Washington as soon as possible for consultation regarding future policies in connection with research work in China. So I am leaving on or about next Wednesday.

Yesterday I took Dr. Granger and Mr. Nelson out to Tsing Hua to see Dr. Li. Nelson took along a few specimens that he had found in Yunnan, and we had a very interesting discussion and luncheon. Li is coming in Saturday to have lunch with Granger at one, and is coming first to our hotel to talk over our future and his own connection with the Smithsonian. I am anxious that you should join us in this discussion, for I think that upon its results will depend a great deal. I want to take back with me a clear and definite plan of operations, and I want you and Li to help formulate it. I believe Granger intends to invite you to the luncheon on Saturday, but I want to see you before that, when we can talk at more freedom and ease.

I think my past work here has made it sufficiently clear

2.

that what I want is to promote the cause of scientific research by the Chinese organizations themselves. It has been in this way that we have worked heretofore, and it is increasingly so, it seems to me, that we should work in the future. One of the best ways of doing this, to my mind, is to subsidize young men of training and ability, like Li for example, and help them in other ways, to do definite pieces of work, in the name of some Chinese organization, but so that the results may be at the service of all. It is things of this sort that I want to talk over with you, and if noon on Saturday won't serve, then I should be glad to have you suggest another date.

    Hoping to see you soon, I remain,

              Sincerely yours,

                    C. W. Bishop.

6 North Compound, P. U. M. C., Peking,

21 April, 1927

Dear Dr. Ting:

You are so elusive around the hotel, that I have despaired of ever seeing much of you there. So I am taking this method of getting in touch with you.

On account of the unsettled state of affairs arising from the sudden death of Dr. Walcott and the resignation of the head of the Freer Gallery, I have been instructed to return to Washington as soon as possible for consultation regarding future polices in connection with research work in China. So I am leaving on or about next Wednesday.

Yesterday I took Dr. Granger and Mr. Nelson out to Tsing Hua to see Dr. Li. Nelson took along a few specimens that he had found in Yunnan, and we had a very interesting discussion and luncheon. Li is coming in Saturday to have lunch with Granger at one, and is coming first to our hotel to talk over our future and his own connection with the Smithsonian. I am anxious that you should join us in this discussion, for I think that upon its results will depend a great deal. I want to take back with me a clear and definite plan of operations, and I want you and Li to help formulate it. I believe Granger intends to invite you to the luncheon on Saturday, but I want to see you before that, when we can talk at more freedom and ease.

I think my past work here had made it sufficiently clear that what I want is to promote the cause of scientific research by the Chinese organization themselves. It has been in this way that we have worked heretofore, and it is increasingly so, it seems to me, that we should work in the future. One of the best ways of doing this, to my mind, is to subsidize young men of training and ability, like Li for example, and help them in other ways, to do definite pieces of work, in the name of some Chinese organization, but so that the results may be at the service of all. It is things of this sort that I want to talk over with you, and if noon on Saturday won't serve, then I should be glad to have you suggest another date.

Hoping to see you soon, I remain,

Sincerely yours
C. W. Bishop

The Geological Survey,
3, Feng-Sheng Hutung,
W. Peking, China.

May 17, 1927.

C. W. Bishop Esq.,

Freer Art Gallery

Smithsonian Institute,

Washington D. C.

Dear Mr. Bishop:-

I hope you have safely arrived at Washington. There is a personal matter of mine for which I hope you will be kind enough to do something. In 1915 I sent to the late Dr. Walcott my collection of Yunnan fossils for preliminary determination. In return I authorised Dr. Walcott to choose from the specimens a set of duplicates for the Smithsonian Institute. Later on Dr. Walcott sent the whole collection to Illinois and thence to China, after having chosen a duplicate set from the Devonian, Silurian and Carboniferous fossils. Unfortunately in shipping the collection from Illinois to China in the absence of some one really interested many specimens were lost and some of the labels mixed up, so that when Dr. Grabau started to describe them, he found many important specimens missing. I then write to Dr. Walcott asking him to send back the duplicates to his hands and promising to return them to the Smithsonian Institute after they have been described. Dr. Walcott was however away at the time I never got any satisfactory reply. I shall be very grateful indeed if

农商部地質調查所
The Geological Survey,
3, Feng-Sheng Hutung,
W. Peking, China.

May 17, 1927.

you will take the matter up with the proper authorities. I will of course pay for the necessary expenses. If the collection is not very large, it can probably be sent through the post.

Apologising for troubling you,

Yours sincerely,

V. K. Ting

P.S. The carboniferous fossils were determined by Mrs. Eula D. McEwan, and those of Silurian and Silurian Devonian by Dr Stanton(?). They were probably responsible for choosing the duplicates.

農 商 部 地 質 調 查 所
The Geological Survey,
3, Feng-Sheng Hutung,
W. Peking, China.

May 17, 1927.

C. W. Bishop Esq.,
Freer Art Gallery
Smithsonian Institute,
Washington D. C

Dear Mr. Bishop:

I hope you have safely arrived at Washington. There is a personal matter of mine for which I hope you will be kind enough to do something. In 1915 I sent to the late Dr. Walcott my collection of Yunnan fossils for preliminary determination. In return I authorized Dr. Walcott to choose from the specimens a set of duplicates for the Smithsonian Institute. Late on Dr. Walcott sent the whole collections to Illinois and thence to China, after having chosen a duplicate set from the Devonian, Silurian and Carboniferous fossils. Unfortunately, in shipping the collection form Illinois to China in the absence of some one really interested many specimens were lost and some of the labels mixed up, so that when Dr. Grabau started to describe them, he found many important specimens missing. I then write to Dr. Walcott asking him to send back the duplicates in his hands and promising to return them to the Smithsonian Institute after they have been described. Dr. Walcott was however away at the time I never got any satisfactory reply. I shall be very grateful indeed if you will take the matter up with the proper authorities. I will of course pay for the necessary expenses. If the collection is not very large, it can probably be sent through the post.

  Apologizing for troubling you,

  Yours sincerely,
  V. K. Ting

P.S. The Carboniferous fossils were determined by Mr. Eula D. McEwan and those Silurian and Devonian by Dr. Stanton (?). They are probably responsible for choosing the duplicates.

Ting, V. K.

17 August, 1927.

Dr. V. K. Ting,
The Geological Survey,
Peking, China.

Dear Dr. Ting:-

I finally reached Washington, after a trip through Egypt, Italy, Austria, Hungary, Germany, France, and England, only a few days ago, and found awaiting me, along with very many others, your good letter of May 17th.

I shall be glad to do all I can about having the duplicate set of fossils sent out to you, of course. But just now everyone is away, and there are few people in town. They will, however, begin coming back about the first of September, and meanwhile I'll see what can be done in regard to the matter. The Acting Secretary, Dr. Abbott, is away in California, but I'll try to see his locum tenens Dr. Wetmore, the ornithologist, today or tomorrow, and get the thing started.

To judge from the paucity of China news in the papers, things must be more or less at a standstill now. About all we hear about is the "Red Spears" movement; I wonder if it will grow into anything on the scale of the great popular risings that have punctuated Chinese history ever since the Eastern Han Dynasty at least? And why is it that we seem to hear of nothing analogous in earlier times?

Please remember me to mutual friends, and let me hear from you often. Will write again shortly. With kindest regards, as ever,

17 August, 1927.

Dr. V. K. Ting,

The Geological Survey,

Peking, China.

Dear Dr. Ting:

I finally reached Washington, after a trip through Egypt, Italy, Austria, Hungary, Germany, France, and England, only a few days ago, and found awaiting me, along with very much others, your good letter of May 17th.

I shall be glad to do all I can about having the duplicate set of fossils sent out to you, of course. But just now everyone is away, and there are few people in town. They will, however, begin coming back about the first of September, and meanwhile I will see what can be done in regard to the matter. The Acting Secretary, Dr. Abbott, is away in California, but I'll try to see his locum tenens, Dr. Wetmore, the ornithologist, today or tomorrow, and get the thing started.

To judge form the paucity of China news in the papers, things must be more or less at a standstill now. About all we hear about is the "Red Spears" movement; I wonder if will grow into anything on the scale of the great popular risings that have punctuated Chinese history ever since the Eastern Han Dynasty at least? And why is it that we seem to hear of nothing analogous in earlier times?

Please remember me to mutual friends, and let me hear from you often. Will write again shortly. With kindest regards, as ever,

[C. W. Bishop]

184, Meikakudai, Dairen,
15, November 1927.

Mr. C. W. Bishop,
Smithsonian Institution,
Freer Art Gallery,
Washington D.C.

Dear Mr. Bishop,

I must apologise for not acknowledging your letter of the 17th August sooner than this. It came to hand about the beginning of October when I left for Japan for a holiday and did not return until the end of that month.

As you can see from the address I am at Dairen. I came here in the beginning of August to escape the heat which was particularly trying this summer, but finding the place so quite and so free from social disturbance I decided to spend the winter here in order to finish the work in hand. I have made already considerable progress and hope to get it in shape suitable for publication early next year. So I am as eager as ever to know whether you have succeeded in negotiating with the Smithsonian authorities to find out the duplicates of fossils and lend them back to me for study. I shall be much obliged if you will kindly let me know the result.

Paucity of China news is by no means the best news. Serious developments have taken place since you wrote last. You ask me why was it that before the time of Han no great popular rising was heard of. Well, I think the reasons are simple enough. These risings are the results of economic distress due to increased population and taxation. In feudal times when every state was making war upon its neighbour the population had no chance for increase.

The above address is probably good for two more months, but the Geological Survey or Peipiao Co, will always reach me.

With best regards,
Yours sincerely,

(V.K.Ting)

184, Meikakadai, Dairen,

15, November, 1927.

Mr. C. W. Bishop,

Smithsonian Institution,

Freer Art Gallery,

Washington D. C

Dear Mr. Bishop,

I must apologize for not acknowledging your letter of the 17th August sooner than this. It came to hand about the beginning of October when I left for Japan for a holiday and did not return until the end of that month.

As you can see from the address I am at Dairen. I came here in the beginning of August to escape the heat which was particularly trying this summer, but finding the place so quiet and so free from social disturbance I decided to spend the winter here in order to finish the work in hand. I have made already considerable progress and hope to get it in shape suitable for publication early next year. So I am as eager as ever to know whether you have succeeded in negotiation with the Smithsonian authorities to find out the duplicates of fossils and lend them back to me for study. I shall be much obliged if you will kindly let me know the result.

Paucity of China news is by no means the best news. Serious developments have been taken place since you wrote last. You ask me why was it that before the time of Han no great popular rising was heard of. Well, I think the reasons are simple enough. These risings are the results of economic distress due to increased population and taxation. In feudal times when very state was making war upon its neighbor the population had no chance for increase.

    The above address is probably good for two more months, but the Geological Survey or Peipiao Co, will always reach me.

With best regards,

Yours sincerely,
V. K. Ting

December 16, 1927.

Dr. V. K. Ting,
184 Meikakudai,
Dairen, Manchuria.

Dear Dr. Ting:-

Your letter of the 15th of November arrived a few days ago, and I was delighted to learn how you have been getting on. I wonder what you know about recent Japanese excavations in Manchuria? I should be glad if you could tell me anything about them.

In regard to the duplicates of fossils here at the Smithsonian, I took up the matter with the Acting Secretary as soon as he returned to town, and supposed that it had already been attended to. I wonder whether the fact of your recent peregrinations may not have something to do with the difficulty? However, I shall get in touch with the proper authorities at once, and see what we can do to carry out your wishes.

Your explanation of the reason why no great popular risings are recorded prior to the Han Dynasty, I fancy, is quite correct. But I wonder whether it covers the whole ground? Is it not likely that the great social changes which were taking place in China during the 4th and 3rd centuries B. C., and which culminated in the great revolution under the Ch'in

2.-

the Ch'in Dynasty, may not have given rise to a wider self-consciousness on the part of the peasantry then was possible under the archaic faudal system?

With kindest regards, I remain,

      Yours sincerely,

        C. W. Bishop.

December 16, 1927.

Dr. V. K. Ting,
184 Meikakudai,
Dairen, Manchuria.

Dear Dr. Ting:

Your letter of the 15th of November arrived a few days ago, and I was delighted to learn how you have been getting on. I wonder what you know about recent Japanese excavations in Manchuria? I should be glad if you could tell me anything about them.

In regard to the duplicates of fossils here at the Smithsonian, I took up the matter with the Acting Secretary as soon as he returned to town, and supposed that it had already been attended to. I wonder whether the fact of your recent peregrinations may not have something to do with the difficulty? However, I shall get in touch with the proper authorities at once, and see what we can do to carry out your wishes.

Your explanation of the reason why no great popular risings are recorded prior to the Han Dynasty, I fancy, is quite correct. But I wonder whether it covers the whole ground? Is it not likely that the great social changes which were taking place in China during the 4th and 3 rd centuries B. C., and which culminated in the great revolution under the Ch'in Dynasty, may not have given rise to a wider self-consciousness on the part of the peasantry then was possible under the archaic feudal system?

With kindest regards, I remain,

Yours sincerely,
C. W. Bishop

1928 年

Ting, V. K.

January 12, 1928.

Dr. V. K. Ting,
Geological Survey of China,
3, Feng-Sheng Hutung,
West City, Peking, China.

Dear Dr. Ting:-

As you requested in your last letter, I have taken up with the Smithsonian Institution the matter of your missing fossils. Just before Christmas I received from Dr. Wetmore, the Assistant Secretary, the accompanying Memorandum. Dr. Wetmore seems to have gone in the matter very thoroughly, and if there is anything further that we can do, I hope you will not hesitate to let me know.

As usual, the American press, preoccupied with affairs of local importance, devotes almost no space to what is going on in China, so I know almost nothing of the progress of events, save what Mr. Tung and Dr. Li tell me. I find, however, a decided growth of interest in Chinese affairs on the part of our more intelligent classes, among whom I trust I may include the staff of the Smithsonian Institution. I am hoping, therefore, that the next two or three years will see great progress in the establishment of cultural contacts of many sorts between our two people. You will no doubt have heard of the appointment of Dr. C. G. Abbot, the well known astrophysicist, as Secretary of the Smithsonian Institution, to take the place of the late Dr. Walcott. Dr. Abbot is a great friend of mine, and I know

2.-

of no one else so well qualified to fill the position.

    I hope ypu will let me hear from you from time to time in regard to your own doings as well as the trend of events in China. With kindest regards, I remain,

                      Sincerely yours,

                      C. W. Bishop.

January 12, 1928.

Dr. V. K. Ting,

Geological Survey of China,

3, Feng-Sheng Hutung,

West City, Peking, China.

Dear Dr. Ting:

    As you requested in your last letter, I have taken up with the Smithsonian Institution the matter of your missing fossils. Just before Christmas I received from Dr. Wetmore, the Assistant Secretary, the accompanying Memorandum. Dr. Wetmore seems to have gone in the matter very thoroughly, and if there is anything further that we can do, I hope you will not hesitate to let me know.

    As usual, the American press, preoccupied with affairs of local importance, devotes almost no space to what is going on in China, so I know almost nothing of the progress of events, save what Mr. Tung and Dr. Li tell me. I find, however, a decided growth of interest in Chinese affairs on the part of our more intelligent classes, among whom I trust I may include the staff of the Smithsonian Institution. I am hoping, therefore, that the next two or three years will see great progress in the establishment of cultural contacts of many sorts between our two people. You will no doubt have heard of the appointment of Dr. C. G. Abbot, the well known astrophysicist, as Secretary of the Smithsonian Institution, to take the place of the late Dr. Walcott. Dr. Abbot is a great friend of mine, and I know of no one else so well qualified to fill the position.

    I hope you will let me hear from you from time to time in regard to your own doing as well as the trend of events in China. With Kindest regards, I remain,

                              Sincerely yours,

                              C. W. Bishop

184, Meikakudai, Dairen
18 Jan. 1928

Dear Mr. Bishop, Tung, V K.

Many thanks for your kind letter of the 16th Dec. and your effort auprès the Secretary. However the delay could not have been due to my peregrinations as I still keep the Geological Survey in Peking as my permanent address and Dr. Wong would of course forward all my mails. However in order to be extra-safe please ask the Secretary to take up the matter with Dr. W. H. Wong at the Geological Survey in case if I again wander away from my present path.

I wish your stenogapher were right about "pregnancy"! In that case I would have been fruitful. However I have been working at my Yunnan material and have made some progress. I hope to get that out of the way in a few months and then start to write a book on Chinese history à la H. G. Wells's. Do you think I will ever be able to get a publisher?

Li Chi passed through here a fortnight ago and spent two pleasant days with me. I tried also to get some introductions for him.

I received at the same time as your letter a booklet on Walcott. Not knowing where it came from I have not been able to acknowledge its receipt. If it comes from Mrs. Walcott will you kindly pass a word to her on my behalf?

    I hope to leave here in April for Peking. Until then the above will my address

    With best wishes,
      Yours sincerely,

[signature] (V.K.Ting)

184, Meikakudai, Dairen

18 Jan, 1928

Dear Mr. Bishop,

Many thanks for your kind letter of the 16th Dec. and your effort aupres the Secretary. However, the delay could not have been due to my peregrinations as I still keep the Geological Survey in Peking as my permanent address and Dr. Wong would of course forward all my mails. However, in order to be extra-safe please ask the Secretary to take up the matter with Dr. W. H. Wong at the Geological Survey in case if I again wander away from my present path.

I wish your stenographer were right about "pregnancy". In that case I would have been fruitful. However, I have been working at my Yunnan material and have made some progress. I hope to get that out of the way in a few months and then start to write a book on Chinese history a la H. G. Wells's. Do you think I will ever be able to get a publisher?

Li Chi passed through here a fortnight ago and spent two pleasant days with me. I tried also to get some introductions for him. I received at the same time as your letter a booklet on Walcott. Not knowing where it came from I have not been able to acknowledge its receipt. If it comes from Mrs. Walcott will you kindly pass a word to her on my behalf?

I hope to leave here in April for Peking. Until then the above will my address.

With best wishes,

Yours sincerely,
V. K. Ting

Ting, V. K.

February 28, 1928.

Dear Dr. Ting:-

Your letter of January 18th reached me a few days ago, and I was glad to learn what you had been doing with yourself. I should imagine that Dairen would be quite frigid as a summer resort, and I cant picture you taking very many sea-baths *in puris naturalibus* among the icebergs. However, I expect that when this letter reaches you, the almonds will be in bloom, and the grass will be turning green.

I hear from Li Chi at frequent intervals. His last letter was written from Hankow, and in it he expressed doubts about the feasibility of the trip which he had planned up the Han and across the mountains to Hsi-an. I hope that his enthusiasm for research will lead him into no unnecessary risks, for he is too valuable a man to lose. I am anxious to have him come on to Washington in the near future, to consult regarding plans for the prosecution of further research in China on a joint Sino-American basis. I have succeeded in interesting the American Council of Learned Societies, the Librarian of Congress, and numbers of other people and organization of influence in this matter, and the first step to be taken would seem to be a comprehensive survey of the work which has already been done and which remains to be done in Chinese archaeological and historical research, both by Chinese and by foreign scholars.

2.-

I am anxious to have Dr. Li Chi take part in the planning of this undertaking.

I shall look forward with real interest to the book on Chinese history which you tell me you are planning, for I know of no one, literally, whom I consider so well qualified as yourself for such a task. You did not state in your letter whether you proposed to write it in Chinese or in English; but if the latter perhaps I could help you to secure a publisher.

I wrote you on January 12th, in care of the Survey, inclosing an official memorandum of the report transmitted to me by the Assistant Secretary of the Smithsonian, after he had given a through investigation to the matter of your missing specimens; I hope that this has safely reached you. I had it sent by registered mail.

Let me hear from you again soon; your letters are always most welcome. With kindest regards, I remain,

       Yours sincerely,

       C. W. Bishop.

February 28, 1928.

Dear Dr. Ting:

Your letter of January 18th reached me a few days ago, and I was glad to learn what you had been doing with yourself. I should imagine that Dairen would be quite frigid as a summer resort, and in can't picture you taking very many sea-baths in puris naturalibus among the icebergs. However, I expect that when this letter reaches you, the almonds will be in bloom, and the grass will be turning green.

I hear from Li Chi at frequent intervals. His last letter was written from Hankow, and in it he expressed doubts about the feasibility of the trip which he had planned up the Han and across the mountains to His-an. I hope that his enthusian for research will lead him into no unnecessary risks, for he is too valuable a man to lose. I am anxious to have him come on to Washington in the near future, to consult regarding plans for the persecution of further research in China on a joint Sino-American basis. I have succeeded in interesting the American Council of Learned Societies, the Librarian of Congress, and numbers of other people and organization of influence in this matter, and the first step to be taken would seem to be a comprehensive survey of the work which has already been done and which remains to be done in Chinese archaeological and historical research, both by Chinese and by foreign scholars. I am anxious to have Dr. Li Chi take part in the planning of this undertaking.

I shall look forward with real interest to the book on Chinese history which you tell me you are planning, for I know of on one, literally, whom I consider so well qualified as yourself for such a task. You did not state in your letter whether you proposed to write it in Chinese or in English; but if the latter perhaps I could help you to secure a publisher.

I wrote you on January 12th, in care of the Survey, inclosing an official memorandum of the report transmitted to me by the Assistant Secretary of the Smithsonian, after he had given a through investigation to the matter of your missing specimens; I hope that this has safely reached you. I had it send by register mail.

Let me hear from you again soon; your letters are always most welcome. With kindest regards, I remain,

Yours sincerely,
C. W. Bishop.

184 Meikakudai, Dairen
30 March 1928

Ting, V. K

Dear Mr. Bishop,

    Your letter of the 28th Feb. has just been forwarded. It came just in time as I am leaving immediately for Peking.

    I am glad to hear that you are so actively interested in the problems of Chinese history and archaeology. I wish I could do something to help you, but at present I am still occupied with my geological work which has taken me longer time than I expected.

    I suppose you have heard that the southern people want Li Chi to go Kuangsi on a scientific expedition organised by the Kuangsi elements in the party. I think he may leave soon for the south west.

    My projected book will be written in Chinese, but if I can find a publisher I will translate it into English.

    Your letter of 12th Jan. reached me sometime ago, but unfortunately the fossils have not been traced.

    With kind regards,
    Yours sincerely,
    (V. K. Ting)

184 Meikakudai, Dairen

March 30, 1928

Dear Mr. Bishop,

Your letter of the 28th Feb. has just been forwarded. I came just in time as I am leaving immediately for Peking.

I am glad to hear that you are so actively interested in the problem of Chinese history and archeology. I wish I could don something to help you, but at present I am still occupied with my geological work which has taken me longer time than I expected.

I supposed you have heard that the southern people want Li Chi to go Kuangsi on a scientific expedition organized by the Kuangsi element in the S. party. I think he may leave soon for the south west.

My projected book will be written in Chinese, but if I can find a publisher I will translate it into English.

Your letter of 12th Jan. reached me sometime ago, but unfortunately the fossils have not been traced.

With kind regards,

Yours sincerely,

V. K. Ting

Ting, V. K.

April 23, 1928.

Dr. V. K. Ting,
Geological Survey of China,
3, Feng-Sheng Hutung,
West City, Peking, China.

Dear Dr. Ting:-

Your letter of March 30th has just arrived and I hasten to answer.

I am sorry that you have been unable to trace the missing fossils; there would seem to be no doubt from our records here that they reached Peking, and I hope that upon your return there you were able to find them.

Regarding the book which you have in prospect, I have very little doubt that you could find a publisher in this country for an English version. I will begin inquires at once and will let you know their outcome. Meanwhile, if you have any definite ideas on this subject, please let me know. I am sure I need not tell you that I shall be only to happy if I can be of any service whatever.

We recently received a cablegram from Li Chi, stating that he was leaving Shanghai for the United States on May 5th. I am looking forward with much interest to his visit, because I feel that it can be made the means of helping to arouse a greater and more intelligently informed interest in this country regarding Chinese affairs in general.

Let me hear from you again soon, and believe me, with all

2.-

good wishes, as well as my kindest regards to Dr. Wong, Dr. Grabau, and my other friends in Peking.

     Very sincerely yours,

     C. W. Bishop.

April 23, 1928.

Dear Dr. Ting:

Your letter of March 30th has just arrived and I hasten to answer.

I am sorry that you have been unable to trace the missing fossils; there would seem to be no doubt from our records here that they reached Peking, and I hope that upon your return there you were able to find them.

Regarding the book which you have in prospect, I have very little doubt that you could find a publisher in this country for an English version. I will begin inquiries at once and will let you know their outcome. Meanwhile, if you have any definite ideas on this subject, please let me know. I am sure I need not tell you that I shall be only to happy if I can be of any service whatever.

We recently received a cablegram from Li Chi, stating that he was leaving Shanghai for the United States on May 5th. I am looking forward with much interest to his visit, because I feel that it can be made the means of helping to arouse a greater and more intelligently informed interest in this country regarding Chinese affairs in general.

Let me hear form again soon, and believe me, with all good wishes, as well as my kindest regards to Dr. Wong, Dr. Grabau, and my other friends in Peking.

Very sincerely yours,

C. W. Bishop.

Ting, V. K.

May 17, 1928.

Dr. V. K. Ting,
Geological Survey of China,
3, Feng-Sheng Hutung,
West City, Peking, China.

Dear Dr. Ting:-

    In pursuance of my promise to try and find you a publisher for the English edition of your forthcoming book on Chinese civilization, I discussed the matter with Mr. Lodge, our curator. He was much interested, and said that it might very probably be the most valuable contribution to the subject that has yet appeared. He further authorized me to tell you that if you would send us your translation, he would be glad to give it his most careful consideration, with a view to its publication by the Freer Gallery of Art. He also suggested, that the English version be as fully documented as possible with references to the original Chinese sources. As you doubtless know, we have here at the Library of Congress a very good and steadily growing Chinese library, which is coming to be more and more used by scholars in that field.

    I have in mind several other possibilities in regard to the publication of your book, and feel assured that you need have no fear about finding a publisher. The main thing of course is, first of all to get your manuscript carefully typed, so that it may receive the most favorable consideration possible.

    I need not tell you how eagerly I should welcome a book such

2.-

as you are sure to write, nor how gladly I shall assist in securing for it the best terms for publication.

With kindest regards and all good wishes, as ever,

Sincerely yours,

C. W. Bishop.

May 17, 1928.

Dr. V. K. Ting,
Geological Survey of China
3, Feng-Sheng Hutung,
West City, Peking, China.

Dear Dr. Ting:

In pursuance of my promise to try and find you a publisher for the English edition of your forthcoming book on Chinese civilization, I discussed the matter with Mr. Lodge, our curator. He was much interested, and said that it might very probably be the most valuable contribution to the subject that has yet appeared. He further authorized me to tell you that if you would send us your translation, he would be glad to give it his most careful consideration, with a view to its publication by the Freer Gallery of Art. He also suggested, that the English version be as fully documented as possible with reference to the original Chinese sources. As you doubtless know, we have here at the Library of Congress a very good and steadily growing Chinese library, which is coming to be more and more used by scholars in that field.

I have in mind several other possibilities in regard to the publication of your book, and feel assured that you need have no fear about finding a publisher. The main thing of course is, first of all to get your manuscript carefully typed, so that it may receive the most favorable consideration possible.

I need not tell you how eagerly I should welcome a book such as you are sure to write, nor how gladly I shall assist in securing for it the best terms for publication.

With kindest regards and all good wishes, as ever,

Sincerely yours,
C. W. Bishop.

Ting, Dr V. K.

THE NATIONAL GEOLOGICAL SURVEY OF CHINA
3 FENGSHENG-HUTUNG W. PEIPING CHINA

21 December 1928

C. W. Bishop Esq.,
Freer Art Gallery,
Smithsonian Institution,
Washington D. C.

Dear Mr. Bishop,

I must apologize for not being able to answer your letter of the 17th May before this. The fact is I left N. China to make a 6 months trip in the south, principally in Kwangsi where I traveled more than 1,500 miles and brought back nearly a ton of fossils. In order to work out the scientific results of my journey I have accepted a fellowship from the China Foundation and am now busily engaged in this unexpected piece of work which is probably my last contribution to geology.

The fellowship offered by the China Foundation lasts till next June when I hope to get all my geological work, including my paper on Yunnan, finished. After that I will start to realize my cherished dream of writing a general history of China. I will however have to find some means to keep my self fed, clothed and housed for at least two if not three years in order to be able to do the work absolutely undisturbed. Please accept my best thanks for your kind interest in my work and when the proper time comes I will not hesitate to turn to you for help to find a publisher.

Li Chi is now back here and all arrangements are made to excavate at Anyang early next year.

With kind regards,
Yours sincerely,

(V. K. Ting)

THE NATIONAL GEOLOGICAL SURVEY OF CHINA
3 Fengsheng-Hutung, W. Peiping, China

21 December 1928

C. W. Bishop Esq.,

Freer Art Gallery,

Smithsonian Institution,

Washington D. C.

Dear Mr. Bishop,

I must apologize for not being able to answer your letter of the 17th May before this. The fact is I left N. China to make a 6 months trip in the south, principally in Kwangsi where I traveled more than 1500 miles and brought nearly a ton of fossils. In order to work out the scientific results of my journey I have accepted a fellowship form the China foundation and am now busily engaged in this unexpected piece of work which is probably my last contribution to geology.

The fellowship offered by the China Foundation lasts till next June when I hope to get all my geological work, including my paper on Yunnan, finished. After that I will start to realized my cherished dream of writing a general history of China. I will however, have to find some means to keep myself fed. Clothed and housed for at least two if not three years in order to be able to do the work absolutely undisturbed. Please accept my best thanks for your kind interest in my work and when the proper time comes I will not hesitate to turn to you for help to find a publisher.

Li Chi is now back here and all arrangements are made to excavate at Anyang early next year.

With kind regards

Yours sincerely,

V. K. Ting

1929 年

2 February, 1929.

Dear Dr. Ting:-

I received your letter of Dec. 21st some days ago, and read it with much interest. It is good to know that you have returned successful from your trip to the Southwest, and I shall look forward to the publication of your report. I hope, too, at no very distant date to discuss your results with you in person, and ask you many questions, particularly in regard to the archaeology and ethnology of the region.

In regard to your proposed general history of China, you already know my own sentiments. But let me repeat once more, that I know of no one whom I believe better qualified to undertake such a work than yourself. I should esteem it a real privilege if I might in any way facilitate your task. As soon as I received your letter, I took it to Mr. Lodge for discussion, and he authorizes me to say that if you will send him an outline or syllabus of your history, as you have planned it, he will give it careful consideration with a view to the possibility of aiding you in carrying the undertaking through. Something tangible of this sort he feels he must have before taking up the matter of devoting to such a purpose a portion of the funds entrusted to him for the encouragement of studies in the historical development of China.

Mr. Lodge is particularly interested in the critical discussion of source material, in the documentation, and in the archae-

2.

ological references and bibliography; also in the exact chronology, the use of Chinese characters for all proper names, quotations from Chinese sources, maps, illustrations, glossaries, and indexes. He of course regards as of still more fundamental importance the general scope and chief divisions of the work; but these would no doubt be indicated in the prospectus in any case.

Quite possibly you have such an outline or prospectus already drawn up, and could send it to Mr. Lodge at once; for June is not so very far away. I would suggest that you address him direct, here at the Freer Gallery; you need no introduction or intermediary. Dr. Li has doubtless already told you of Mr. Lodge's active interest in the promotion of Chinese studies, and I need not assure you that any undertaking to which he decides to lend his effective assistance will be carried through in the best possible manner, in all respects.

Your intimation that Dr. Li had completed arrangements to excavate at Anyang was the first that I had received, but a few days later there came a letter from Dr. Li, telling me more in detail of the results of his negotiations. He seems to have handled the matter capitally, and I have no doubt he will conduct the actual excavation just as ably. What we find there may well clear up many dark places in early Chinese History, and throw much light on questions to which we in vain seek an answer from literary sources. The discovery of inscribed bones there justifies the hope that fresh contemporary documentary evidence may be found.

2.

As I have already intimated, I may have the pleasure of seeing you again in the near future. Some months ago I told Mr. Lodge that I was commencing to feel the urge for the field once more. It is now almost two years since I left China, and more than that since my last field trip, when I traveled over Shansi from end to end. And the political situation in China has given such marked evidence of improvement in recent months that I feel little doubt about the feasibility of field work. Dr. C. C. Wu, the newly appointed Minister to Washington, is an old friend, of over a dozen years' standing, and we have had several interesting conversations regarding archaeological research in China. I told him one day that I considered effective, friendly, and mutually advantageous scientific investigation one of the best means of promoting a good understanding between our two countries. He replied that I didn't have to convince him of that,---that he was convinced already.

It is impossible as yet for me to say definitely when I shall be sailing for China again, as there are a few things that I must finish before I can think of leaving. These, however, are already well under way, and I look forward to starting at the earliest possible date. In view of the improbability of a letter from you finding me still here, I would repeat my suggestion that you write direct to Mr. Lodge. Thanks again for your letter, and believe me, with my kindest regards and all good wishes,

Yours sincerely,

2 February, 1929.

Dear Dr. Ting:

I received your letter of Dec. 21st some days ago, and read it with much interest. It is good to know that you have returned successful from your trip to the Southwest, and I shall look forward to the publication of your report. I hope, too, at no very distant date to discuss your results with you in person, and ask you many questions, particularly in regard to the archeology and ethnology of the region.

In regard to your proposed general history of China, you already know my own sentiments. But let me repeat once more that I know of no one whom I believe better qualified to undertake such a work than yourself. I should esteem it a real privilege if I might in any way facilitate your task. As soon as I received your letter, I took it to Mr. Lodge for discussion, and he authorizes me to say that if you will send him an outline or syllabus of your history, as you have planned it, he will give it careful consideration with a view to the possibility of aiding you in carrying the undertaking through. Something tangible of this sort he feels he must have before taking up to matter of devoting to such a purpose a portion of the funds entrusted to him for the encouragement of studies in the historical development of China.

Mr. Lodge is particularly interested in the critical discussion of source material, in the documentation, and in the archaeological references and bibliography; also in the exact chronology, the use of Chinese characters for all proper names, quotations from Chinese sources, maps, illustrations, glossaries, and indexes. He of course regards as of still more fundamental importance the general scope and chief divisions of the work; but these would no doubt be indicated in the prospectus in any case.

Quite possibly you have such an outline or prospectus already drawn up, and could sent it to Mr. Lodge at once; for June is not so very far away. I could suggest that you address him direct, here at the Freer Gallery; you need to introduction or intermediary. Dr. Li has doubtless already told you of

Mr. Lodge's active interest in the promotion of Chinese studies, and I need not assure you that any undertaking to which he decides to lend his effective assistance will be carried through in the best possible manner, in all respects.

Your indication that Dr. Li had completed arrangements to excavate at Anyang was the first that I have received, but a few days later there came a letter from Dr. Li, telling me more in detail of the results of his negotiations. He seems to have handled the matter capitally, and I have no doubt he will conduct the actual excavation just as ably. What we find there may well clear up many dark places in early Chinese history, and throw much light on questions to which we in vain seek an answer from literary sources. The discovery of inscribed bones there justifies the hops that fresh contemporary documentary evidence may be found.

As I have already intimated, I may have the pleasure of seeing you again in the near future. Some months ago I told Mr. Lodge that I was commencing to feel the urge for the field once more. It is now almost two years since I left China, and more than that since my last field trip, when I traveled over Shansi from end to end. And the political situation in China has given such marked evidence of improvement in recent months that I feel little doubt about the feasibility of field work. Dr. C. C. Wu, the newly appointed Minister to Washington, is an old friend, of over a dozen years' standing, and we have had several interesting conversations regarding archaeological research in China. I told him one day that I considered effective, friendly and mutually advantageous scientific investigation one of the best means of promoting a good understanding between our two countries. He replied that I didn't have to convince him of that—that he was convinced already.

It is impossible as yet for me to say definitely when I shall be sailing for China again, as there are a few things that I must finish before I can think of leaving. These, however, are already well under way, and I look forward to starting at the earliest possible date. In view of the improbability of a letter from you finding me still here, I would repeat my suggestion that you write about to Mr. Lodge. Thanks again for your letter, and believe me, with my kindest regards and all good wishes.

Yours sincerely,
[C. W. Bishop]

31 May, 1930.

Dr. V. K. Ting,
Geological Survey of China,
West City, Peiping, China.

Dear Dr. Ting:-

    To my great delight, Dr. Li told me yesterday that you had at last returned from your arduous trip, and I hasten to write to you to ask if you will come to an informal little "stag" dinner that I am giving at the Hotel du Nord at 6.30 on the evening of June 10th, to enable my former junior assistant, Mr. A. G. Wenley, to meet some friends. Dr. Li has already promised to be present, and I have invited two or three others. I sincerely hope you can come also, for I have long looked forward to seeing you again and renewing our old acquaintance; and I am anxious to hear at first-hand about your latest trip.

    As you may have heard, I spent most of the spring in Shanghai and Nanking, where I met a number of friends, both old and new, and had the pleasure of helping excavate a couple of what seem to be Six Dynasties tombs. I also inquired about you, hoping you might come down river while I was still there; but in this I was disappointed.

    Hoping to see you on the evening of the 10th prox., and with all good wishes, I remain,

                  Sincerely yours,

                    C. W. Bishop,
                    Culty Chambers,
                      Legation Quarter.

31 May, 1930.

Dr. V. K. Ting,

Geological Survey of China,

West City, Peiping, China.

Dear Dr. Ting:

To my great delight, Dr. Li told me yesterday that you had at last returned from your arduous trip, and I hasten to write to you to ask if you will come to an informal little "stag" dinner that I am giving at the Hotel du Nord at 6.30 on the evening of June 10th, to enable my former junior assistant, Mr. A. G. Wenley, to meet some friends. Dr. Li has already promised to be present, and I have invited two or three others. I sincerely hope you can come also, for I have long looked forward to seeing you again and renewing our old acquaintance; and I am anxious to hear at first-hand about your latest trip.

As you may have heard, I spent most of the spring in Shanghai and Nanking, where I met a number of friends, both old and new, and had the pleasure of helping excavate a couple of what seem to be six dynasties tombs. I also inquired about you, hoping you might come down river while I was still there; but in this I was disappointed.

Hoping to see you on the evening of the 10th prox. And with all good wishes, I remain,

Sincerely yours

C. W. Bishop

Culty Chambers,

Legation Quarter

1931 年

Ting, V. K

THE NATIONAL GEOLOGICAL SURVEY OF CHINA
9 PING MA SSU, WEST CITY, PEIPING, CHINA

13 Jan 1931

Dear Mr Bishop,

Are you free tomorrow (Wednesday) night? I have invited Hedin & Lessing and a few others to a dinner that night at 8 at the Nord Hotel. Shall be glad if you can join us.

Yours,
V. K. Ting

THE NATIONAL GEOLOGICAL SURVEY OF CHINA

9 Ping Ma Ssu, West City, Peiping, China

13 Jan, 1931

Dear Mr. Bishop,

Are you free tomorrow (Wednesday) night? I have invited Hedin and Lechery (?) and a few others to a dinner that might at 8 at the Nord Hotel. Shall be glad if you can join us.

Yours,
V. K. Ting

Ting, V. K.

THE NATIONAL GEOLOGICAL SURVEY OF CHINA
9 PING MA SSU, WEST CITY, PEIPING, CHINA

13 Jan. 1931.

Mr. C. Bishop,
   3, Kweiloti Buildings,
      Legation Quarter.

Dear Mr. Bishop:-

      I am writing a book for the Cresset Press of London entitled "China, a Study of the Growth of a Civilisation". For the purpose of making illustrations I should like to have photographs of the Pao-Chi bronzes originally belonged to Tuan-fan and sold to the Metropolitan Museum through Dr. Ferguson. A series similar to those published by Siren in his "History of Chinese Art" Vol. I plate 34 - 27, 39, 41 and 45 will be very welcome. As I do not know any body personally in the Museum, may I trouble you to write to them on my behalf? I shall of course pay for the copies in questions.

      With kind regards,

               Yours sincerely,

               (V. K. Ting).

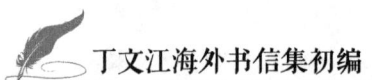

THE NATIONAL GEOLOGICAL SURVEY OF CHINA
9 Ping Ma Ssu, West City, Peiping, China

13 Jan, 1931

Mr. C. Bishop,
3, Kweiloti Buildings,
Legation Quarters,

Dear Mr. Bishop,

    I am writing a book for the Cresset Press of London entitles "China, a Study of the Growth of a Civilization". For the purpose of making illustrations I should like to have photographs of the Pao-Chi bronzes originally belonged to Tuan-fan and sold to the Metropolitan Museum through Dr. Ferguson. A series similar to those published by Siren in his "History of Chinese Art" Vol. I plate 34-37, 39, 41 and 45 will be very welcome. As I do not know anybody personally in the Museum, may I trouble you to write to them on my behalf? I shall of course pay for the copies in questions.

With kind regards,

Yours sincerely
V. K. Ting

Ting, V. K.

THE NATIONAL GEOLOGICAL SURVEY OF CHINA
9 PING MA SSU, WEST CITY, PEIPING, CHINA

2 March 1931

Dear Mr Bishop,

Enclosed is a letter from Mr Fu to you. He has signed it to save trouble. But in case if you find it not satisfactory, please let me know.

Yours sincerely,
V. K. Ting

THE NATIONAL GEOLOGICAL SURVEY OF CHINA
9 Ping Ma Ssu, West City, Peiping, China

2 March, 1931

Dear C. W. Bishop,

Enclosed is a letter you from Mr. Fu to you. He has singed it to save trouble. But in case if you find it not satisfactory, please let me know.

Yours sincerely
V. K. Ting

Ting, V. K

5 March, 1931.

Dr. V. K. Ting,
The Geological Survey,
West City, Peiping.

Dear Dr. Ting:-

Thanks very much for your cordial note of the 2nd instant, accompanied by the letter from Mr. Fu. I should have acknowledged them both but for the serious illness of Mrs. Bishop's mother, who has been critically ill at the German Hospital for the past few days. She is slightly better today, however, and I am able to give a little attention to routine matters.

I enjoyed our recent talk very much, and can quite sympathize with Mr. Fu's position and his reasons for desiring that the entire credit of the An-yang "dig" should go to the Academia Sinica. I have written him today to that effect, going into the whole matter in detail.

As I stated in my letter to him, the Freer Gallery spent, not counting Dr. Li's and Mr. Tung's salaries and Dr. Li's trip around the world in 1928 but on actual field work alone, nearly four thousand dollars gold. Moreover, from Dr. Li's regular reports while engaged on the "dig", the Freer Gallery was naturally led to believe that it would in time receive a full report of the work, accompanied by photographs. These it has not had up to date.

Consequently I have made certain suggestions to Mr. Fu which I believe will, if complied with, dispose my superiors at Washington to acquiesce in Mr. Fu's wishes. These suggestions are as fol-

2.

lows.

Firstly, that Dr. Li return to us all the material with which he was entrusted by the Freer Gallery while he was in its employ, and which he still retains, although his resignation took effect on June 30th last.

Secondly, I suggested that the Freer Gallery should have two complete sets of photographs of the work at An-yang and the finds made there, for study purposes. Inasmuch as the Gallery paid for the taking of these photographs, I feel sure that Mr. Fu will agree to the justice of this suggestion.

Lastly, I felt that Mr. Lodge would like a statement from Dr. Li as to the approximate date at which he could expect the comprehensive report by the latter of which Mr. Fu speaks.

Of course I can not guarantee that there will not be a detailed statement in the Annual Financial Report of the Smithsonian Institution of the amounts spent by the Freer Gallery in connection with its expenditures at An-yang; and indeed I am not sure that such a public statement is not required by law. Nor can I say how much they will wish to have appear in our Annual Report regarding the share of the Freer Gallery in the excavation at An-yang.

However, I am writing to Mr. Fu and to Dr. Li both in regard to the above points, and have little doubt that if we act promptly, everything can be arranged satisfactorily to all concerned. The Annual Report of the Smithsonian Institution is published about the end of June (our fiscal year terminates on June 30th), and I presume will not go to press for another month or two. Hence if Mr. Fu can cooperate with me in the matter of my suggestions, I shall be glad to do all I can on my part.

3.

    The only point, however, is that we act as soon as possible in regard to satisfying the fair expectations of the Freer Gallery, either in the way of photographs and some reasonable expectation of a report on the results of their effort in connection with the An-yang site, to be published later; or else of full and immediate public announcement of their share in that excavation.

    However, I feel sure that if I explain the situation thoroughly to my superiors in Washington, and accompany my recommendation with something tangible, I shall be able to accede to Dr. Fu's suggestions, provided Mr. Fu acts very soon. But <u>periculum in morâ</u>, as they used to say in my Latin class; we have but little time to lose if we are to write to Washington and arrange matters there.

    I am glad to say that since I have been writing this note, Mrs. Bishop has come back from the German Hospital with the news that her mother is somewhat better, and we feel much more encouraged than we have for several days. But for her mother's illness, I should have attended to the matter of the photographs for you---the phallus, the oldest dated cannon at T'ai-yuan, and the Yün-kang carvings. If I can dig up anything decent from Lung-mên, I'll include that too. Did I ever tell you of the time I was up at Yün-kang with Mr. Wenley, and caught him out early one morning with our little field "movie" camera, taking a moving picture of the great stone Buddha there? I often rally him about that episode.

    I can't tell you how much I enjoyed our talk of the other night. I feel much more clearly what Dr. Fu's position is, although our past relations have invariably been most cordial. Hoping to see you again soon, I remain,

                  Sincerely yours,   C. W. Bishop

5 March, 1931.

Dr. V. K. Ting,
The Geological Survey,
West City, Peiping.

Dear Dr. Ting:

Thanks very much for your cordial note of the 2nd instant, accompanied by the letter from Mr. Fu. I should have acknowledged them both but for the serious illness of Mrs. Bishop's mother, who has been critically ill at the German Hospital for the past few days. She is slightly better today, however, and I am able to give a little attention to routine matters.

I enjoyed our recent talk very much, and can quite sympathize with Mr. Fu's position and his reason for desiring that the entire credit of the An-yang "dig" should go to the Academia Sinica. I have written him today to that effect, going into the whole matter in detail.

As I stated in my letter to him, the Freer Gallery spent, not counting Dr. Li's and Mr. Tung's salaries and Dr. Li's trip around the world in 1928 but on actual field work alone, nearly four thousand dollars' gold. Moreover, from Dr. Li's regular reports while engaged on the "dig", the Freer Gallery was naturally led to believe that it would in time receive a full start of the work, accompanied by photographs. These it has not had up to date.

Consequently, I have made certain suggestions to Mr. Fu which I believe will, if complied with, dispose my superiors at Washington to acquiesce in Mr. Fu's wishes. These suggestions are as follows.

Firstly, that Dr. Li returns to us all the material with which he was entrusted by the Freer Gallery while he was in its employ, and which he still retains, although his resignation took effect on June 30th last.

Secondly, I suggested that the Freer Gallery should have two complete sets of photographs of the work at An-yang and the finds made there, for study purpose. Inasmuch as the Gallery paid for the taking of these photographs, I feel sure that Mr. Fu will agree to the justice of this suggestion.

Lastly, I felt that Mr. Lodge would like a statement from Dr. Li as to the approximate date at which he could expect the comprehensive report by the latter of which Mr. Fu speaks.

Of course I cannot guarantee that there will not be a detailed statement in the Annual Financial Report of the Smithsonian Institution of the amounts spent by the Freer Gallery in connection with its expenditures at An-yang; and indeed I am not sure that such a public statement is not required by law. Nor can I say how much they will wish to have appearing our Annual Report regarding the share of the Freer Gallery in the excavation at An-yang.

However, I am writing to Mr. Fu and to Dr. Li both in regard to the above point, and have little doubt that if we act promptly, everything can be arranged satisfactorily to all concerned. The Annual Report of the Smithsonian Institution is published about the end of June (our fiscal year terminates on June 30th), and I presume will not go to press for another month or two. Hence if Mr. Fu can cooperate with me in the matter of my suggestions, I shall be glad to do all I can on my part.

The only point, however, is that we act as soon as possible in regard to satisfying the fair expectations of the Freer Gallery either in the way of photographs and some reasonable expectation of a report on the results of their effort in connection with the An-yang site, to be published later; or else of full and immediate public announcement of their share in that excavation.

However, I feel sure that if I explain the situation thoroughly to my superiors in Washington, and accompany recommendation with something tangible, I shall be able to accede to Dr. Fu's suggestions, provided Mr. Fu acts very soon. But periculum in mora as they used to say in my Latin class; we have but little time to lose if we are to write to Washington and arrange matters there.

I am glad to say that since I have been writing this note, Mrs. Bishop has come back from the German Hospital with the news that her mother is somewhat better, and we feel much more encouraged than we have for several days. But for her mother's illness, I should have attended to the matter of the photographs for you—the phallus, the oldest dated cannon at T'ai-yuan, and the Yun-kang carvings. If I can dig un anything decent from Lung-men, I will include that too. Did I ever tell you of the time I was up at Yun-kang with Mr. Wenley, and caught him out early one morning with our little field movie camera, taking moving picture of the great stone Buddha there?

I can't tell you how much I enjoyed out talk of the other night, I feel much more clearly what Dr. Fu's position is, although our past relations have invariably been most cordial. Hoping to see you again soon, I remain,

Sincerely yours

C. W. Bishop

Ting V. K.

7 March, 1931.

Dr. V. K. Ting,
Geological Survey,
West City, Peiping.

Dear Dr. Ting:-

In accordance with your request, I am enclosing a carbon copy of my letter to Mr. Fu, although I fancy that my letter to him, which I mailed personally at the same time that I mailed mine to yourself, will eventually reach him, for I have found the Postal Service in Peiping exceedingly good.

I am particularly anxious, for the immediate present, to have returned to me the property of the Freer Gallery of Art which has remained in Dr. Li's possession hitherto, but which was entrusted to him solely for use in connection with the Field work of the Freer Gallery. This includes several books, some ten gallons or so of high grade shellac, and other material, of which I sent Dr. Li a list. Fortunately I registered his letter, so that I need have no apprehension that it might not reach him.

I should also like to have the photographs for which the Freer Gallery has paid; and there should also be some statement from Dr. Li, as definite as possible, in regard to the approximate date when the Freer Gallery may expect his report.

As soon as these suggestions are complied with, I shall feel in a position to take the matter up with the Freer Gallery; but I can hardly approach them with empty hands, and meanwhile there is little time to lose unless we all, collectively and individually do our share.

2.

    Let me say again that I am as anxious as possible to comply with Mr. Fu's wishes in this matter to the extent of my power. I have always valued Mr. Fu's friendship, and trust that matters may so shape themselves that we can look forward to long years of co-operation in the elucidation of the fascinating questions met with in the study of China's wonderful past.

    Hoping to hear from you and Mr. Fu and Dr. Li as soon as possible, I remain,

        Very sincerely yours,

           C. W. Bishop.

P. S. As I was writing the above, a letter came in which was written here in Peiping on February 27th, and postmarked the 28th; so I feel more certain than ever that the delay in the delivery of my letter to Mr. Fu must have taken place in the mails.

7 March, 1931.

Dr. V. K. Ting,
Geological Survey,
West City, Peiping

Dear Dr. Ting:

In accordance with your request, I am enclosing a carbon copy of my letter to Mr. Fu, although I fancy that my letter to him, which I mailed personally at the same time that I mailed mine to yourself, will eventually reach him, for I have found the Postal Service in Peiping exceedingly good.

I am particularly anxious, for the immediate present, to have retuned to me the property of the Freer Gallery of Art which has remained in Dr. Li's possession hitherto, but which was entrusted to him solely for use in connection with the field work of the Freer Gallery. This includes several books, some ten gallons or so of high grade shellac, and other material, of which I send Dr. Li a list. Fortunately, I registered his letter, so that I need have no apprehension that it might not reach him.

I should also like to have the photographs for which he Freer Gallery has paid; and there should also be some statement from Dr. Li, as definite as possible, in regard to the approximate date when the Freer Gallery may expect his report.

As soon as these suggestions are complied with, I shall feel in a position to take the matter up with the Freer Gallery; but I can hardly approach them with empty hands, and meanwhile there is little time to lose unless we all, collectively and individually do our share.

Let me say again that I am as anxious as possible to comply with Mr. Fu's wishes in this matter to the extent of my power. I have always valued Mr. Fu's friendship, and trust that matters may so shape themselves that we can look forward to long years of cooperation in the elucidation of the fascinating questions met with in the study of China's wonderful past.

　　Hoping to hear from you and Mr. Fu and Dr. Li as soon as possible, I remain,

Very sincerely yours,

C. W. Bishop.

　　P.S. As I was writing the above, a letter came in which as written here in Peiping on February 27th, and postmarked the 28th; so I feel more certain than ever that the delay in the delivery of my letter to Mr. Fu must have taken place in the mails.

Ting, V. K.

8 March, 1931.

Dear Dr. Ting:-

Last night I received a very nice letter from Dr. Li, clearing up a number of matters on which I had lacked precise information, and telling me that he expected to have his report ready before the end of the present calendar year. So that part of the matter is entirely satisfactory, as far as I am concerned, and I am sure it will be to the people at Washington.

I can not write more, for Mrs. Bishop's mother is very low at the German Hospital, and I must go back in a few minutes. However, I shall be glad if you will tell Mr. Fu for me that I have every expectation that the whole matter may be arranged to the full satisfaction of all concerned.

With good wishes, I remain,

Very sincerely yours,

C. W. Bishop

Dr. V. K. Ting,
Geological Survey,
West City, Peiping.

8 March, 1931.

Dear Dr. Ting:

Last night I received a very nice letter from Dr. Li, clearing up a number of matters on which I had lacked precise information, and telling me that he expected to have his report ready before the end of the present calendar year. So that part of the matter is entirely satisfactory, as far as I am concerned, and I am sure it will be to the people at Washington.

I cannot write more, for Mrs. Bishop's mother is very low at the German Hospital, and I must go back in a few minutes. However, I shall be glad if you will tell Mr. Fu for me that I have every expectation that the whole matter may be arranged to the full satisfaction of all concerned.

With good wishes, I remain,

Very sincerely yours,
C. W. Bishop

Dr. V. K. Ting,
Geological Survey,
West City, Peiping.

Tang, V. K

21 March, 1931.

Dr. V. K. Ting,
The Geological Survey,
West City, Peiping.

Dear Dr. Ting:-

  I am enclosing herewith a print of the pottery phallus, which I had Mr. Tung photograph for me. He has written the description on the back.

  A few days ago I received a cordial letter from Mr. Kent, the Secretary of the Metropolitan Museum, in which he says he is sending the photographs for which I asked him on your behalf, and which, he says, he hopes "may be exactly what Dr. Ting wants". So far they have not reached me, and it occurs to me that he may have sent them to you direct. But perhaps they are a bit slower in coming than his letter, and will arrive in the near future.

  The prints of the dated early Ming cannon and of the Yunkang sculptures I hope to have for you in a few days.

  I wonder if you could tell me where I could get, or if you could get for me, a copy of the paper you told me of, the evening you were here, about the ox-drawn plow not having appeared in China till about the Ch'in Dynasty; I should like to see it very much.

  Sincerely,

21 March, 1931.

Dr. V. K. Ting,

The Geological Survey,

West City, Peiping

Dear Dr. Ting:

I am enclosing herewith a print of the pottery phallus, which I had Mr. Tung photograph for me. He has written the description on the back.

A few days ago I received a cordial letter from Mr. Kent, the Secretary of the Metropolitan Museum, in which he says he is sending the photographs for which I asked him on your behalf, and which, he says, he hopes "may be exactly what Dr. Ting wants". So far they have not reach me, and it occurs to me that he may have sent then to you direct. But perhaps they are a bit slower in coming than his letter, and will arrive in the near future.

The prints of the dated early Ming cannon and of the Yun-kang sculptures I hope to have for you in a few days.

I wonder if you could tell me where I could get, or if you could get for me, a copy of the paper you told me of, the evening you were here, about the ox-drawn plow not having appeared in China till about the Ch'in Dynasty; I should like to see it very much.

Sincerely,

C. W. Bishop

THE NATIONAL GEOLOGICAL SURVEY OF CHINA

9 PING MA SSU, WEST CITY, PEIPING, CHINA

March 24, 1931.

Mr. C. W. Bishop,

 Peking.

Dear Mr. Bishop:-

  Many thanks for your kind letter of the 21st with the photograph of the pottery phallus. I cannot make out from Mr. Tung's romanised locality the Chinese characters. Can you ask him to send me a note? Some more details about the "Neolithic" that contains the specimen would be welcome, for I am not sure if it is the Mongolian neolithic found by Teilhard and Nelson, or is it the typical Yangshao. What is the scale of the photo?

  No, I have received nothing from Mr. Kent.

  I no longer need any photos of Yunkang or Lungmen, for I have got a magnificent set from Yamamoto here.

  I will of course be very grateful for the prints of the dated cannon.

  The paper on the ox-drawn flow shall be sent to you in a few days.

        Yours sincerely,

        (V. K. Ting).

THE NATIONAL GEOLOGICAL SURVEY OF CHINA
9 Ping Ma Ssu, West City, Peiping, China

March 24, 1931.

Mr. C. W. Bishop,
Peking.

Dear Mr. Bishop:

Many thanks for your kind letter of the 21st with photography of the pottery phallus. I cannot make out from Mr. Tung's Romanized locality the Chinese characters. Can you ask him to send me a note? Some more details about the "Neolithic" that contains the specimen would be welcome, for I am not sure if it is the Mongolian Neolithic found by Teilhard and Nelson, or is it the typical Yangshao. What is the scale of the photo?

No, I have received nothing from Mr. Kent.

I no longer need any photos of Yunkang or Lungmen, for I have got a magnificent set from Yamamoto here.

I will of course be very grateful for the prints of the dated cannon.

The paper on the ox-drawn flow shall be sent to you in a few days.

Yours sincerely,
V. K. Ting

Ting, V. K.

3 April, 1931.

Dr. V. K. Ting,
Geological Sirvey,
West City, Peiping.

Dear Dr. Ting:-

I am sending you herewith the photographs you wanted from the Metropolitan, and also the photograph I took of an old bombard in the Museum at T'ai-yuan, in Shansi, in the autumn of 1926.

As you will see, Dr. Kent has sent you the pictures with his compliments, which I think was very decent of him, particularly as exchange is what it is. Dr. Kent also wrote me a very cordial letter, thanking me for enabling him to be of service to you. I shall of course write him in reply, and if you wish to thank him direct, you will find his address on the enclosed card.

The inscription on the bombard states that the piece was cast in Shansi in the 10th year of Ming Hung Wu (1377 A.D.). So far as I know, it is the oldest definitely datable cannon in the world, and seems to be not at all in the European tradition. I believe the theory has been propounded that the Mongols used cannon. This piece, as you see, comes very near the close of the Mongol period, and several of its details indicate that it had already a considerable period of development behind it.

In regard to Wan Ch'üan (   ), you will find it in extreme

2.

southwestern Shansi, just south of the Fên Ho, very near where it debouches into the Huang Ho. The phallus, so far as I know, was discovered in that locality, apparently in connection with remains of the local Painted Pottery culture. More than that I can not tell you at present, as Mr. Tung is out of reach.

Please let me know if there is anything else in which I can be of service to you. I know your book is going to be an extremely valuable one. With good wishes, I remain,

Sincerely yours,

C. W. Bishop.

3 April, 1931

Dr. V. K. Ting,
Geological Survey,
West City, Peiping.

Dear Dr. Ting:

I am sending you herewith the photographs you wanted from the Metropolitan, and also the photography I took of an old bombard in the Museum at T'ai-yuan, in Shansi, in the autumn of 1926.

As you will see, Dr. Kent has sent you the picture with his compliments, which I think was very decent of him, particularly as exchange is what it is. Dr. Kent also wrote me a very cordial letter, thanking me for enabling him to be of service to you. I shall of course write him in reply, and if you wish to thank him direct, you will find his address on the enclosed card.

The inscription on the bombard states that the piece was cast in Shansi in the 10th year of Ming Hung Wu (1377 A. D). So far as I know, it is the oldest definitely datable cannon in the world, and seems to be not at all in the European tradition. I believe the theory has been propounded that the Mongols used cannon. This piece, as you see, comes very near the close of the Mongol period, and several of its details indicate that it had already a considerable period of development behind it.

In regard to Wan Ch'uan (), you will find it in extreme southwestern Shansi, just south of the Fen Ho, very near where it debouches into the Huang Ho. The phallus, so far as I know, was discovered in that locality, apparently in connection with remains of the local Painted Pottery culture. More than that I can not tell you at present, as Mr. Tung is out of reach.

Please let me know if there is anything else in which I can be of service to you. I know your book is going to be an extremely valuable one. With good wishes, I remain,

Sincerely yours,

C. W. Bishop.

Tung, Dr. V.K.

14 May, 1931.

Dr. V. K. Ting,
Geological Survey,
West City, Peiping.

Dear Dr. Ting:-

In accordance with my promise to you last night, I have checked up our book lists, and find that the book to which you had reference, "Ur Excavation, 1927", by Hall and Woolley, purchased by Dr. Li here in Peiping on behalf of the Freer Gallery of Art, is now in the possession of Mr. Tung, who as you know is conducting work for us in Shansi.

I fancy Mr. Tung will be back in town by the end of June, or possibly sooner, and I shall be glad at that time to lend you the book. I am sorry it is not available just now.

Sincerely yours,

C. W. Bishop.

14 May, 1931.

Dr. V. K. Ting,
Geological Survey,
West City, Peiping.

Dear Dr. Ting:

In accordance with my promise to you last night, I have checked up our book lists, and find that the book to which you had reference, "Ur Excavation, 1927", by Hall and Woolley, purchased by Dr. Li here in Peiping on behalf of the Freer Gallery of Art, is now in the possession of Mr. Tung, who as you know is conducting work for us in Shansi.

I fancy Mr. Tung will be back in town by the end of June, or possibly sooner, and I shall be glad at that time to lend you the book. I am sorry it is not available just now.

Sincerely yours,

C. W. Bishop.

Ting, Dr. V. K.

THE NATIONAL GEOLOGICAL SURVEY OF CHINA
9 PING MA SSU, WEST CITY, PEIPING, CHINA

19 Sept. 1931

Dear Mr Bishop,

Many thanks for your note of yesterday. My paper is entitled "How China acquired her Civilisation" and is being printed by the Institute of Pacific Relations. It should be ready in a few days' time. As soon as I receive a copy, I will send it to you, for I no longer possess the manuscript which was sent to the printer in a great hurry.

With kind regards,
Yours V. K. Ting

THE NATIONAL GEOLOGICAL SURVEY OF CHINA

9 Ping Ma Ssu, West City, Peiping, China

19 Sept, 1931

Dear Mr. Bishop,

Many thanks for your note of yesterday. My paper is entitled "How Chinese acquired the Civilization" and is being printed by the Institution of Pacific Relations. It should be ready in a few days' time. As soon as I receive a copy, I will send it to you. But I no longer possess the manuscript when it was sent to the Institute in a great hurry.

With kind regards,

Yours,

V. K. Ting

Ting, Dr. V. K.

29 October, 1931.

Dr. V. K. Ting,
The Geological Survey,
West City, Peiping.

Dear Dr. Ting:-

I had supposed that you were still in the South, and only learned by accident, a day or two ago, that you were back in Peiping. A few days back I happened to be in the Language School Library, and saw in the current issue of Pacific Affairs that your article on "How China acquired her Civilization" had at last appeared. I wonder if you can tell me how I can procure a copy.

I have just returned from the Wan-ch'üan region, where Mr. Tung and his colleagues of the Women's Normal University and the Shansi Provincial Library made such interesting discoveries last spring and the previous autumn, and was impressed, among other things, by the quantities of what seems to be a sort of vitreous slag associated, apparently, with the Neolithic deposits. I wonder if you could tell me where we could get specimens of this analyzed? I fancy it would be just in the line of the Geological Survey, and the amount of this slag shows that it is a feature of some importance.

No doubt you have seen a recent Kuo Wên despatch to the effect that the Commission for the Preservation of Antiquities has requested the Shansi Provincial Government to stop

2.

our work in the Wan-ch'üan region. I am writing an open letter to the Press, expressing my disbelief in the accuracy of this news item, for I know several of the gentlemen on the Commission, and feel sure they would not stoop to anything so underhanded as to try to stop our work without saying anything to me first. Such an action would moreover, as I do not need to point out to you, constitute a direct and gratuitous insult to the Smithsonian Institution, and through it to the people of the United States, whose interest and sympathy in everything that concerns China have so often and so strikingly been manifested.

Now that you are back, I shall hope to see you soon. In the meantime, with kindest regards, I remain,

Sincerely yours,

C. W. Bishop.

29 October, 1931.

Dr. V. K. Ting,
The Geological Survey,
West City, Peiping.

Dear Dr. Ting:

I had supposed that you were still in the South, and only learned by accident, a day to two ago, that you were back in Peiping. A few days back I happened to be in the Language School Library, and saw in the current issue of Pacific Affairs that your article on "How China acquired her Civilization" had at last appeared. I wonder if you can tell me how I can procure a copy.

I have just returned form the Wan-ch'uan region, where Mr. Tung and his colleagues of the Women's Normal University and the Shansi Provincial Library made such interesting discoveries last spring and previous autumn, and was impressed, among other things, by the quantities of what seems toe be a sort of vitreous slag associated, apparently, with the Neolithic deposits. I wonder if you could tell me where we could get specimens of this analyzed? I fancy it would be just in the line of the Geological survey, and the amount of this slag shows that it is a feature of some importance.

No doubt you have seen a recent Kuo Wen dispatch to the effect that the Commission for the Preservation of Antiquities has requested the Shansi Provincial Government to stop our work in the Wan-ch'uan region. I am writing an open letter to the Press, expressing my disbelief in the accuracy of this news item, for I know several of the gentlemen on the Commission, and feel sure they would not stoop to anything so underhanded as to try to stop our work without saying anything to me first. Such an action would moreover, as I do not need to point out to you, constitute a direct and gratuitous insult to the Smithsonian Institution, and through it to the people of the United States, whose interest and sympathy in everything that concerns China have so often and so strikingly been manifested.

Now that you are back, I shall hope to see you soon. In the meantime, with kindest regards, I remain,

Sincerely yours,

C. W. Bishop.

Ting, V. K

THE NATIONAL GEOLOGICAL SURVEY OF CHINA
9 PING MA SSU, WEST CITY, PEIPING, CHINA

30 Oct. 1931

Dear Mr Bishop,

Many thanks for your letter of yesterday. My article is published in the "Symposium" on Chinese Culture printed by the China Council of the Institute of Pacific Relations, 20, Museum Road Shanghai where I suppose you ought to be able to buy a copy. No reprints so far has been received.

Yours sincerely,
V K Ting

THE NATIONAL GEOLOGICAL SURVEY OF CHINA

9 Ping Ma Ssu, West City, Peiping, China

30 Oct., 1931

Dear Mr. Bishop,

Many thanks for your letter of yesterday. My article is published in the "Symposium" on Chinese culture printed by the China Council of the Institute of Pacific Relations, 20 Museum Road, Shanghai where I suppose you ought to be able to buy a copy. No reprint so far has been received.

Yours sincerely,

V. K. Ting

1932 年

Ting, V. K.

21 April, 1932.

Dr. V. K. Ting,
The Geological Survey,
West City, Peiping.

Dear Dr. Ting:-

    I have wanted to get in touch with you for some time past, but have been working almost night and day to get out a preliminary report on our work in southwestern Shansi, and so have been hindered.

    It would give me great pleasure to have you look at the material, especially of a skeletal nature, from our "dig", if you can spare the time to run out with me and look at it. I believe I told you that both Stevenson and Shellshear said that, judging from photographs, one or two of the skulls we found seemed to differ somewhat from the usual North China type, such as Andersson found.

    I saw Père Teilhard at Dr. Grabau's last night, and we arranged to go out and see the material on Monday, May 2nd, if he is back from Chou Kou Tien by that time. The plan is for me to pick him up at the Survey and bring him down here for lunch, and then go on out in the early afternoon. If you could join us, I should be delighted. But if any other date would suit you better, I shall be glad to go out with you at any time. As ever,

                Yours sincerely,

21 April, 1932.

Dr. V. K. Ting,
The Geological Survey,
West City, Peiping.

Dear Dr. Ting:

I have wanted to get in touch with you for some time past, but have been working almost night and day to get out a preliminary report on our work in southwestern Shansi, and so have been hindered.

It would give me great pleasure to have you look at the material, especially of a skeletal nature, from our "dig", if you can spare the time to run out with me and look at it. I believe I told you that both Stevenson and Shellshear said that, judging from photographs, one or two of the skulls we found seemed to differ somewhat from the usual North China type, such as Andersson found.

I saw Pere Teilhard at Dr. Grabau's last night, and we arranged to go out and see the material on Monday, May 2nd, if he is back from Chou Kou Tien by that time. The plan is for me to pick him up at the Survey and bring him down here for lunch, and then go on out in the early afternoon. If you could join us, I should be delighted. But if any other date would suit you better, I shall be glad to go out with you at any time. As ever,

Yours sincerely
[C. W. Bishop]

Ting, V. K.

THE NATIONAL GEOLOGICAL SURVEY OF CHINA
9 PING MA SSU, WEST CITY, PEIPING, CHINA

22 April 1932

My dear Mr. Bishop,

Many thanks for your letter of yesterday. I shall be delighted to join you on Monday, but as I have a lecture from 11–12, I shall not be at the Survey until 12:30.

Yours sincerely,
V. K. Ting

THE NATIONAL GEOLOGICAL SURVEY OF CHINA

9 Ping Ma Ssu, West City, Peiping, China

22 April, 1932

My dear Mr. Bishop,

Many thanks for your letter of yesterday. I shall be delighted to join you on Monday, but as I have a lecture from 11-12, I shall work at the Survey until 12:30.

Yours sincerely,

V. K. Ting

Ting, V. K.

23 April, 1932.

Dear Dr. Ting:-

Your note of yesterday is just at hand, and I am delighted to learn that you can come out and see out things on Monday, the second of May.

Père Teilhard told me that there were some things he wanted to show me at the Survey before I brought him home for lunch, and if you are free by 12.30 that will fall in nicely with our plans. We can all come here for lunch then, and go out in the early afternoon to see the material at the Laboratory of the Normal University.

There are a great many points which I look forward to discussing with you then besides the skeletal material---among other things, for example, whether our site belongs to the Yang Shao or to some one of Andersson's other phases.

I shall look forward to seeing you at the Survey a week from Monday. As ever,

Sincerely yours,

C. W. Bishop.

23 April, 1932.

Dear Dr. Ting:

Your note of yesterday is just at hand, and I am delighted to learn that you can come out and see out things on Monday, the second of May.

Pere Teilhard told me that there were some things he wanted to show me at the Survey before I brought him home for lunch, and if you are free by 12:30 that will fall in nicely with our plans. We can all come here for lunch then, and go out in the early afternoon to see the material at the Laboratory of the Normal University.

There are a great many points which I look forward to discussing with you then besides the skeletal materials—among other things, for example, whether our site belongs to the Yang Shao or to some one of Andersson's other phases.

I shall look forward to seeing you at the Survey a week from Monday. As ever,

Sincerely yours,

C. W. Bishop.

THE NATIONAL GEOLOGICAL SURVEY OF CHINA
9 PING MA SSU, WEST CITY, PEIPING, CHINA

Ting, V. K

27 April 1932

Dear Mr Bishop,

Teilhard is going to Choukoutien tomorrow and will not be back until Monday. I am also going there with 30 students and very likely cannot come back until Monday. So please postpone our lunch party after our return.

Yours sincerely,
V. K. Ting

THE NATIONAL GEOLOGICAL SURVEY OF CHINA

9 Ping Ma Ssu, West City, Peiping, China

27 April, 1932

Dear Mr. Bishop,

Teilhard is going to Choukoutien tomorrow and will not be back until Monday. I am also going there with 30 students and very likely cannot come back until Monday. So please postpone our lunch party after our return.

Yours sincerely,

V. K. Ting

Ting, V. K.

13 may, 1932.

Dr. V. K. Ting,
The Geological Survey,
Peiping, China.

Dear Dr. Ting:-

The article on a Glacial Period in northern and central Asia about which I told you is reviewed at some length in the April/1932 number of the Geographical Review, pp. 322 et seq. It is written by V. A. Obruchev, and appears in the Byulleten Kommissii po Izucheniyu Chetvertichnogo Perioda, 1931, No. 3, pp. 43-120.

The review, by J. V. Fuller, concludes with the following words:

"The total picture presented is of anQuaternary Ice Age in Asia corresponding generally with that in Europe but marked by a more restricted extension southward of the main northern mass. The difference, amounting to 10 or 12 degrees of latitude, is accounted for by the greater dryness of the climate, which, while not precluding entirely the development of a continental ice sheet, as alleged by Voeikov, did impose a limitation on its size."

I hope the above may be of some service to you.

Sincerely yours,

13 May, 1932.

Dr. V. K. Ting,
The Geological Survey,
Peiping, China.

Dear Dr. Ting:

The article on a Glacial Period in northern and central Asia about which I told you is reviewed at some length in the April, 1932 number of the Geographical Review, pp. 322 et seq. it is written by V. A. Obruchev, and appears in the Byulleten Kommissii po Izucheniyu Chetvertichnogo Perioda, 1931, No. 3, pp. 43-120.

The review, by J. V. Fuller, concludes with the following words:

"The total picture presented is of a Quaternary Ice Age in Asia corresponding generally with that in Europe but marked by a more restricted extension southward to the main northern mass. The difference, amounting to 10 or 20 degrees of latitude, is accounted for by the greater dryness of the climate, which, while not precluding entirely the development of a continental ice sheet, as alleged by Voeikov, did impose a limitation on its size."

I hope the above may be of some service to you.

Sincerely yours,
[C. W. Bishop]

Ting, V. K.

7 May, 1932.

Dr. V. K. Ting,
Geological Survey,
West City, Peiping.

Dear Dr. Ting:-

Mrs. Woodland has just telephoned to say that you and Père Teilhard will be able to go out Tuesday afternoon to see our skeletal and other material from Wan Ch'üan. So if it is all right with you both, I shall plan to come out to the Survey around eleven o'clock and see the things that Père T. wanted to show me, and then bring you both home with me for lunch, and afterward we can go out and see our stuff. Both Shellshear and Stevenson thought from the photographs that one or two of our skulls differed from the usual North China type found in Painted Pottery deposits; hence I shall be particularly glad if you will confirm or refute this from an examination of the skulls themselves.

A little problem has come up recently upon which I should like to consult you. As you must be aware, a find of bronze vessels was made some years ago in northern Shansi, some of which, I believe, passed into the hands of M. Wannieck, the French dealer. I believe it is claimed that these vessels are of Eastern Chou date. But so far as I am aware, the Eastern Chou kings, fainéant rulers as they were, exercised no power in northern Shansi at any time. That region, I believe, was part

2.

of the Chin state until well on in the 5th century B. C., when that state split up into three, and thereafter northern Shansi belonged to the Chao state down to Ch'in times. Hence while the vessels may date from the Eastern Chou period, that they were every used by the kings of that dynasty themselves in conducting the official state worship seems to me inherently improbable.

M. Wannieck says, in part, in his note on the "Bronzes de Li-Yu",

"Le Trésor de Li-Yu fut découvert en Mars 1923. Le village de Li-Yu est situé à 120 lis sud/sud-est de T-Toung-Fou at à 12 lis ouest de la sous-préfecture de Huan-Yn-Chou, située dans le nord du Shansi.

Les villes de Li-Yu et Huan-Yn-Chow se trouvent au pied du versant nord du Ho-Chan, l'une des cinq montagnes sacrées de la Chine."

I find a place called Hun-yüan Chou (now Hsien) 120 li southeast of Ta-T'ung, while 18 li southwest of Hun-yüan Hsien is a place called Li-yu Do you suppose these are the places Wannieck means?

And how about "Ho-chan" being one of the Five Sacred Mountains? The only sacred mountain of importance that I know of in Shansi is Wu-t'ai Shan, and this isn't one of the five as usually enumerated.

All I know about the find is what I have heard rumored about town, mostly by dealers, and what Wannieck says. I have a suspicion that the latter simply threw in the little flourish about it having been made "at the foot of one of China's

3.

sacred mountains" just to make it sound better. It seems to me that the find must belong either to the Chin state or to the subsequent Chao, and that it may probably be of the Eastern Chou period, though having nothing to do with the ruling house itself, which so far as I know exercised no power so far north. On the other hand, it can hardly have been earlier, for to the best of my recollection, northern Shansi was only brought under Chinese control, by the China state, about the seventh or sixth century B. C.

If you can throw any light on the points I have mentioned I shall be grateful, for I can't believe that the various statements made, by M. Wannieck and others, are altogether accurate.

I understand that the Academia Sinica has the matter of the disposition of the find in hand, and I trust the bronzes will soon be properly and scientifically cared for.

Looking forward to seeing you Tuesday, I remain,

Sincerely yours,

7 May, 1932.

Dr. V. K. Ting,
Geological Survey,
West City, Peiping.

Dear Dr. Ting:

Mrs. Woodland has just telephoned to say that you and Pere Teilhard will be able to go out Tuesday afternoon to see our skeletal and other material from Wan Ch'uan. So if it is all right with you both, I shall plan to come out to the Survey around eleven O'clock and see the things that Pere T. wanted to show me, and then bring you both home with me for lunch, and afterward we can go out and see our stuff. Both Shellshear and Stevenson thought from the photographs that one or two of our skulls differed from the usual North China type found in Painted Pottery deposits; hence I shall be particularly glad if you will confirm or refute this from an examination of the skulls themselves.

A little problem has come up recently upon which I should like to consult you. As you must be aware, a find of bronze vessels was made some years ago in northern Shansi, some of which, I believe, passed into the hands of M. Wannieck, the French dealer. I believe it is claimed that these vessels are of Eastern Chou date. But so far as I am aware, the Eastern Chou kings, fainéant rulers as they were, exercised no power in northern Shansi at any time. That region, I believe, was part of the Chin state until well on in the 5th century B. C. when that state split up into three, and thereafter northern Shansi belonged to the Chao state down to Ch'in times. Hence while the vessels may date from the Eastern Chou period, that they were every used by the kings of that dynasty themselves in conducting the official state worship seems to me inherently improbable.

M. Wannieck says, in part, in his note on the "Bronzes de Li-Yu",

"Le Tresor de Li-Yu fut decouvert en Mars 1923. Le village de Li-Yu est situe a 120 lis sud/sud-est de T-Toung-Fou at a 12 lis oust de la sous-prefecture de Huan-Yn-Chou, situee dans le nord du Shansi.

Les villes de Li-Yu et Huan-Yn-Chow se trouvent au pied du versant nord du Ho-Chan, l'une des cinq montagnes sacrees de la Chine."

I find a place called Hun-yuan Chou (now Hsien) 12 li southeast of Ta-T'ung, while 18 li southwest of Hunyuan Hsien is a place called Li-yu, do you suppose these are the places Wannieck means?

And how about "Ho-chan" being one of the Five Sacred Mountains? The only sacred mountain of importance that I know of in Shansi is Wu-t'ai Shan, and this isn't one of the five as usually enumerated.

All I know about the find is what I have heard rumored about town, mostly by dealers, and what Wennieck says. I have a suspicion that the latter simply threw in the little flourish about it having been made "at the foot of one of China's sacred mountains" just to make it sound better. It seems to me that the find must belong either to the Chin state or to the subsequent Chao, and that it may probably be of the Eastern Chou period, though having nothing to do with the ruling house itself, which so far as I know exercised no power so far north. On the other hand, it can hardly have been earlier, for to the best of my recollection, northern Shansi was only brought under Chinese control, by the China state, about the seventh or sixth century B.C

If you can throw any light on the points I have motioned I shall be grateful, for I can't believe that the various statements made, by M. Wannieck and others, are altogether accurate.

I understand that the Academia Sinica has the matter of the disposition of the find in hand, and I trust the bronzes will soon be properly and scientifically cared for.

Looking forward to seeing you Tuesday, I remain,

Sincerely yours,

[C. W. Bishop]

1933 年

Warszawa
Aleje Jerozolimskie Nr. 39
vis-a-vis Dworca Głównego.

4. Oct. 1933

Telefon: Polonia-Warszawa.
Telegraf: Poloniahotel-Warszawa.

My dear Barbour,

At last I have come out of U.S.S.R.! I entered Russia on the 30th Aug. & left it on the 3rd Oct. In 34 days I travelled some 8,000 kms. I was at Moscow, Leningrad, Tula, Baku, Tiflis — Vladikavkas (across n. Caucasus), Rostov, Donetz Basin, Dnieprostroy (the big hydro-electrical station) and Kiev. I saw a great deal of the oil, iron & coal industry of U.S.S.R.

Everywhere I saw new buildings (à l'Américaine), and in the mining districts new development works. They have increased their petroleum production by 100%, & coal & iron 50%. If nothing unforseen happens, U.S.S.R. will probably attain the economic level of W. Europe in 25-30 years time.

That does not mean that life in U.S.S.R. is in any way easy. Thanks to the good harvest this year, bread is no longer scarce, but everything else is! All the food and clothing which the people needed but did not get have gone into the heavy industry.

I think the Communist regime is going to stay. The young generation is quite reconciled to it; the old is not, but the latter does not count.

I was everywhere received with great courtesy. The Russian Geological Service actually sent a man to go with me at their own expense (amounting to some 3,000 R). Nor did anybody try to restrict my freedom of movement. Nevertheless the journey has been a rather strenuous one and I arrive at Warsaw with the sense of relief.

In a few days I will sail from Venice for China.

With kind regards to Mrs. Barbour,

Yours ever

V-K. Ting

POLONIA PALACE HOTEL

Warszawa

Aleje Jerozolimskie Nr. 39

vis-à-vis Dworca Glownego.

4 Oct, 1933

My dear Barbour,

At last I have come out of U. S. S. R!

I entered Russia on the 30th Aug. and left it on the 3rd Oct. In 34 days I traveled some 8,000 miles. I was at Moscow, Leningrad, Tula, Baku, Tiffin-Vladikavkaz (across N. Caucasus), Rostov, Donets Basin, Dnieperkstrg (the big hydro-electrical station) and Kiev. I saw a great deal of the oil, iron and coal industry of U. S. S. R.

Everywhere I saw new buildings (Américaine), and in the mining districts new development works. They have increased their petroleum production by 100%, and coal and iron 50%. If nothing unforeseen happens, U. S. S. R. will probably attain the economic level of W. Europe in 25-30 years' time.

That does not mean their life in U. S. S. R. is in any way easy. Thanks to the good harvest this year, bread is no longer scarce, but everything else is! All the food and clothing which the people needed but did not get have gone into the heavy industry.

I think the Communist regime is going to stay. The young generation is quite reconciled to it, the old is not, but the latter dos not count.

I was everywhere received with great country. The Russian geological service actually sent a man to go with us at their own expenses (accounting to some 3,000 R). Nor did anybody try to restrict my freedom of movement. Nevertheless, the journey has been a rather strenuous one and I arrive at Warsaw with the sense of relief.

In a few days, I will sail from Vania for China.

With kind regards to Mrs. Barbour,

Yours ever
V. K. Ting

ACADEMIA SINICA

HEAD OFFICE
48 CHEN HSIEN KAI
NANKING, CHINA

TELEPHONE NO. 31556 / 31491

October 29, 1934

Private and Confidential

R. S. Greene, Esq.
P. U. M. C.
P e i p i n g.

ans. 11ґ1-34

My dear Mr. Greene:

  Many thanks for your letter of the 16th. I have not answered you promptly because I was hoping that I might see you in Peiping on the 30th when the meeting of the Board of Trustees was to take place. As you know this is to be postponed.

  I had a talk with Y. T. Tsur when he passed through. I agreed with him that the Board of Trustees should take joint responsibility with the Director in any measure to which New York takes exception, since all such measures have been passed by the Board.

  I saw J. H. Liu's letter also. I think there is no need of fearing that the Board will antagonize New York. For in that case the members of the Board can and should resign to make room for those who enjoy the confidence of New York.

  This is my considered view. Of course I do not expect you to express any opinion about it. But if you think that I am quite wrong and may unwittingly cause the P.U.M.C. any harm, please let me know.

  Yours sincerely,

(V. K. Ting)

P. S. -
  I have wired to Dr. W. H. Wong voicing my approval of Weidenreich.

國 立 中 央 研 究 院
ACADEMIA SINICA
HEAD OFFICE
48 CHEN HSIEN KAI
NANKING, CHINA

October 29, 1934

Private and Confidential
R. S. Greene, Esq.
P. U. M.C
Peiping.

My dear Mr. Greene:

Many thanks for your letter of the 16th. I have not answer you promptly because I was hoping that I might see you in Peiping on the 30th when the meeting of the Board of Trustees was to take place. As you know this is to be postponed.

I had a talk with Y. T. Tsur when he passed through. I agreed with him that the Board of Trustees should take joint responsibility with the Director in any measure to which New York takes exception, since all such measures have been passed by the Board.

I saw J. H. Liu's letter also. I think there is no need of fearing that the Board will antagonize New York. For in that case the members of the Board can and should resign to make room for those who enjoy the confidence of New York.

This is my considered view. Of course I do not expect you to express any opinion about it. But if you think that I am quite wrong and may unwittingly cause the P. U. M. C. any harm, please let me know.

Your sincerely,

V. K. Ting

P. S.

I have wired to Dr. W. H. Wong voicing my approval of Weidenreich.

ACADEMIA SINICA
HEAD OFFICE
48 CHEN HSIEN KAI
NANKING, CHINA

TELEPHONE NO. 31556
31491

November 1, 1934

Dr. G. B. Barbour
Queen's Gate Hotel
Queen's Gate
South Kensington
L o n d o n.

Dear Barbour,

Many thanks for your letter of 14th of October.

Here is my answer to your questionaires: —

(1) My views about Yunnan have been considerably changed - not due to Gregory or Credner but due to careful working out of field notes (when I wrote the Congress paper I had no time to work the thing out), and to my observations in Kwangsi. The main point is that most of the overthrusts are really unconformities - the Permian (and possibly Moscovian) limestone overlies all sorts of Strata. Deprat thought these to be overthrusts. So did I. But now I am convinced that they are due to Hercynian (Premoscovian) folding.

(2) Yes, The articles contain some physiographical material. I have written to have these sent to you directly from the Independent Review office.

(3) Yes, In fact the idea was originally mine - I told Gregory in 1911 before I went to Yunnan when we were looking at Davie's map together.

(4) Pay no attention to Credner who certainly talks through his hat.

(5) Heim's mapping is worthless. The supposed Cretaceous Red Beds are mainly Devonian. Hence the supposed overthrusts do not exist.

(6) I see no evidence whatsoever of Himalayan folding in China at all. Its general absence for Burma confirms my view that folding in Yunnan is largely Yenshanian.

ACADEMIA SINICA

HEAD OFFICE
48 CHEN HSIEN KAI
NANKING, CHINA

TELEPHONE NO. 31556 / 31491

- 2 -

(7) On the evidence of Yunnan alone it is not possible to date the folding very accurately. No beds older than Pliocene and younger than Jurassic have been discovered.

(8) Both fault scarp and fault-line scarp may exist. Most if not all the basins are true basins of subsidence.

   I have told Wong about your idea of publishing your report on Lushan. He must finally decide.

   Please do not forget to let me know the price of the lettering machine which I bought from you.

   With best regards,

    Yours sincerely,

     (V. K. Ting)

P. S. - Remember me to your family and Wordie.

Memorandum on Yunnan and adjoining Yangtze reaches.
Please answer b. brief comment in spaces left:

(1) Have later published researches of other men (Gregory, Credner etc) or rumination or inspiration led to serious modification of ideas put forward in International Congress Paper?   Yes
                                                                                                                                                                  No

(2) I cannot yet get a copy here of the two articles by VKT published in the Chinese Independent Review (in Chinese) so cannot find out whether they embody important physiographic conclusions except VK's support of the theory that the Yangtze once drained south. Can I leave it at that, or is there much more in them?   Yes   No

(3) Am I correct in understanding that VK more or less subscribes to Gregory's idea of that drainage as going through the Chienchuan basin to Red River?   Yes   No

(4) Credner attacks Deprat and Gregory insisting that the earlier pre-entrenchment valleys of Yunnan are themselves erosional, and originally subsequent where not actually consequent to uplift, rather than tectonic (i.e. block-fault); the latter Credner assumes only for a few of the larger valleys e.g. Tali lake. Does not Credner do alot of talking through his hat? Even granting that Deprat sees more in the evidence than it will stand and that (a) faulting may be only one of several controls and (b) that the minor substages in the rejuvenation cannot be corroborated as widely as he thinks, does not the truth lie somewhere between?

(5) Credner's mapping does not seem to give strong support to Gregory's ideas as to trend of extension of Himalayas, but rather supports Deprat. Is Credner wrong here too? I believe he is right in some of his criticisms of Heim, whose work seems hasty.

(6) Who knows anything about the date, extent and limitations of the Himalayan movement as one of folding in China?

(7) Gregory thinks of orogenesis only in terms of Hercynian and Himalayan and entirely neglects possibility of Yenshan effects. Have you evidence of preHimalayan post-Jurassic movements; the folding of margins of Yangtze arc you mention are "midTertiary or older"; how much older? Or is precise stratigraphic evidence wanting; if so, is not the physiographic evidence of use?   Many Thanks

GBB

Postscript.
(8) Gregory (Phil Trans. p.243) lists criteria used to detect tectonic, i.e. faulted, basins. But entirely overlooks the possiblity of fault-line scarps as distinct from fault-scarps. A straight cliff may be a fault feature or an erosional-feature- developed-along-a-fault-line-by erosion-of-nonresistent-block-surface (Cf. W.M.Davis or D.Johnson). Deprat similarly ignores this alternative. Credner does not, though his allowance for it is implicit rather than explicit. The real argument for their being fault-scarps seems to be rather the present day seismic history. Granting fault-control in either case, did your observations support the idea of the depressions being actually subsided strips or differentially eroded surfaces etched in a rifted terrain of unequally resistent materials?

(presence of lakes, or depth of alluvium)

國立中央研究院
ACADEMIA SINICA
HEAD OFFICE

48 CHEN HSIEN KAI

NANKING, CHINA

November 1, 1934

Dr. G. B. Barbour

Queen's Gate Hotel

Queen's Gate

South Kensington

London.

Dear Barbour,

Many thanks for your letter of 14th of October.

Here is my answer to your questionnaires:

(1) My views about Yunnan have been considerably changed, not due to Gregory or Credner but due to careful working out of field notes (when I wrote the Congress paper I had no time to work the thing out), and to my observations in Kwangsi. The main point is that most of the overthrusts are really unconformities-the Permian (and possibly Moscovian) limestone overlies all sorts of Strata. Deprat thought these to be overthrusts. So did I. But now I am convinced that they are due to Hercynian (Premoscovian) folding.

(2) Yes, the articles contain some physiographical material. I have written to have these sent to you

directly from the Independent Review Office.

(3) Yes, in fact the idea was originally mine --I told Gregory in 1911 before I went to Yunnan when we were looking at Davie's map together.

(4) Pay no attention to Credner who certainly talks through his hat.

(5) Heim's mapping is worthless. The supposed Cretaceous Red Beds are mainly Devonian. Hence the supposed overthrusts do not exist.

(6) I see no evidence whatsoever of Himalayan folding in China at all. Its general absence for Burma confirms my view that folding in Yunnan is largely Yenshianian.

(7) On the evidence of Yunnan alone it is not possible to date the folding very accurately. No beds older than Pliocene and younger than Jurassic have been discovered.

(8) Both fault scarp and fault-line scarp may exist. Most if not all the basins are true basins of subsidence.

I have told Wong about your idea of publishing your report on Lushan. He must finally decide.

Please do not forget to let me know the price of the lettering machine which I bought from you.

With best regards,

Yours sincerely,

V. K. Ting

P. S. Remember me to your family and Wordie.

Memorandum on Yunnan and adjoining Yangtze reaches.

Please answer by briefly comment in spaces left:

(1) Have later published researches of other men (Gregory, Credner etc) or rumination or inspiration led to serious modification of ideas put forward in International Congress Paper? Yes/No

(2) I cannot yet get a copy here of the two articles by VKT published in the Chinese Independent Review (in Chinese) so cannot find out whether they embody important physiographic conclusions except VK's support of the theory that the Yangtze once drained south. Can I leave it at that, or is there much more in them? Yes/No

(3) Am I correct in understanding that VK more or less subscribes to Gregory's idea of that drainage as going through the Chienchuan basin to Red River?

(4) Credner attacks Deprat and Gregory insisting that the earlier pre-entrenchment valleys of Yunnan are themselves erosional, and originally subsequent where not actually consequent to uplift, rather than tectonic (i. e. block-fault); the latter Credner assumes only for a few of talking through his hat? Even granting that Deprat sees more in the evidence than it will stand and that (a) faulting may be only one of several controls and (b) that the minor substages in the rejuvenation cannot be corroborated as widely as he thinks, does not the truth lie somewhere between?

(5) Credner's mapping does not seem to give strong support to Gregory's ideas as to trend of extensions, but rather supports Deprat. Is Credner wrong here too? I believe he is right in some of his criticisms of Heim, whose work seems hasty.

(6) Who knows anything about the date, extent and limitations of the Himalayan movement as one of folding in China?

(7) Gregory thinks of orogenesis only in terms of Hercynian and Himalayan and entirely neglects possibility of Yenshan effects. Have you evided of pre-Himalayan post-Jurassic movements; the

folding of margin of Yangtze are you mention are mid-Tertiary or older; how much older? Or is precise stratigraphic evidence wanting; if so, is not the physiographic evidence of use?

Many Thanks

GBB

Postscript

(8) Gregory lists criteria used to detect tectonic, i.e. faulted, basins. But entirely overlooks the possibility of fault-line scarps as distinct from fault-scarps. A straight cliff may be a fault feature or an erosinal-feature-developed-along-a-fault-line-by erosion-of-nonresistent-block-surface. Deprat similarly ignores this alternative. Credner does not, though his allowance for it is implicit rather than explicit. The real argument for their being fault-scarps seems to be rather the present day seismic history. Granting fault-control in either case, did your observations support the idea of the depressions being actually subsides strips or differentially eroded surfaces etched in a rifted terrain of unequally resistant materials?

DIRECTOR'S OFFICE FILE

April 16, 1935

Dear Dr. Ting:

I suppose that within the next two or three weeks there will be news from New York which will make it necessary for the College to consider what is to be done about the post which I now hold. If the news is such as to make it seem desirable that I leave shortly, the question of a successor will immediately come up.

According to the By-Laws, the initiative must be taken by the Committee of Professors, who make recommendations to the Trustees. If the Trustees are not pleased with the first nomination, they have the right to send it back and ask for another.

There is room for a good deal of difference of opinion as to the type of person to be secured to relieve me. I do not claim to be wiser than all others on this subject, but you may be interested in my views.

As regards whether we should attempt to appoint a Chinese, as I believe Dr. Houghton would prefer, or an American, I have this to say:

1. The post is not an easy one, involving complicated relationships both here in China and in the United States.

2. The selection among Chinese is rather restricted, at least if one considers only persons well known to the Professors and Trustees, as I think one must.

3. The coming year is one of exceptional difficulty, since various outstanding questions, such as future relationships between the Peiping Union Medical College, The China Medical Board, Inc., and the Rockefeller Foundation, have to be settled, and some agreement must be reached as to the future budget of the institution, which I fear may have to suffer a further cut. In other words, the new executive would not know precisely under what conditions he would have to work, and what money he would have at his disposal.

4. The Chinese who might be considered are persons occupying important

Dr. Ting - 2   April 16, 1935

posts, and it is not certain whether their services would be more valuable in
an executive post or in the scientific posts which they are now holding.

    5. If a Chinese is to be appointed to such a difficult post, it seems to me desirable that he should have every possible advantage in the way of a clear understanding of relationships, and knowledge of the money at his disposal. A man who had it in him to produce good results over a long period might well fail to give satisfaction during the coming year.

    The above considerations have led me to favor a temporary appointment, preferably of some one who has an assured position and influence at home to which he can return. Dr. Gregg, Director for Medical Sciences in the Rockefeller Foundation, has two associates, Dr. R. A. Lambert, who has had long experience in the United States, Europe, and South America, and I think would give satisfaction during a year's service if he is available. There is another associate, Dr. Bradley M. Patten, whose experience has been only in the United States, but I think would be able to hold the position satisfactorily for a year with the help that he could obtain from the professors, Dr. Tsur, and the secretarial staff. It is not certain that either of these men will be available, as the Foundation may hesitate to give them leave for the purpose, particularly for the very reason for which I should like to see them come, namely, that they would thereby acquire a special interest in the College.

    It is barely possible that Dr. Canby Robinson, formerly Dean of the Cornell Medical School, and previously of the Vanderbilt University Medical School, might consider staying for a year. He is a highly experienced administrator, and with the introduction which he will have had during six months work in our department of medicine as visiting professor, he should be able to hold the fort for a year. Whether he would care to take the position is another question. He has become much attached to the College and to the life in Peiping, but one of the attractions has been the opportunity to devote himself to actual professional work, i.e., the teaching of general medicine. He may not care to take on another taxing administrative post.

DIRECTOR'S OFFICE FILE

Dr. Ting - 3   April 16, 1935

However, I should not consider it entirely out of the question, as I do not believe he has any other position in prospect.

According to my present state of mind, I should be disposed to lay these suggestions before the Committee of Professors, and I should hope that in doing so, I could feel that my course would be acceptable to the Trustees.

I attach great weight to your opinion, and shall therefore be much obliged if you will write me frankly as to how the points which I have made impress you.

If the various uncertainties can be eliminated in the course of the next fifteen months, and if a suitable Chinese is available then, he could take up the work with much better prospects for success than if he were to assume this coming fall the thankless task of preparing a budget for 1936-37, with so many fundamental questions unsettled.

I am extremely sorry that I cannot attend the meeting of the Trustees of the China Foundation in Shanghai, but our affairs here are in such a critical position that it is necessary for me to remain in Peiping to deal with the situation which is constantly changing, and to assist in the preparation of our defense in the various cases which have been brought against us.

I hope very much that you will be disposed to favor some of the proposed appropriations in which I am particularly interested, i.e., that of Cheeloo University Medical School, a highly useful institution, Yenching University, and the Mass Education Movement. I realize that you are not particularly sympathetic with the type of work in which Mr. James Yen is engaged, and to a certain extent I have shared your point of view, but at the present time when the Movement for rural reconstruction is arousing so much interest, it seems to me highly desirable that such an organization as ours show its sympathetic interest and help to make the enterprise as efficient as possible. I should be very happy if you could talk with Mr. Gunn about this matter before the meeting of the China Foundation, though my letter may arrive too late to permit this.

Dr. Ting - 4   April 16, 1935

       With kindest regards, I am,

                Yours sincerely,

                Roger S. Greene
                Acting Director

Dr. V. K. Ting,
c/o Academia Sinica,
Nanking. (Express letter)

Copy to Shanghai via air mail

Dr. V. K. Ting,
c/o Mr. H. C. Zen, Director
China Foundation,
Park Hotel, Shanghai (to await arrival)

RSG:RP

April 16, 1935

Dear Dr. Ting,

I suppose that within the next two or three weeks there will be news from New York which will make it necessary for the College to consider what is to be done about the post which I now hold. If the news is such as to make it see desirable that I leave shortly, the question of a successor will immediately come up.

According to the By-Laws, the initiative must be taken by the Committee of Professors, who make recommendations to the Trustees. If the trustees are not pleased with the first nomination, they have the right to send it back and ask for another.

There is room for a good deal of difference of opinion as to the type of person to be secured to relieve me. I do not claim to be wiser than all others on this subject, but you may be interested in my views.

As regards whether we should attempt to appoint a Chinese, as I believe Dr. Houghton would prefer, or an American, I have this to say:

1. The post is not an easy one, involving complicated relationships both here in China and in the United States.

2. The selections among Chinese is rather restricted, at least if one considers only persons well known to the Professors and Trustees, as I think one must.

3. The coming year is one of exceptional difficulty, since various outstanding questions, such as future relationships between the Peiping Union Medical College, The China Medical Board, Inc., and the Rockefeller Foundation, have to settled, and some agreement must be reached as to the future budget of the institution, which I fear may have to suffer a further cut. In other words, the new executive would not know precisely under what conditions he would have to work, and what money he

would have at his disposal.

4. The Chinese who might be considered are person occupying important post, and it is not certain whether their services would be more valuable in an executive post or in the scientific posts which they are now holding.

5. If a Chinese is to be appointed to such as a difficult post, it seems to me desirable that he should have every possible advantage in the way of clear understanding of relationships, and knowledge of the money at his disposal. A man who had it in his to produce good results over a long period might well fall to give satisfaction during the coming year.

The above consideration has led me to favor a temporary appointment, preferably of someone who has an assured position and influence at home to which he can return. Dr. Gregg, Director for Medical Sciences in the Rockefeller Foundation, has two associates, Dr. R. A. Lambert, who has had long experience in the United States, Europe, and South America, and I think would give satisfaction during a year's services if he is available. There is another associate, Dr. Bradley M. Patten, whose experience has been only in the United States, but I think would be able to hold the position satisfactorily for a year with the help that he could obtain from the professors, Dr. Tsur, and the secretarial staff. It is not certain that either of these men will be available, as the Foundation may hesitate to give them leave for the purpose, particularly for the every reason for which I should like to see them come, namely, that they would thereby acquire a special interest in the College.

It is barely possible that Dr. Canby Robinson, formerly Dean of the Cornell Middle School, and previously of the Vanderbilt University Medical School, might consider staying for a year. He is highly experienced administrator, and with the introduction which he will have had during six months' work in our department of medicine as visiting professor, he should be able to hold the fort for a year. Whether he would care to take the position is another question. He has become much attached to the College and to the life in Peiping, but one of the attractions has been the opportunity to devote himself to actual professional work, i.e., the teaching of general medicine. He may not care to take on another taxing administrative post.

However, I should not consider it entirely out of the question, as I do not believe he has any other position in prospect.

According to my present state of mind, I should be dispose to lay these suggestions before the Committee of Professors, and I should hope that in doing so, I could feel that my course would be acceptable to the Trustees.

I attach great weight to your opinion, and shall therefore be much obliged if you will write me frankly as to how the points which I have made impress you.

If the various uncertainties can be eliminated in the course of the next fifteen months, and if a suitable Chinese is available then, he could take up the work with much better prospects for success than if he were to assume his coming fall the thankless task of preparing a budget for 1933-37, with so many fundamental questions unsettled.

I am extremely sorry that I cannot attend the meeting of the Trustees of the China Foundation in Shanghai, but our affairs here are in such a critical position that it is necessary for me to remain in Peiping to deal with the situation which is constantly changing, and to assist in the preparation of our defense in the various cases which have been brought against us.

I hope very much that you will be disposed to favor some of the proposed appropriations in which I am particularly interested, i. e., that of Cheeloo university Medical School, a highly useful institution, Yenching University, and the Mass Education Movement. I realize that you are not particularly sympathetic with the type of work in which Mr. James Yen is engaged, and to a certain extent I have shared your point of view, but at the present time when the Movement for rural reconstruction is arousing so much interest, it seems to me highly desirable that such an organization as ours show its sympathetic interest and help to make the enterprise as efficient as possible. I should be very happy if you could talk with Mr. Gunn about this matter before the meeting of the China Foundation, though my letter may arrive too late to permit this.

                With kindest regards, I am,
                Yours sincerely,

                Roger S. Greene,
                Acting Director

Dr. V. K. Ting,

c/c Academia Sinica,

Nanking. (Express letter)

Copy to Shanghai via air mail

Dr. V. K. Ting

c/c Mr. H. C. Zen, Director

China Foundation,

Park Hotel, Shanghai (to await arrival)

1936 年

NEW YORK TIMES,

DR. V. K. TING DEAD; CHINESE GEOLOGIST

Jan. 7, 1936

Former Mayor of Shanghai and Noted Author Studied in European Universities.

SUCCUMBS WHILE ON TOUR

Had Directed Mining Survey of Ministry of Agriculture and Commerce From 1913 to '21.

CHANGSHA, China, Jan. 6 (Æ).— Dr. V. K. Ting, eminent Chinese geologist, died here today from pneumonia, following a severe attack of carbon monoxide poisoning. He suffered his attack while sleeping in a closed room, where a charcoal stove was burning, during an inspection tour of Hunan Province coal mines.

Dr. Ting was born 48 years ago at Tai-hsing, Kiangsu. He attended Cambridge University, England; the University of Glasgow, Scotland, and the University of Freiberg, Germany. He was director of the bureau of geological survey of the Ministry of Agriculture and Commerce from 1913 to 1921, and managing director of the Peipiao Cola Mining Company, Tientsin, from 1922 to 1925. He also was a member of the British Boxer Indemnity Advisory Committee in 1924, a trustee of the China Foundation for Promotion of Education and Culture since 1925 and a former associate director of the Shanghai and Woosung Port Administration and a former Mayor of Greater Shanghai. He wrote several important geological books, including "Fifty Years of Mining in China" and "Geology of the Yangtse Delta."

New York Times

Dr. V. K. TING DEAD; CHINESE GEOLOGIST

Jan7, 1936

Former Mayor of Shanghai and Noted Author Studied in European Universities.

SCCUMBS WHILE ON TOUR

Had Directed Mining Survey of Ministry of Agriculture and Commerce from 1913 to '21

CHANGSHA, CHINA, Jan. 6---Dr. V. K. Ting, eminent Chinese geologist, dies here today from pneumonia, following a severe attack of carbon monoxide poisoning. He suffered his attack while sleeping in a closed room, where a charcoal stove was burning, during an inspection tour of Hunan Province coal mines.

Dr. Ting was born 48 years ago at Tai-hsing, Kiangsu. He attended Cambridge University, England; the University of Glasgow, Scotland, and the University of Freiberg, Germany. He was director of the bureau of geological survey of the Ministry of Agriculture and Commerce from 1913 to 1921, and managing director of the Peipiao Cola Mining Company, Tientsin, from 1922 to 1925. He also was a member of the British Boxer Indemnity Advisory Committee in 1924, a trustee of the China Foundation for Promotion of Education and Culture since 1925 and a former associate director of the Shanghai and Woosung Port Administration and a former Mayor of Greater Shanghai. He wrote several important geological books, including "Fifty Years of Mining in China"

The death of Dr. V. K. Ting, the eminent Chinese geologist, which was reported in the New York Times January 7th, ~~1936,~~ ~~deserves~~ deserves much more than passing notice, for he was one of ~~the little~~ a select group, none too numerous in any nation, who combined high qualifications in ~~his~~ their chosen fields with broad culture ~~formed~~ and exceptional vigor.

In his early youth at home Dr. Ting received a sound literary training according to the Chinese classical standards of the time, and then while still a boy made his way to Japan in search of a modern education. Japan was at that time swamped by a flood of Chinese students, many of whom, like Dr. Ting himself, were unprepared for admission to the best Japanese schools and consequently were compelled to attend inferior institutions. Dr. Ting's alert and critical mind soon made him aware that he was wasting his time, and he therefore decided after some months to go to England, all this while still a half grown youth. Nevertheless he gained from this experience an introduction to the Japanese language and some appreciation of the new Japanese civilization which later served him well. In Britain, besides pursuing his scientific studies he found time to acquire a familiarity with the best of English literature superior to that gained by most of our own college graduates. A shorter period of study in Germany further widened his horizon, so that when he returned to China he was already mature and prepared for the heavy responsibilities which then awaited Chinese youths coming home after study abroad.

The direction of the National Geological Survey of China which had recently been established then was entrusted to Dr. Ting some twenty-two years ago. Starting with almost nothing in the way of exact knowledge about Chinese geology, with no experienced staff and with the most modest resources, Dr. Ting rapidly developed the Survey into a serious scientific institution which commanded the respect of the local mining industry and visiting geologists, and made itself favorably known

-2-

to the geological world abroad by the number and quality of its publications. During this period he served also as a professor in the National University of Peking where he trained a little body of students who learned by his example not to fear the hardships and dangers of field work which in China involves, and to apply in the laboratory the same devotion and the severe critical standards which he required of himself.

One of the most striking qualities which Dr. Ting possessed was his ability to select able co-workers and to give them the support that they needed. Since the number of competent Chinese geologists was too small to meet the immediate need Dr. Ting secured the cooperation for longer or shorter periods of a number of distinguished foreign scientists, such as Dr. J. G. Andersson, former head of the Swedish Geological Survey, and Professor A. W. Grabau, formerly of Harvard and Columbia Universities, who has been for many years in charge of invertebrate palaeontology at the Survey and professor of palaeontology at the National University of Peking. In this connection it is appropriate to mention that, though warmly patriotic as a Chinese, Dr. Ting was singularly free from Chauvinism and never allowed political feeling to warp his judgment or to interfere with his personal or professional relations with those whose character and scientific work entitled them to respect. It was largely due to him that it was possible to organize the successful search for the so-called Peking Man, Sinanthropus Pekinensis, which was conducted by the Caenozoic Laboratory of the Geological Survey under the leadership of the late Professor Davidson Black, F.R.S., of the Peiping Union Medical College, with funds provided by the Rockefeller Foundation.

In 1921 Dr. Ting having become convinced that Dr. Wong Wen-hao, the present head of the Geological Survey, was better qualified than himself to head the organization, and since the scanty budget made it difficult for both to remain and still to provide properly for the younger geologists, insisted on resigning in favor of Dr. Wong, and took up a position as manager of the Peipiao Coal Mining Company, but continued to work actively for the Survey, both in an advisory ca

-3-

capacity and occasionally by heading parties for field explorations.

Extremely modest in his own manner of life, and well acquainted through his field trips and his industrial experience with conditions of life among Chinese farmers and laborers, Dr. Ting had in recent years been much interested in social and political questions. When General Sun Chuan-fang was governor of Kiangsu Province in   he appointed Dr. Ting as Mayor of Shanghai, a post formerly regarded as a merely a political plum. Dr. Ting regarded it as an opportunity for showing what could be done in the way of improving the city by devoting attention to the reform of the technical services of the municipality on a purely non-partisan basis, starting with the selection of the men whom he considered to have the best professional qualifications for their several posts. In this he was so successful that even after the fall of the governor compelled his own retirement, some of the chiefs of bureaus whom he had appointed were retained by his successors of quite opposite political affiliations solely because of their proved efficiency and devotion.

Some two years ago, after a period of retirement devoted largely to geological studies, and to a resumption of his service as professor of geology at the National University of Peking, Dr. Ting was called upon to become the executive head of the Academia Sinica, the National Research Institute of China, under the chairmanship of Dr. Tsai Yuan-pei, the post which he held at the time of his death. This national academy has a wide variety of departments, including history and linguistics, social sciences, physics, chemistry and biology, geology, meteorology and engineering. Probably no one could have been found in any country better qualified by education, experience and interests to direct such an important enterprise, and in the short period during which he had been in charge Dr. Ting had already effected important reforms in the way of coordination of effort among various institutions engaged in similar work, elimination of unproductive activities and provision of more adequate support for the productive.

In recent years Dr. Ting has been one of a group in Peiping including Dr. Hu Shih, the well known philosopher, Dr. Wong Wen-hao, Mr. H. C. Zen and Mrs. Sophia Chen Zen, which has published a highly interesting and

-4-

increasingly influential journal called the "Independent Critic" dealing with social and political affairs, and has himself contributed to it.

Dr. Ting's sudden death will be mourned by many friends in the United States and in Europe as well as in China where he can so ill be spared. Many who have not had the good fortune of intimate association with him in a common work will remember him as a delightful companion ready to contribute something of interest and usually something significant, no matter what the subject of conversation. Those who have been more closely associated with him will remember the inspiration of his complete devotion to the interests of his work, his frankness, the severe limitation which he placed on his few prejudices, his modesty combined with courage and decision when called for, and his capacity for friendship.

For many years Dr. Ting served as a trustee of the China Foundation for the Promotion of Education and Culture which administers the American Boxer Indemnity funds, and when in 1924 the British Government appointed a commission under the chairmanship of Lord Willingdon, later Viceroy of India, to consider the application of the British indemnity funds Dr. Ting was appointed and served as a member of that commission. He was also a trustee of Nankai University and of the Peiping Union Medical College.

Statement about Dr. V. K. Ting (Draft)

By Roger S. Greene

The death of Dr. V. K. Ting, the eminent Chinese geologist, which was reported in the New York Times January 7th deserves much more than passing notices, for he was one of a select group, none too numerous in any nation, who combined high intelligence qualifications in their chosen fields with broad culture and exceptional vigor.

In his early youth at home Dr. Ting received a sound literary training according to the Chinese classical standards of the time, and then while still a boy made his way to Japan in search of a modern education. Japan was at that time swamped by a flood of Chinese students, many of whom, like Dr. Ting himself, were unprepared for admission to the best Japanese schools and consequently were compelled to attend inferior institutions. Dr. Ting's alert and critical mind soon made him aware that he was wasting his time, and he therefore decided after some months to go to England, all this while still a half grown youth. Nevertheless, he gained from this experience an introduction to the Japanese language and some appreciation of the new Japanese civilization which later served him well. In Britain, besides pursuing his scientific studies he found time to acquire a familiarity with the best of English literature superior to that gained by most of our own college graduates. A shorter period of study in Germany further widened his horizon, so that when he returned to China he was already mature and prepared for the heavy responsibilities which then awaited Chinese youths coming home after study abroad.

The direction of the National Geological Survey of China which had recently been established was then entrusted to Dr. Ting some twenty-two years ago. Starting with almost nothing in the way of exact knowledge about Chinese geology, with no experienced staff and with the most modest resources, Dr. Ting rapidly developed the Survey into a serious scientific institution which commanded the respect of the local mining industry and visiting geologists, and made itself favorably known to the geological world abroad by the number and quality of its publications. During this period, he served also as a professor in the National University of Peking where he trained a little body of students who learned by his example not to fear the hardships and which field work in China involves and to apply in the laboratory the same devotion and the severe critical standards which he required of himself.

One of the most striking qualities which Dr. Ting possessed was his ability to select able co-worker and to give them the support that they needed. Since the number of competent Chinese geologist was too small to meet the immediate need Dr. Ting secured the cooperation for longer or shorter periods of a number of distinguished foreign scientists, such as Dr. J. G. Andersson, former head of the Swedish Geological Survey, and Professor A. W. Grabau, formerly of Harvard and Columbia Universities, who has been for many years in charge of invertebrate paleontology at the Survey and professor of paleontology at the National University of Peking. In this connection it is appropriate to mention that, though warmly patriotic as a Chinese, Dr. Ting was singularly free from Chauvinism and never allowed political feeling to warp his judgment or to interfere with his personal or professional relations with those whose character and scientific work entitled them to respect. It was largely due to him that it was possible to organize the successful search for the so-called Peking Man, Sinanthropus Pekinensis, which was conducted by the Cenozoic Laboratory of the Geological Survey under the leadership of the late Professor Davidson Black, F. R. S., of the Peiping Union Medical College, with funds provided by the Rockefeller Foundation.

In 1921 Dr. Ting having become convinced that Dr. Wong Wen-hao, the present head of the Geological Survey, was better qualified than himself to head the organization, and since the scanty budget made it difficult for both to remain and still to provide properly for the younger geologists, insisted on resigning in favor of Dr. Wong, and took up a position as manager of the Peipiao Coal Mining Company, but continued to work actively for the Survey, both in an advisory on capacity and occasionally by heading parties for field explorations.

Extremely modest in his own manner of life, and well acquainted through his field trips and his industrial experiences with conditions of life among Chinese farmers and laborers, Dr. Ting had in recent years been much interested in social and political questions. When General Sun Chuan-fang was governor of Kiangsu Province in--, he appointed Dr. Ting regarded it as an opportunity for showing what could be done in the city by devoting attention to the reform of the technical services of the municipality on a purely non-partisan basis, starting with the selection of the men who he considered to have the best professional qualifications for their several posts. In this he was so successful that even after the fall of the governor compelled his own retirement, some of the chiefs of bureaus whom he had appointed were retained by his successors of quite opposite political affiliations solely because of their proved efficiency and devotion.

Some two years ago, after a period of retirement devoted largely to geological studies, and to a resumption of his service as professor of geology at the National University of Peking, Dr. Ting was called upon to become the executive head of the Academia Sinica, the National Research Institute of China under the chairmanship of Dr. Tsai Yuan-pei, the post which he held at the time of his death. This national academy has a wide variety of departments, including history and linguistics, social sciences, physics, chemistry and biology, geology, metrology and engineering. Probably no one could have been found in any country better qualified by education, experience and interests to direct such an important enterprise, and in the short period during which he had been in charge Dr. Ting had already effected important reforms in the way of coordination of effort among various institutions engaged in similar work, elimination of unproductive activities and provision of more adequate support for the productive.

In recent years Dr. Ting has been one of a group in Peiping including Dr. Hu Shih, the well-known philosopher, Dr. Wong Wen-hao, Mr. M. C. Zen and Mrs. Sophia Chen Zen, which has published highly interesting and increasingly influential journal called the "Independent Critic" dealing with social and political affairs, and has himself contributed to it.

Dr. Ting's sudden death will be mourned by many friends in the United States and in Europe as well as in China where he can so ill be spared. Many who have not had the good fortune of intimate association with him in a common work will remember him as a delightful companion ready to contribute something of interest and usually something significant, no matter what the subject of conversation. Those who have been more closely associated with him will remember the inspiration of his complete devotion to the interests of his work, his frankness, the severe limitation which he placed on his few prejudices, his modesty combined with courage and decision when called for, and his capacity for friendship.

For many years Dr. Ting served as a trustee of the China Foundation for the Promotion of Education and Culture which administers the American Boxer Indemnity funds, and when in 1924 the British Government appointed a commission under the chairmanship of Lord Willingdon, later Viceroy of India, to consider the application of the British indemnity funds Dr. Ting was appointed and served as a member of that commission. He was also a trustee of Nankai University and of the Peiping Union Medical College.

Ting, Dr. V. K.

24 January, 1936.

Dr. V. K. Ting, Secretary,
The Academia Sinica,
Nanking, China.

Dear Dr. Ting:-

It gives me great pleasure to introduce to you Dr. Karl Gustav Izikowitz, of Sweden.

Dr. Izikowitz wishes to devote himself to a study of the older forms of social organization occurring in China, both among the Chinese people themselves and also among some of the less completely assimilated aboriginal tribes of the south. I have told him that I know of no one so well qualified as yourself to advise him in all such matters; and I know from my own experience how much he will profit by your assistance.

With renewed thanks for your innumerable kindnesses, and with cordial remembrances, I remain,

Very sincerely yours,

C. W. Bishop.

24 January, 1936.

Dr. V. K. Ting, Secretary,
The Academia Sinica,
Nanking, China.

Dear Dr. Ting:

It gives me great pleasure to introduce to you Dr. Karl Gustav Izikowitz, of Sweden.

Dr. Tzikowitz wishes to devote himself to a study of the older forms of social organization occurring in China, both among the Chinese people themselves and also among some of the less completely assimilated aboriginal tribes of the south. I have told him that I know of no one so well qualified as yourself to advise him in all such matter; and I know form my own experience how much he will profit by your assistance.

With renewed thanks for your innumerable kindnesses, and with cordial remembrances, I remain,

Very sincerely yours,

C. W. Bishop.

With the Author's compliments

DR. V. K. TING
1887—1936

By

G. B. BARBOUR

[*Reprinted from the* QUARTERLY JOURNAL *of the* GEOLOGICAL SOCIETY OF LONDON, *vol.* xcii, 1936, *pp.* xcv–xcix.]

[*From the* QUARTERLY JOURNAL *of the* GEOLOGICAL SOCIETY, Vol. xcii, part 3, 1936.]

Dr. V. K. TING (TING VEN-KIANG) died on January 5th, 1936, at the age of 49.

Few of the Glasgow undergraduates in the years 1907 to 1911 can have sensed the significance in their midst of a smiling, slightly built, Chinese student whom they accepted first for his good company and ability to stand a joke. Their opinion of " V. K." grew when, after taking the medal in advanced zoology, he turned to geology and repeated the process first in Part I and then in Part II.

Born in northern Kiangsu, Ting had come to school in England with another boy—the odyssey of these two young orientals from Shanghai to Tilbury would have tried stouter hearts—and submitted with unfailing, if tongue-tied, good nature to the intolerance with which the British schoolboy treats all that is alien to his world. Of this early chapter of his life Ting seldom spoke, but it gave his mind food for thought beyond its years.

Towards Graham Kerr and J. W. Gregory, Ting felt a life-long gratitude for " awakening an oriental mind to the truth of western science". Professor Kerr used to take his students for dredging trips on the West Coast. "Ven-kiang Ting was an immense favourite," he writes. "I can see him now, with his friendly smile, at the foot of the table at Carsaig Manse, carrying out the duty imposed on him of carving for the evening meal. Whether clambering on the hills, pulling a heavy dredge, or camping by the loch side in a snell east wind, he seemed to radiate happiness." A fellow student adds, "One day the water was rough, the boat none too comfortable and Ting felt very seedy. But he refused to succumb, continuing to sort specimens till we reached shore. Later that year he returned to dredge on his own. We saw a good deal of him. He often sat discussing education, morals and religion, and indicated that he was preparing himself for what might be an important task in his own country." Just how true this was to be, even Ting himself could not have foreseen.

After visiting Germany, Ting returned to Peking in 1912, travelling across Yunnan where he made his first important scientific contribution. (While still in Glasgow he had made suggestions that Professor Gregory admitted were valued contributions to the success of his own Yunnan expedition a decade later.) As Professor at the National University and as Director of the newly organized Geological Survey, Ting at once gathered round him a group of keen young men whom he inspired with some of his own enthusiasm. Dr. Wong Wen-hao, his close friend and his successor as Director, is not exaggerating when he speaks of Ting as "the founder of scientific geology in China". The Geological Survey of China is his creation.

Ting was keenly alive to the value of the scientific view we sometimes mistakenly tend to regard as a Western prerogative. Recognizing the vital need of a sound stratigraphic basis for all future work he invited Dr. A. W. Grabau to join the Survey as Chief Palæontologist. Among the results of this co-operation were a body of keen young stratigraphers, the appearance of the *Palæontologia Sinica*, and the foundation of the Geological Society of China. The need for reliable estimates of the Republic's resources led to plans for the training overseas of young prospectors and research students. With his colleague, Dr. Wong, he equipped laboratories for

part 3] OBITUARY NOTICES xcvii

soil survey, fuel research, and seismological study. He organized topographic and geological mapping on a regional scale and laid plans for the publication of the first 1/M sheets which his successor has ably carried on. The superb *New Atlas of China* recently issued under the names of Ting and Wong is a fitting last testimony to his patient effort in a field on which he had been engaged for years. Working under the handicaps of inadequate support, officialist obstruction, and political unrest, any survey might be proud of a seventeen-years' achievement which includes the publication of 36 bulletins, 23 memoirs, and 80 palæontological fascicles, besides 14 volumes of society transactions and a hardly less impressive list of miscellaneous issues.

Ting himself published little in English, his longest work being a study of the Yangtze estuary. But the breadth of his interests is shown by the range of subjects dealt with in shorter papers—copper-mines at Tungchwen, manganese at Hsihutsun, the coalfields of Yuhsien, tectonics of eastern Yunnan, width-height ratios in *Spirifer*, droughts and desiccation, stratigraphy of the Fengning system, orogenic movements in China, etc. But from the *Geology of the Western Hills*, the first memoir, onwards, his hand is seen in the writings of the men he trained.

His genius for handling difficult situations was partly the result of an unusual understanding of both Western and Oriental psychology. His fellow members on the British Boxer Indemnity Commission came to place special reliance on his judgment. His wise enlisting of foreign co-operation through Dr. J. Gunnar Andersson led to the finding of Peking Man. The plans for the Cenozoic Laboratory evolved with the late Dr. Davidson Black were well laid by Ting long before Mr. Pei's momentous discovery.

Though to the scientific world Ting was a geologist, to his own countrymen he meant much more. His return to China coincided with the birth of the Literary Renaissance. It is not always realized that 25 years ago the printed page in China was virtually reserved for the official written language; the spoken language of every day was thought too vulgar for such permanence. It was as if in Europe nothing but Latin might appear in print. Ting was one of the inner group of half a dozen who led in the reform that made possible a vernacular literature of science, history, philosophy, romance, and even the newspaper. This new vehicle of expression, fashioned in the first years of the Republic, became the vital factor in the spread of new ideas. Traditional patterns of life and thought had to be re-valued under modern conditions. It was here that Ting's influence was greatest. He read widely in English, French, and German, and had a sound grasp of economics, sociology, and political science. Acknowledging an early debt to Huxley and Galton, he found special stimulus in the writings of Keynes, Laski, Wells, Bertrand Russell, and Julian Huxley. But he never lost the keenly critical attitude that marked all his thinking. He deplored the lack of character among the rank and file in Chinese politics as much as the blind obstinacy of foreign diplomats, and constantly urged the younger scientists to show their patriotism by " contributing what they were good for " to improve the condition of their country. " If China cannot be saved from the destroying hand of the invader, at least let us toughen the fibre of the race so as to make it imperishable."

He repeatedly refused urgent calls to political office, until the Japanese invasion of Manchuria destroyed all prospects of the further development of Peipiao coalfield, to which he had devoted his energy after resigning from the Survey. Then, believing that the one hope of unifying his country lay in finding a common ground upon which the people of North and South could agree to unite, he accepted the directorship of the Shanghai Port Administration. A motor accident, from which he escaped only with his life, put a sudden end to these hopes. On recovery, he threw himself again into scientific work—the long-delayed working up of the important results of his expeditions into Kwangsi, Kweichow, and Yunnan, and a book on the influence of climatic and geological factors on the contact between the East and the West across central Asia—only to be interrupted again by a call to Nanking as Secretary-General of the Academia Sinica with its ten departments of scientific research. Any time he could snatch from executive duties was devoted to giving practical help on problems in his own field. It was on one such errand to a coalfield in Hunan that death overtook him. On a cold blustery night the window of his room was left closed and he was overcome by fumes from a stove.

It is characteristic of Ting that he had used moments of delay in his last week's field-work to compose a series of short Chinese poems of real merit and beauty.

G. B. Barbour

Dr. V. K. Ting
1887–1936

By G. B. Barbour

The Quarterly Journal of the Geological Survey of London, Vol. xcii, part 3, 1936, pp. xcv-xcix

Dr. V. K. Tsing (TING Ven-KIANG) died on January 5th, 1936, at the age of 49.

Few of the Glasgow undergraduate in the years 1907 to 1911 can have sensed the significance in their midst of a smiling, slightly built, Chinese student whom they accepted first for his good company and ability to stand a joke. Their opinion of "V. K." grew when, after taking the medal in advanced zoology, he turned to geology and repeated the process first in Part I and then in Part II.

Born in northern Kiangsu, Ting had come to school in England with another boy-the odyssey of these two young orientals from Shanghai to Tilbury would have tried stouter hearts-and submitted with unfailing, if tongue-tied, good nature to the intolerance with which the British schoolboy treats all that is alien to his world. Of this early chapter of his life Ting seldom spoke, but it gave his mind food for thought beyond its years.

Towards Graham Kerr and J. W. Gregory, Ting felt a lifelong gratitude for "awakening an oriental mind to the truth of western science". Professor Kerr used to take his students for dredging trips on the West Coast. "Ven-kiang Ting was an immense favorite," he writes. "I can see him now, with his friendly smile, at the foot of the table at Carsaig Manse, carrying out the duty imposed on him of carving for the evening meal. Whether clambering on the hills, pulling a heavy dredge, or camping by the loch side in a snell east wind, he seemed to radiate happiness." A fellow student adds, "One day the water was rough, the boat none too comfortable and Ting felt very seedy. But he refused to succumb, continuing to sort specimens till we reached shore. Later that year he returned to dredge on his own. We saw a good deal of him. He often sat discussing education, morals and religion, and indicated that he was preparing himself for what might be an important task in his own country." Just how true this was to be, even Ting himself could not have foreseen.

After visiting Germany, Ting returned to Peking in 1912, traveling across Yunnan where he made his first important scientific contribution. (While still in Glasgow he had made suggestion that Professor Gregory admitted were valued contributions to the success of his own Yunnan expedition a decade later.) As professor at the National University and as Director of the newly organized Geological Survey, Ting at once gathered round him a group of keen young men whom his inspired with some of his own enthusiasm. Dr. Wong Wen-hao, his close friend and his successor as Dirctor, is not exaggerating when he speaks of Ting as "the founder of scientific geology in China". The Geological Survey of China is his creation.

Ting was keenly alive to the value of the scientific view we sometimes mistakenly tend to regard as a western prerogative. Recognizing the vital need of a sound stratigraphic basis for all future work he invited Dr. A. W. Grabau to join the Survey as Chief Paleontologist. Among the results of this co-operation were a body of keen young stratigraphers, the appearance of the Paleontologia Sinica, and the foundation of the Geological Society of China. The need for reliable estimates of the Republic's resources led to plans for the training overseas of young prospectors and research students. With his colleague, Dr. Wong, he equipped laboratories for soil survey, fuel research, and seismological study. He organized topographic and geological mapping on a regional scale and laid plans for the publication of the first 1/M sheets which his successor has ably carried on. The superb New Atlas of China recently issued under the names of Ting and Wong is a fitting last testimony to his patient effort in a field on which he had been engaged for years. Working under the handicaps of inadequate support, officialist obstruction, and political unrest, any survey might be proud of a seventeen years' achievement which includes the publication of 36 bulletins, 23 memoirs, and 80 paleontological fascicles, besides 14 volumes of society transactions and a hardly less impressive list of miscellaneous issues.

Ting himself published little in English, his longest work being a study of the Yangtze estuary. But the breadth of his interests is shown by the range of subjects dealt with in shorter papers-cooper mines at Tungchwen, manganese at Hsihutsun, the coalfields of Yuhsien, tectonics of eastern Yunnan, width-height ratios in Spirifer, droughts and desiccation, stratigraphy of the Fengning system, orogenic movements in China, etc. But from the Geology of the Western Hills, the first memoir, onwards, his hand is seen in the writings of the men he trained.

His genius for handling difficult situations was partly the result of an unusual understanding of both Western and Oriental psychology. His fellow members on the British Boxer Indemnity Commission came to place special reliance on his judgment. His wise enlisting of foreign co-operation through Dr. J. Gunnar Andersson led to the finding of Peking Man. The plans for the Cenozoic Laboratory evolved with the late Dr. Davidson Black were well laid by Ting long before Mr. Pei's momentous discovery.

Though to the scientific world Ting was a geologist, to his own countrymen he meant much more. His return to China coincided with the birth of the Literary Renaissance. It is not always realized that 25 years ago the printed page in China was virtually reserved for the official written language; the spoken language of every day was thought too vulgar for such permanence. It was as if in Europe nothing but Latin might appear in print. Ting was one of the inner group of half a dozen who led in the reform that made possible a vernacular literature of science, history, philosophy, romance and even the newspaper. This new vehicle of expression, fashioned in the first years of the Republic, became the vital factor in the spread of new ideas. Traditional patterns of life and though had to be re-valued under modern conditions. It was here that Ting's influence was greatest. He read widely in English, French and German, and had a sound grasp of economics, sociology, and political science. Acknowledging an early debt to Huxley and Galton, he found special stimulus in the writings of Keynes, Laski, Wells, Bertrand Russell, and Julian Huxley. But he never lost the keenly critical attitude that marked all his thinking. He deplored the lack of character among the rank and file in Chinese politics as much as the blind obstinacy of foreign diplomats, and constantly urged the younger scientists to show their patriotism by "contributing what they were good for" to improve the condition of their country. "If China cannot be saved from the destroying hand of the invader, at least let us toughen the fibre of the race so as to make it imperishable."

He repeatedly refused urgent calls to political office, until the Japanese invasion of Manchuria destroyed all prospects of the further development of Peipiao coalfield, to which he had devoted his energy after resigning from the Survey. Then, believing that the one hope of unifying his country lay in finding a common ground upon which the people of North and South could agree to unite, he accepted the directorship of the Shanghai Port Administration. A motor accident, from which he escaped only with his life, put a sudden end to these hopes. On recovery, he threw himself again into scientific work-the long-delayed working up of the important results of his expeditions into Kwangsi, Kweichow, and Yunnan, and a book on the influence of climatic and geological factors on the contact between the East and the West across central Asia-only to be interrupted again by a call to Nanking as Secretary-Central of the Academia Sinica with its ten department of scientific research. Any time he could snatch from executive duties was devoted to giving practical help on problems in his own field. It was on one such errand to a coalfield in Hunan that death overtook him. On a cold blustery night the window of his room was left closed and he was overcome by fumes from a stove.

It is characteristic of Ting that he had used moments of delay in his last week's field-work to compose a series of short Chinese poems of real merit and beauty.

G. B. Barbour

1955 年

SINO-BRITISH CULTURAL ASSOCIATION

62, NEW CAVENDISH STREET,
LONDON, W.1.

Telephone:
LANgham 1675.

Earl Russell,
c/o Messrs. Allen & Unwin Ltd.,
40, Museum Street,
LONDON, W.C.1.

27th October, 1955.

Dear Lord Russell,

    Dr. V.K. Ting died in January 1936, at a most critical time in the history of China when he was on the eve of entering the Cabinet. I have sometimes wondered whether if V.K. had not died, the history of China during the last twenty years might not be somewhat different.

    V.K.'s brother, Dr. W.Y. Ting and some of V.K.'s old friends, in Hongkong and elsewhere, are contemplating the publication of a commemorial volume to mark the 20th anniversary of V.K.'s decease to be issued at the end of the year. Knowing that V.K. admired you more than any other thinker of the age during his lifetime, and became a close friend of yours during your visit to Peiping, they think that you must have something interesting and revealing to tell about him. They asked me to make a request to you. They would be most grateful if you would write a short article of your recollection of him.

    I have not met you again since one of the UNESCO General Conferences in Paris, but I have listened to your broadcast talks with great interest. A short article of this nature will greatly preserve the memory of a remarkable man of the age. I should also be very glad to hear of any other Englishmen or women who were V.K.'s friends.

Yours sincerely,

Chen Yuan
(L.Y. Chen)

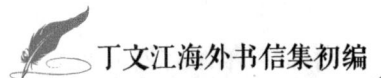

SINO–BRITISH CULTURAL ASSOCIATION

62. NEW CAVENDISH STREET.

LONDON. W. 1

Earl Russell,

c/o Messrs. Allen & Unwin Ltd.,

40, Museum Street,

London, W. C.1   27th October, 1955

Dear Lord Russell,

  Dr. V. K. Ting died in January 1936, at a most critical time in the history of China when he was on the eve of entering the Cabinet. I have sometimes wondered whether if V. K. had not died, the history of China during the last twenty years might not be somewhat different.

  V. K's brother, Dr. W. Y. Ting and some of V. K's old friends, in Hong Kong and elsewhere, are contemplating the publication of a commercial volume to mark the 20th anniversary of V. K. decease to be issued at the end of this year. Knowing that V. K admired you more than any other thinker of the age during his lifetime, and became a close friend of yours during your visit to Peiping, they think that you must have something interesting and revealing to tell about him. They asked me to make a request to you. They would be most grateful if you would write a short article of your collection of him.

  I have not met you again since one of the UNESCO General Conferences in Paris, but I have listened to your broadcast talks with great interest. A short article of this nature will greatly preserve the memory of a remarkable man of the age. I should also be very glad to hear of any other Englishmen or women who were V. K's friends.

                  Yours sincerely

                  Chen yuan

                  (L. y, Chen)

Copy

2 November, 1955.
41 Queen's Rd., Richmond

Dear Mr. Chen,

Thank you for your letter of October 27. I am sorry that my recollections of V. K. Ting are not sufficiently extensive to make an article. There is, however, cone fact which is interesting and possibly not known to you: When Ramsey Macdonald was Prime Minister in L924 he appointed a Committee to consider the Boxer Indemnity payments and to suggest methods by which they could be made useful to China. Lowes Dickinson and I were to be members of this Committee. There were to be two Chinese members and I was asked who I should recommend. I recommended V. K. Ting and Hu Shi. Before anything could be done Macdonald's Government fell. The Conservative Bovernment which succeeded hi refused to confiem the appointment of Dickinson and myself on the Committee and asked the Chinese Government to recommend any two Chinese except Hu S hi and V. K. Ting. The Chinese Government replied that they must have these or nobody. I was removed by the British Government from membership on the Committee on the ground that I was ignorant of China.

I have extremely pleasant recollections of V. K. Ting whom I much admired and whose friendship I valued highly, but I cannot remember such incidents as would make an article.

Yours sincerely,

2 November, 1955

41 Queen's Rd., Richmond

Dear Mr. Chen,

Thank you for your letter of October 27. I am sorry that my recollections of V. K. Ting are not sufficiently extensive to make an article. There is, however, one fact which is interesting and possibly not known to you: When Ramsey Macdonald was Prime Minister in 1924 he appointed a Committee to consider the Boxer Indemnity payments and to suggest methods by which they could be made useful to China. Lowes Dickinson and I were to be members of this Committee. There were to be two Chinese members and I was asked who I should recommend. I recommended V. K. Ting and Hu Shi. Before anything could be done Macdonald's Government fell. The Conservative Government which succeeded it refused to confirm the appointment of Dickinson and myself on the Committee and asked the Chinese Government to recommend any two Chinese except Hu Shi and V. K. Ting. The Chinese Government replied that they must have these or nobody. I was removed by the British Government from membership on the Committee on the ground that I was ignorant of China.

I have extremely pleasant recollections of V. K. Ting whom I much admired and whose friendship I valued highly, but I cannot remember such incidents as would make an article.

Yours sincerely

[Bertrand. Russell]

Nord Hotel Sunday.

Dear Barbour,

You are the very man I wanted to see, but unfortunately your note did not strike my eye until one o'clock this morning so there was no means of telephoning according to your instructions. Besides I am engaged all day today and it will be difficult to find a convenient time and place to meet. I think the best way is to come here to lunch any day you are coming up town. I am usually at home for lunch, but please telephone before hand to make sure.

Yours sincerely,

Undated

Nord Hotel Sunday

Dear Barbour,

You are the very man I wanted to see, but unfortunately your note did not strike my eye until one o'clock this morning so there was no means of telephoning according to your instructions. Besides I am engaged all day today and it will be difficult to find a convenient time and place to meet. I think the best way is to come here to lunch any day you are coming up town. I am usually at home for lunch, but please telephone before hand to make sure.

Yours sincerely

V. K. Ting

附 录

The Correspondence of G. E. Morrison II, 1912-1920

Edited by Lo Hui-min, Cambridge University Press, Cambridge, 1978, pp. 621-622

Peking, 8 August 1917

Dear Mr. Ting,

Some little time ago you asked me if my library had been sold. At that time it had not been. It was under offer to the Japanese, but it was of course uncertain whether the offer would be acceptable or not. To-day, however, the transaction has been completed, and my library in due course will be transferred to Tokyo.

I have made it a condition that the Library shall be open as in the past to all serious students. It will remain intact and will be called after me. More than this it will be kept up to date.

Its purchaser is the famous Baron Iwasaki, who purchased Max Muller's Library, although that is a very inferior one.

I am sorry to part with my library, but the strain of keeping it up is too severe both upon my time and my pocket. I should have liked if it could have remained in Peking, but that is not possible.

The climate here is ideal for book collecting.

I have kept my catalogue, and if ever the Government should decide upon starting a Library of their own I will be very glad indeed to help in acquiring one. But to keep a library worth &35000 in Peking uninsured with incidents such as those of the 12th July occurring round about one is a risk that ought to be borne not by an individual but by a corporation.

       With kind regards
       Believe me

       Very sincerely yours
       [G. E. Morrison]

附 录

The Correspondence of G. E. Morrison II, 1912-1920

Edited by Lo Hui-min, Cambridge University Press, Cambridge, 1978, pp. 756-758

Paris 14 May 1919

My dear Dr. Morrison,

I went to MacMahon Hotel a few days ago and to my grief I found that you had gone back to England. Let us hope that the pure air of Sussex will do you good and make you recover rapidly.

You asked me the other day the economic consequences of the Japanese victory—Well I think they are more important than many people can imagine and will certainly affect other countries than China. Japan, in spite of her organization, is a country without resources. Nothing made her realize her importance more than when America prohibited the export of steel in entering the War. As you well know, in recent years great efforts have been made to secure her needs at the expense of China. The Peace Conference has given her-3-4,000,000 tongs of good iron ore and more than one billion tons of good coal, all near to the railway, the extension of which will traverse three more coal fields, containing billions of tons of coking coal. Thus Japan has secured her monopoly of Chinese iron industry.

There can be no doubt that in the near future Japan will be able to build as many ships as he likes with her own steel. The she will assume a different attitude towards such questions as racial equality. Besides for the first time the Powers give formal recognition to what is known as the Japanese equivalent to the Monroe doctrine. Here in a treaty to be signed by practically all the countries of the world Japan is allowed to act as arbitrator between China and Germany. Kiouchow is to be returned to China not directly by Germany with whom China is also at War, but through the hands of Japan. Henceforth Japan can regard herself as the only spokesman of Asia.

I wonder how many Englishmen understand the mental attitude of the Japanese towards India. I remember vividly that in 1903 the Indian students in Tokyo organized an evening party at which I was fortunate enough to be present. There many prominent Japanese spoke openly against England and told the Indians that as soon as Japan was strong enough India would be cleared of Englishmen. And they were prolonged applauded. During the whole period of the World War, every little incident in India was carefully exaggerated in the Japanese express. Even after the armistice many articles on India appeared in the Japanese papers which were extremely unfriendly to England (to put it mildly). You yourself must have been aware of the intimate connections between the prominent Indian agitators and many responsible Japanese statesmen, notably Count Okuma. Now so far Japan has remained passive (apparently at least) because she is fully aware of her weakness in resources, but when she can produce 5,000,000 tons of steel instead of 500,000 she will only wait for a favorable opportunity to become your enemy instead of your ally, and not only India, but even Australia will not be safe without a large navy.

In thinking over these things I cannot help becoming a fatalist. It seems that fate is with Japan in her effort to dominate Asia, for at the Paris conference Great Britain, who, of all nations, should have opposed Japan in her own interests, vigorously supported her claims. It is Fate that has whispered to Lloyd George in favor of her protégé or is it simply ignorance?

I am leaving Paris tomorrow for Normandy and hope to go to Bilbao afterwards. But I am compelled reluctantly to give up my projected trip to Rio Tinto as the communication is too difficult.

Hoping to have good news from you soon.

Yours sincerely

V. K. Ting

George B. Barbour, *Memories of Three Continents*, Manuscript, George B. Barber Papers, Cincinnati University Special Collection p.78

Geological Survey
Ministry of Agriculture and Commerce
Peking

30 April 1921

Dear Mr. Barbour,

Many thanks for your letter of the 27th Inst. And the Invitation. I can promise definitely now that I will come to dinner Wednesday, because I have decided to go to Tientsin on Monday.

Please do not take any notice of Van der Veen's remarks. I think he meant well, and certainly everyone else on the committee appreciated your report. Van der Veen is chiefly interested in the irrigation of the plain by means of wells. That is why he was anxious to know something of the wells farther from the hills.

If you care to write a short paper for our bulletin you can put in the important geological facts.

Yes, please do send me the maps you made of the district.

Very sincerely,
V. K. Ting
Director, Geological Survey

后 记

  丁文江书信的收集是我在美国做博士论文寻找档案的过程中一个副产品 (By-product)。自 2011 年开始收集,足迹遍及纽约、华盛顿、芝加哥、波士顿、辛辛那提。同时,还从美国加州、澳大利亚以及英国各档案馆购买了部分书信。四五年来,集腋成裘,竟集有近百封。不过欧洲部分,特别是瑞典的安德生档案和斯文·赫定档案,没有机缘一睹其容,此为一憾。

  拜读丁文江的书信之后,感受其博大。同时又感叹丁氏手写英文的飘逸,判读着实不易,不知不觉竟前后耗时三年。在解读之中,葛熹宁教授(Sydney L. Greenblatt)和 Geraldine Forbes 教授伉俪给予了莫大帮助,在此谨表致谢。

  2014 年春,在张九辰老师牵线下,曾计划与中国科学院自然科学史所合作出版这部书信,但后来因为各自日程问题,不了了之。2016 年夏,在杨雷编辑努力之下,与学苑出版社达成协议,得以在丁文江诞辰一百三十周年(2017 年)之际出版此编。

  本文特别致谢美国 Smithsonian Institute 档案部,美国自然历史博物馆档案部,美国洛克菲勒档案中心,美国芝加哥 Field 博物馆档案部,美国 Huntington 图书馆特藏部,美国哈佛大学 Houghton 图书馆,美国辛辛那提大学档案馆,英国 McMaster 图书馆特藏部,英国格拉斯哥大学档案馆,澳大利亚南威尔士大学图书馆特藏部提供珍贵档案资料及授权出版。

后 记

同时感谢美国雪城大学、美国洛克菲勒档案中心、日本松下集团、美国 Dim 东亚科技史研究基金提供资助，以及美国哈佛大学提供 Houghton Library Fellowship。

最后感谢香港岭南大学予以的支持。

丰邑 张雷

2017 年 10 月 28 日

定稿于香港

作者简介

张雷，江苏丰县人。

北京大学硕士，美国雪城大学（Syracuse University）博士，香港岭南大学历史系助理教授，主要研究中国历史地理。